The Urban School:
A Factory for Failure

The MIT Press
Cambridge, Massachusetts, and London, England

The Urban School:
A Factory for Failure

A Study of Education in American Society

Ray C. Rist

371.82996073
R597u

This book was set in Linotype Helvetica
by New England Typographic Service, Inc.,
printed on Mohawk Neotext Offset
and bound in G.S.B. S/535/30 "Granite"
by The Colonial Press, Inc.
in the United States of America.

Library of Congress Cataloging in Publication Data

Rist, Ray C
  The urban school.

  Bibliography: p.
  1. Negroes—Education. 2. Education, Urban—United States. I. Title.
LC2771.R57   372.9'73   73–15580
ISBN 0–262–18064–2

171253

In memory of
Jules Henry, whose passion for truth was matched by
his compassion for children, and
Patricia Roberts, a colleague on this study of schools
whose life was cut short

Alle Menschen werden Brüder

Contents

Foreword

Each generation of Americans spends more time in school than the previous one. It looks as if coming generations will both start school earlier, given the growth in the day-care movement, and stay in school longer, given the enthusiasm for college for everyone. Yet we know much less than we ought about what schooling actually does for and to students. Aside from test results, educational research has remarkably little to say (other than impressionistically) about what being in school means to children, about how their experiences in school foster or frustrate their efforts to make satisfying lives for themselves and develop in ways that are meaningful to them and those around them.

One way to begin the development of a more systematic understanding of what events in the classroom do to students is to bring to bear the skills of participant-observation field work on this problem.

In this book, Ray Rist uses these skills to make us understand the first few years of school experience of one group of children. He shows us in fine-grained detail how teachers shape and direct some of the children toward academic success and others toward failure. Because most of these children are poor and black, and because their teachers, though black themselves, nevertheless expect most of their charges to do poorly, the principal training that goes on in the classroom seems to be training for a life of failure rather than success.

This work is one of the fruits of a line of investigation to which Jules Henry devoted a major portion of his professional career. Henry sought to demonstrate through his research and writing the ways in which anthropological methods could reveal our culture and its workings to us more sharply and incisively than other social science methods. For almost two decades he trained his students, the author of this study among them, to observe school milieus and to understand classroom teaching as not simply the imparting of objective knowledge but rather as a system for "drilling children in cultural orientations." He reported some of his findings concerning the average, middle-class school in his book *Culture Against Man*. Then he turned his attention to the urban school, particularly the ghetto schools which seemed to him to realize most fully the potential for destructiveness he saw in American culture. His untimely death meant that he was not able to complete the work that he had started, but in this report of his own part of that larger research, Ray Rist adumbrates what are probably the most essential findings from the larger enterprise.

Rist's analysis shows with what unremitting though unconscious effect teachers in ghetto schools shape most of the children in their classrooms to low achievement. By now we have enough results from experimental teaching programs with children from these same backgrounds to know that with proper stimulation these children can achieve as well as the average child, and that in these schools, too, the potentials for extraordinary accomplishment are there if facilitated by the school environment. Whatever cognitive disadvantages these children may bring with them to kindergarten can readily be overcome by highly motivated teachers who relate to children in such a way that the children find learning rewarding. Such experimental programs provide dramatic disproof of the ability of genetic factors to explain poor achievement on the part of lower-status or black children.

But Rist quite properly does not extrapolate his findings concerning the way the lower-class children are mistaught into a prescription for expanded remedial programs. He understands that what goes on in the classroom is but the face-to-face level of a complex system which operates to keep the poor poor and the black oppressed. He understands that the schools, though perpetuating and reinforcing patterns of social inequality, have little potential for compensating for the inequalitarian forces in other institutions in society. What he has observed in the classroom is one of the more poignant symptoms of the inhumanity of our system of social stratification. In his last chapter, Rist presents closely reasoned implications of his study, emphasizing on the one hand the necessity to change inequalitarian patterns in the productive institutions of the society (the economic institutions rather than the educational ones) and on the other hand the necessity of reform in the schools. What he offers is not the vain hope of converting them into a spearhead for equality (because that they cannot be) but rather the prospect of making them into institutions that at least deal with their charges in more humane ways, working to encourage self-realization rather than self-destruction.

Lee Rainwater
Harvard University

Preface

I write this brief preface as three American astronauts streak home from the moon in their Apollo 17 spacecraft. This flight portends to be the last moon voyage for the United States during this decade and perhaps this century. Apollo 17 represents the demise of a special fantasy that has nurtured the members of this society for some years now. Succinctly, in spite of the ills and turmoil in America, we have had the grandeur and daring of the space missions to reaffirm the uniqueness of ourselves as a people. But with this latest fiery launch went the last of the spectacular diversions from the national realities of politicians being shot, of fifty thousand lives lost in jungles halfway around the globe, of babies dying from malnutrition, of heroin spreading beyond the confines of the contained black community, of the powerless chafing under the continued refusal of the powerful to peacefully grant them admission—the last illusion of America as a peace-loving, nonaggressive, and tolerant society. We are up against the wall. We now can no longer turn to the moon to find America.

This book describes what has happened to one group of young black children in an urban school during the Age of Apollo. The narrative of their school experience, individually and collectively, begins with their

first day of kindergarten and continues through to their second grade
Christmas party. During these few brief years, white America had given
up on the ideals of Camelot and the Great Society to opt for a period
of benign neglect. Either way, though, it did not seem to matter much
to the children. They continued to attend an all-black school inside a
black community persistently and doggedly contained by surrounding
whites. Even beyond the realities of racism, their education was influenced by the pervasive impact of schools in perpetuating the existing
inequalities of American society—whether those inequalities be in the
white or black community. What is to follow, then, is an account of how
one school began to shape the lives and options of one group of black
children, and how the children responded at different times with compliance, defiance, or simple withdrawal.

The data for this study were gathered in St. Louis between September
1967 and January 1970. The endeavor was funded by a grant (No.
6–2771) to the Social Science Institute of Washington University by the
United States Office of Education. A much earlier draft of this book
served as my doctoral dissertation, entitled "The Socialization of the
Ghetto Child into the Urban School System," which I completed under
Dr. Helen P. Gouldner. The larger research project, of which I am
reporting one aspect, was begun by Professor Jules Henry and remained under his direction until his death. It was thereafter carried on
by Irving Louis Horowitz and David Pittman and finally brought to frui-
tion by John Bennett and Helen Gouldner. All of these principal inves-
tigators have left their mark on this study. In addition, I profited from
the contributions and criticisms of David Carpenter, Lee Rainwater,
and George Rawick. I would also acknowledge my fellow graduate
students, Steven Jones, Marco Pardi, Patricia Roberts (deceased), and
Carol Talbert, who participated in other aspects of the larger project.

Parts of the data presented here have appeared previously in the
Harvard Educational Review, Journal of Higher Education, Phylon, and
Urban Education, and in my own edited volume, *Restructuring Ameri-
can Education* (Transaction Books, 1972). I am grateful for consent to

include it here. Marjorie Lundell, Roslyn MacDonald, and Anne Morris have all borne the brunt of typing on the several drafts. Finally, the debt of gratitude to my intellectual compatriot and wife, Marilee, is of a special order.

Introduction

Myths die hard in America. Most tenacious are those that pertain to notions about our national character, our role in international affairs, and the kind of society we envision ourselves as having built. Common to all of them is the aggrandizement of a supposed virtue that sets us apart as a distinct and unique people. Where other nations are warlike, we are peaceful; where others distribute power by means of conflict, we do it by consensus; and where others reinforce inequality, we know all men to be equal. As a consequence of what we believe ourselves to be, we have effectively blocked or ignored that which might demythologize what we know to be "real."

But despite our best efforts, reality continues to intrude. Militarism continues to dominate foreign policy, violence remains integral to the political process, and the gap between rich and poor grows wider than ever before. When confronted with these realities, we tend to cast them off as aberrations, as not really representative of American society and life. They are seen to exist in spite of what America is rather than because of what she is.

This book will tackle one such myth and offer an analysis which will show that the outcome is opposite of what the myth might suggest;

that this outcome is what is really sought, despite disclaimers. Succinctly, it may be said that the system of public education in the United States is specifically designed to aid in the perpetuation of the social and economic inequalities found within the society. In spite of the notion that schools are, in the term of Horace Mann, the "great equalizer," they affirm, reflect, and strengthen the social system which created them. As Michael Katz suggests (1971, p. xviii), "Schools are not great democratic engines for identifying talent and matching it with opportunity. The children of the affluent by and large take the best marks and the best jobs."

What this line of analysis ultimately implies is that any discussion of a "crisis" in American education is applicable only if one believes that the current social and economic system is in need of change. For so long as the United States maintains its current structural and institutional arrangements, then the schools are functioning quite well. Indeed, it might be asked how it is that each generation moves with relatively little difficulty into the slots prepared for it by the previous generation. The answer is in large measure found in an examination of the purpose and function of American public education. Schooling has basically served to instill the values of an expanding industrial society and to fit the aspirations and motivations of individuals to the labor market at approximately the same level as that of their parents. Thus it is that some children find themselves slotted toward becoming workers and others toward becoming the managers of those workers.

I think it worth reiterating: *There is no crisis in American education if we accept American society as is.* But one must recognize that inherent in its very existence are aspects of racism, class schisms, coercion, the continual erosion of freedom and destruction of the "humanness" in those insufficiently strong to resist. This book seeks to document that all of these evils find clear expression in our public schools. The last part of the book addresses itself to the social ramifications and policy implications of a reevaluation of the role of schools in American society, focusing on what can be done with and to an institution which reinforces inequality.

On Success and Failure in School: Some Historical Notes

If schools reinforce the inequality present in this society, then also they are actively engaged in creating winners and losers. The schools reward some students in such a manner that these students are able to reap the benefits of American society while simultaneously punishing others in such a way that they find themselves unable to partake of the American feast. This has not occurred by accident. Though Charles Silberman (1970) suggests that the creation of winners and losers most likely results from the "mindlessness" of the schools, I would reply that such a suggestion is more benign than is warranted. The process whereby some take nearly all and others are left with nothing is, as Katz (1971, p. xviii) avers

... the historical result of the combination of purpose and structure that has characterized American education for roughly the last hundred years. ... There is a functional relationship between the way in which schools are organized and what they are supposed to do. That relation was there a century ago and it exists today.

One of the most disconcerting aspects of the fact that schools make winners and losers is that it strikes deeply at the myth of what schools are supposed to be about. Schooling has become the secular religion of America. Central to the articles of faith of that religion are the twin notions of enhanced individual social and economic mobility and the further strengthening of the democratic process through the creation of an enlightened citizenry. This religion has its roots deep in the American past. As Joseph White wrote more than 120 years ago in a report to the Massachusetts Board of Education (quoted in Katz, 1971, p. 40),

The children of the rich and poor, of the honored and the unknown, meet together on common ground. Their pursuits, their aims and aspirations are one. No distinctions find place, but such as talent and industry and good conduct create. In the competitions, the defeats, and the successes of the schoolroom, they meet each other as they are to meet in the broader fields of life before them; they are taught to distinguish between the essential and true, and the fractious and false, in character and condition. . . . Thus a vast and mutual benefit is the result. Thus, and only thus, can the rising generations be best prepared for the duties and responsibilities of citizenship in a free commonwealth. No foundation will be laid in our social life for the brazen walls of caste; and our political life, which is but the outgrowth of the social, will pulsate in harmony with it, and so be kept true to the grand ideals of the fathers and founders of the republic.

Though the aspirations manifest in this creed remain in the current beliefs about schools, there is no indication that fulfillment is any closer. Schools never have worked very well in equipping lower-class youngsters for mobility within the social and economic spheres of American society. It is an erroneous and romanticized notion to assume that at some point in the past schools did in fact achieve their goals and only recently have begun to lag. As Stephan Thernstrom (1964) has so aptly demonstrated, the Boston schools of the nineteenth century served to "cool out" the poor from aspirations for mobility and effectively maintained the class system that existed. What function the schools did accomplish quite well was to provide a means by which students could be socialized to accept the demands of capitalist employment. Schools became agents of social control by which the bourgeois sought to create a disciplined and skilled labor force to fill the rapidly expanding factories. To use the analogy of the factory, the unskilled immigrant child was perceived as a form of raw material that was to be transformed into an efficient end product. The product was to be a disciplined, punctual, obedient, and willing worker.

Perhaps an assessment more realistic than that of Joseph White of what was believed to be the function of the early public education in this country was voiced in a letter to the Massachusetts State Board of Education by an industrialist who wrote in 1841 (Bowles, 1972):

I have never considered mere knowledge . . . as the only advantage derived from a good education . . . [workers with more education possess] a higher and better state of morals, are more orderly and respectful in their deportment, and more ready to comply with the wholesome and necessary regulations of an establishment. . . . In times of agitation, on account of some change in regulations or wages, I have always looked to the most intelligent, best educated, and the most moral for support. The ignorant and uneducated I have generally found the most turbulent and troublesome, acting under the impulse of excited passion and jealousy.

Under the guise of creating an enlightened citizenry, schools for the poor and the immigrant child were organized so as to resemble closely the conditions of the factory and prepare young people to perceive the inevitability of the capitalist division of labor. Public schools were conceived to serve as an integral link in the larger sphere of interinstitutional relations by reinforcing the conditions of unequal power and wealth. Historically one can trace the development of class stratification within the emerging education apparatus of the United States. Elites continued to send their children to private schools, which provided these children with training for the power and prestige they would later possess as adults. Working-class children, on the other hand, would have to leave public school early to contribute to the earnings of the family; Thernstrom (1964) estimates that in the nineteenth-century working-class family in Boston, nearly 20 percent of all family income was earned by children under the age of fifteen.

When the working-class students did begin to enter high schools, the system responded with the vocational school and the development of various academic tracks which continued effectively to socialize the working-class and poor student for occupations that did not provide upward mobility. As Katz (1971, p. 121) suggests:

It [vocational school] was also a solution fit for poor children; it would permit them to attend secondary school without inhibiting aspirations beyond their class. It would continue to instill in them the attitudes and skills appropriate to manual working-class status. Regardless of the rhetoric of its sponsors, vocational education has proved to be an ingenious way of providing universal secondary schooling without disturbing the shape of the social structure and without permitting excessive amounts of social mobility.

The contentions of Katz deserve serious consideration in light of the comments of the superintendent of the Boston public schools who summarized his views on vocational education in 1908 (Bowles, 1972):

Until very recently, they [the schools] have offered equal opportunity for all to receive one kind of education, but what will make them democratic is to provide opportunity for all to receive such education as will fit them equally well for their particular life work.

The reinforcement of the class system occurred when others decided for the student what his "particular life work" was going to be.

One can argue in opposition that the schools were not merely sorting bins for the class system, but were in fact innovative and creative institutions seeking through a variety of ways to overcome the pressures of a class system. One might point to the establishment of the kindergarten, of intelligence testing, or to the introduction of guidance counselors as attempts to make the schooling experience more equitable for all students. Admittedly, such innovations represent no small attempts on the part of the educational system to meet the needs of a changing world. But I am less sure that their consequences were what the reformers assumed. For example, the introduction of kindergarten can be seen as an attempt by middle-class reformers (and industrialists) to counteract what they perceived as the negative effects of the home. The sooner the socialization of the school could begin, the less the influence of the unfavorable conditions of the home. Likewise, the use of ability testing may well sort students on criteria that come closer to measuring class interests and values than innate cognitive ability. The introduction of guidance counselors in the schools may well be a beneficial aid to students uncertain about their future, but the guidance given may be steering the child toward assumed needs and interests —class linked, of course.

Charles Silberman (1970, p. 80) offers a more contemporary example to reinforce this contention:

A black student does poorly in a Northern high school for three years. When he expresses interest in college, his guidance counselor assures him that he is not "college material." Through the intercession of some white friends, and over the objection of the guidance counselor, he is admitted into the federally financed Upward Bound program at a nearby college, which provides an intensive remedial program during the summer and special tutoring during his senior year. His grades shoot up so rapidly that the Upward Bound officials recommend him for a special Transitional Year program at Yale University, designed to give "underachieving students" with high potential the academic skills and self-confidence they need to realize their potential. The counselor begrudgingly supplies the necessary transcripts, after re- marking to the boy, "What, you at Yale? Don't make me laugh." But when the student is admitted—one of sixty selected, out of 500 appli- cants—the school system's public relations apparatus swings into action. The boy's picture appears in the local newspaper in an article reporting the high school's success story; the superintendent intro- duces him to the public at an open meeting of the board of education; and when a group of local black leaders meet with school officials to press some of their complaints about the system, they are told that the boy's admission to the Yale program shows how well the school was serving black students.

Success and Failure: More Recent Interpretations

Within the past decade, two prominent explanations have emerged for the continued school failure of large numbers of poor children. Both place the responsibility on the student for his own failure. Behind such explanations lies a belief in the immutability of the school itself and the need for the child to accommodate himself to the organization of the school. The first, the "culture of poverty" notion, posits that chil- dren fail because of the environmental obstacles they face in their homes and poverty-stricken communities. The other explanation sug- gests that the basis for failure is to be found in genetic differences among groups of children. This has been most recently elaborated upon in some detail in the work of Jensen (1969). Neither perspective, however, is acceptable. Both go to great pains to avoid any analysis of the school systems themselves and by default consent to the myth that schools are egalitarian, classless, humane institutions interested in the potential of individual children.

Central to the culture of poverty concept is the idea that there is such an early and pervasive destruction of the cognitive and creative ability of poor children by their environment that by the time they are ready to enter the public school system they are irreparably damaged. The children are seen as lacking sufficient motivation, self esteem, awareness of the world around them, acceptable language patterns, and knowledge of various social roles in the family, for instance, of the "missing father." Schools then are faced with the nearly impossible task of resurrecting from a smashed organism a lively and vibrant human being. In such circumstances, who could possibly assume that schools would do very well? Failure is considered inevitable for many of the children so afflicted.

What the culture of poverty concept does very nicely is not only to relieve the school system of any blame for the failure of children, but also to take away any guilt from the society at large. We are assured that it is not poverty per se that creates the conditions of failure (for we all know of poor children who are not like the ones described above), but it is the *values and culture* of that particular segment of the poor, passed on from generation to generation, that breed apathy and a fatalistic view of life. Children who live in a culture such as this are assumed to be incapable of planning for the future, delaying gratification, utilizing abstract reasoning, or curtailing their sexual expression.

One of the more notable spin-offs from the culture of poverty concept has been the development of an "inadequate mother" hypothesis, an assumption that mothers from a "culturally deprived" background produce deficient children. It is suggested that the incapacity of the mother creates a destructive environment in which linguistic development is thwarted, cognitive processes are impaired, and self esteem is destroyed. The mother is viewed as failing to provide the social, sensory, and aesthetic stimulation produced by talking and reading to the child and organizing the schedule of events in the home so as to give the child a notion of the importance of time and space. Baratz and Baratz (1970) have provided an excellent critique of this hypothesis and suggest that the basic assumption of a deficit in children from low-income families is both erroneous and pejorative. They note that a difference is not to be equated with a deficit.

With the culture of poverty notion as the dominant theoretical guideline of the "War on Poverty" launched by President Johnson, massive federal funding went into programs seeking to intervene in the lives of the poor in such a manner as to provide them with the motivation and skills necessary for occupational success in American society. Though the "war" was in reality little more than a protracted skirmish, there is little indication that the programs would have succeeded, particularly those dealing with the educational processes. The assumptions guiding such intervention are simply untrue. There appear to be several interrelated ones in particular that are grounded more in the biases of the educational system than in the actual potentialities of poor children. One assumption is that when poor children enter school, they are unable to deal with the curriculum as organized because of deficits in their families and environment. Secondly, the longer the child remains in a "deprived" environment, the more pervasive and permanent his "damage." Third, schools will never succeed with such children as long as the parents live as they do. And fourth, given that some environments are believed to be better than others, it is the obligation of the "betters" to offer assistance to the "lessers."

The pernicious nature of such notions is that they do contain half-truths that, if not carefully scrutinized, leave some who are involved in working with the poor feeling justified in their assumptions about why the poor stay poor. Teachers can claim that they have tried to teach but that some students were simply unable to respond; social workers can comment on the failure of lower-class persons to follow the directives they suggest; and poverty warriors can throw up their hands in resignation because the poor do not "appreciate all that is being done for them." Under the guise of providing motivation and aspiration for self-improvement, these individuals harbor a hegemony of cultural values that labels any others as deviant, deficient, or deprived. The affluent have laid exclusive claim to a set of attributes that supposedly distinguish them from the poor. Such characteristics as neatness, punctuality, orderliness, and aspirations for a decent life are held up to outsiders willing to conform. Schools are viewed as sacred guardians of such virtues, whose obligation it is to pass them on to the deserving poor. Students must conform if the very fabric of civilization is not to be threatened by the mindless antics of an ignorant *lumpenproletariat.*

In retrospect, it may be that the recent theories concerning the inadequacies of the poor are no more than the pouring of old wine into new bottles. Consider the definition by the Boston School Committee of the task set before it in the creation of a city-wide public school system in the early nineteenth century (Katz, 1971, p. 40):

. . . taking children at random from a great city, undisciplined, uninstructed, often with inveterate forwardness and obstinacy, and with the inherited stupidity of centuries of ignorant ancestors; forming them from animals into intellectual beings, and, so far as a school can do it, from intellectual beings into spiritual beings; giving to many their first appreciation of what is wise, what is true, what is lovely, and what is pure; and not merely their first impressions, but what may possibly be their only impressions.

The Boston Committee was concerned at the time with large numbers of recent immigrants to the city, Irish in particular; but the cultural arrogance and incipient racism reflected in this passage have not diminished. The minorities that schools are seeking to serve have different national origins and skin color, but the attitudes remain. Such a view of the poor and the nonwhite is central, not peripheral, to the system of public education.

To oppose theories that environmental factors influence academic success or failure, there periodically emerges a study suggesting that the most significant variable in evaluating academic achievement is the heredity component. One of the more recent is an article published by Arthur Jensen in the Winter 1969 issue of the *Harvard Educational Review* under the title"How Much Can We Boost IQ and Scholastic Achievement?" Opening with a statement that "compensatory education has been tried and apparently has failed," the article brings together data from a large number of previous experiments variously concerned with issues of genetics, intelligence, heredity, and with compensatory programs that seek to modify the influences of all these.

Jensen proposes that individuals with low Intelligence Quotients (IQ) were typically different in their genetic makeup from those who possessed high IQs. Christopher Jencks has noted in a review (1969) of Jensen's work that very few people would dispute such a statement on the surface. The issue is where one goes with it. Jensen does admit that environmental factors can influence IQ differences. He concludes from studies conducted in the United States and England that 80 percent of one's intelligence as measured by IQ tests is due to heredity and 20 percent due to environment.

To this point, Jensen's conclusions are not particularly controversial, although there may be some dispute over the relative percentages of influence of heredity and environment. What provides fuel for controversy is his subsequent argument that the overwhelming influence of genetic factors (.80 versus .20) can explain not only the IQ differences among individuals *within* the same group, but also differences *between* groups as aggregates.

It is at this point that he introduces the issue of race and black-white IQ differences (which he says have held fairly steady at an average fifteen-point gap, though both have numerically increased over time). Jensen concludes that blacks as a group do less well in areas such as abstract reasoning and problem solving when compared with whites and Orientals. He equates ability in these areas with that measured by intelligence tests and, noting that blacks do persistently less well on IQ tests than do whites, imputes these differences to factors of inheritance—matters of genetic structure and brain formation. He then suggests that educational compensatory programs that have been tried to date have ignored the impact of heredity upon performance, and the forced exposure to cultural events, compensatory programs, trips to the country, and properly spoken English will have little if any effect.

(He is correct in arguing that compensatory programs have failed, but for reasons, I suggest, quite different from those he offers.)

In violent disagreement with Jensen, Silberman (1970, p. 77) accuses him of raising an "ugly question." Silberman suggests that Jensen has gone far beyond the boundaries of his data in drawing conclusions, particularly with reference to cross-racial comparisons. He argues that Jensen's data are insufficient to imply a distinctive role for heredity in whatever differences there might be between the scores of black and white children on intelligence tests. Silberman also attacks Jensen's treatment of environmental issues, calling it "simplistic, almost to the point of caricature."

Morris, writing for the Center for Afro-American Studies at U.C.L.A. (1971), takes a somewhat different tack, focusing on Jensen's super-ficial treatment of the conditions in which black children grow up. Morris suggests that Jensen makes an error of immense proportions in assuming that there exists a relatively similar environment for blacks and whites. This assumption, Morris contends, underplays the impact on blacks of coping with a racist environment and ignores the *capacity* of the person versus his performance. Any interpretation from IQ tests that goes beyond the acknowledged problematic nature of such tests, he states, "is simply wrong."

Though the two positions just outlined are but a small sample of the vigorous dissent against Jensen, their proponents share with him an erroneous assumption. Before one can discuss the differences among "races," one must decide what precisely is meant by the term "race." The general response to Jensen's position has taken issue with his interpretation of data, his apparent insensitivity to the differences be-tween black and white culture, and his willingness to place firm faith in IQ tests as accurate measures of intelligence. Little if any attention has been directed toward explicitly defining the categories being com-pared. In short, the argument of black-white differences is meaning-less until there is some notion of what is meant by "black" and "white."

To suggest that there are clearly definable parameters between gene pools of various "racial" groupings which allow for no overlap and for the making of clear distinctions is a debatable presumption at best. The family of man has physical characteristics that exist on a continuum: tall to short, light to dark, straight hair to kinky hair, large nasal passages to small nasal passages, and so on. *To decide along that continuum to create various categories and label them "races" is to perform an act that has its foundations in political, ideological, and cultural considerations, not biogenetic ones.* In fact, many geneticists have come to this conclusion first, and, ironically, the social sciences now stubbornly hold to genetic theories that geneticists have discarded. Ashley Montague, in his recently edited book entitled *The Concept of Race* (1970), brings together a number of geneticists and physical anthropologists who have sought to demythologize the concept of race. Several authors in the volume even suggest the term "race" itself is so value-laden and imprecise that it needs to be dropped from discourse.

With this in mind, it is difficult to take seriously the whole Jensen debate in the framework in which it is now being discussed. To suggest that "blacks as a group differ genetically in intelligence from whites as a group" is to make a statement that implies so many subtle assumptions about what we all "know" to be meant by black and white and what we "know" about how the boundaries were drawn between the two groups that it becomes meaningless. (To add confusion to chaos, there is the debate over what is meant by "intelligence.") Meanwhile, as scholars expend time, energy, and emotions discussing the pros and cons of Jensen's position regarding the genetic merits of groups that have only a social reality, schools—free from any responsibility—continue to produce winners and losers because they "know" that white middle-class children are the superior genetic group. The fact that the winners take both "the best marks and the best jobs" becomes no more than the acting out of a historical inevitability that was decided at conception. Schools can only serve to expedite the upward movement of the genetically endowed and to insure that the less endowed do not develop aspirations beyond their capacity.

The Perpetuation of Inequality

It can be granted that children come to school possessing differences in cultural backgrounds and states of cognitive development. Nevertheless, schools appear to be deliberately organized so as to persist in implementing policies and practices that each year create a continual stream of losers. The reason schools are organized in this fashion is that they have a direct complicity in maintaining the current patterns of inequality in the society, and those who benefit from such inequalities are not clamoring for change. Regardless of rhetoric, the schools serve as sorting mechanisms which legitimate the present structures in American society, insuring that the upper classes preserve their privileged positions and that the lower classes have little or no opportunity to reach them.

Though there have been some blatant manifestations of this sorting process that insures inequality in the society—for example, tracking by social class—the general process is more subtle. Schools do not have to reinforce the structure overtly; *they can merely proceed in such a manner as not to create the conditions for change.* This I take to be the major message of the report prepared by James Coleman (1966, p. 325) for the United States government entitled *Equality of Educational Opportunity.* Coleman notes:

One implication stands out above all: That schools bring little influence to bear on a child's achievement that is independent of his background and general social context; and that this very lack of independent effect means that the inequalities imposed on children by their home, neighborhood, and peer environment are carried along to become the inequalities with which they confront adult life at the end of school. For equality of educational opportunity through the schools must imply a strong effect of schools that is independent of the child's immediate social environment, and that strong independent effect is not present in American schools.

By failing to provide the conditions in which children might overcome the inequalities imposed on them, the schools insure that the *status quo* is preserved. It is the goal of this book to demonstrate how one particular school did operate so as to reinforce the inequalities found in the larger society. The consequence was to contribute to the ranks of both winners and losers.

The findings of the Coleman Report have been disputed, but reanalysis of the data by a group of social scientists and educators at Harvard University indicates that the initial findings are largely correct. The Harvard group has published its conclusions in a book edited by Mosteller and Moynihan (1972). The significant findings of Coleman, substantiated by reanalysis, are several:

(1) The vast majority of black and white children attend schools that are segregated by color. (Eighty percent of white children in the first and twelfth grades attend schools that are more than 90 percent white. For black children, the figures for first and twelfth grades are 65 percent and 48 percent respectively in schools more than 90 percent black.) One would be justified in stating that in 1965 the elementary and secondary schools of the United States had nearly reached the racially "separate" state outlawed by the Supreme Court in 1954.

(2) Though Coleman showed that schools for black and white children were "separate," he also stated that, contrary to the general assumption, they were nearly "equal" in physical facilities, formal curricula, and teacher characteristics, given controls for regional differences. The Report found that the assumed black-white school differences were simply not there. White schools scored higher on some variables (physics and chemistry laboratories) while black schools scored higher on others (full-time librarians and language laboratories). In short, black and white schools were nearly "separate but equal."

(3) Even where there were measured differences between the facilities, curricula, and teacher characteristics, they had, according to the Report, very little effect on the performance of either white or black students as measured by standardized tests. The implications of this

and (2) taken together are important, for they suggest that merely providing an equalization of any unequal facilities, curricula, or teacher characteristics will not be sufficient to overcome the patterns of inequality imposed upon the schools from the home, the environment, and the peer group. The United States has, in large measure, reached equality of opportunity if that is measured by what is offered to children when they attend school, that is, by input. But if one focuses on the *output* of the schools instead, the gap remains as wide.

(4) The two most significant variables which displayed a consistent relation with test performance were those of social class of the parents and social class of fellow students. Thus low-income children came to the school with a double handicap in terms of variables influencing achievement—they themselves were poor and the majority of their classmates could also be expected to be poor. It was found that in those situations where few low-income children were placed with many middle-income children, their performance rose appreciably. Cohen, Pettigrew, and Riley (1972) evaluated the Coleman data to test for the influence of race independent of class on the achievement of black students and concluded that the variable of race most likely varies with social class, though "decisive conclusions about the effects of racial composition . . . are not possible. . . ." Minority-group students, with the exception of Oriental-Americans, on the average scored lower on the administered tests than their white classmates. But when controls for the influence of social class were imposed, the impact of racial differences became nearly nonexistent. This is probably explained by the fact that the majority of nonwhite students also are lower class. There were also variations in test achievement within the group of white students by social class. This finding would suggest that in the future the continued gap of black-white academic achievement will not be closed solely by upgrading schools or by racial integration if the gap in socioeconomic status is ignored.

Overall, the findings of the Coleman Report allow one to make a number of important negative inferences concerning the impact of schools on achievement (for example, teacher training does not appear to make a significant difference in pupil learning; the ratio of teachers to pupils does not appear to make a significant difference in pupil learning; the presence or absence of language laboratories does not appear to make a significant difference in pupil learning). But when one begins to make positive inferences about effects of schools on pupil achievement, the data become less abundant. One can infer from Coleman that the mixing of students from different social classes is of benefit to children of the lower class, so long as the percentage of lower-class students does not reach X percent. For example, low-income black students in largely middle-class schools were about twenty months ahead of low-income black students in largely low-income schools, while those in intermediate social class schools fell in between. Similar results were also found for low-income white students. The question to be pursued from these data is, what social class mix constitutes the "tipping point" at which the performance of lower-class students stops rising? Or, what is the point of diminishing returns on class integration?

This question is crucial, for the data suggest that there is greater pupil variability *within* the same school than *between* schools. Consequently, if the desired outcome of the educational process is to create means whereby one equalizes the outcomes of schooling for children, the efforts to reduce between-school differences will have little impact. Smith (1972), in his reanalysis of the Coleman data, found that 90 percent of all variation in the range of test performance could be located within any typical school for the urban North. One would conclude from this finding that the students who performed the best were often in the same school with those who performed least well. Speaking to this same point, Jencks (1972a, p. 86) comments:

The implications of this are in many ways more revolutionary than anything else in the Equality of Educational Opportunity Survey (EEOS). In the short run it remains true that our most pressing political problem is the achievement gap between Harlem and Scarsdale. But in the long run it seems that our primary problem is not the disparity between Harlem and Scarsdale but the disparity between the top and the bottom of the class in both Harlem and Scarsdale. Anyone who doubts this ought to spend some time talking to children in the bottom half of a "good" middle-class suburban school.

What the findings of the Coleman Report and the reanalysis offered by Jencks and Smith, among others, make clear are that the heated debates over what were assumed to be the critical variables of physical facilities, teacher training, curriculum, and the like, have, in large part, missed the mark. *The inequality in American education is accounted for, not so much by differences between schools, but by how the same school treats different children.* By defining the learning situation in a certain fashion and rewarding some forms of behavior and performance to the exclusion of others, the schools create conditions for differential treatment.

It is important to move one step beyond the analysis provided in the Coleman data. Succinctly, though the Coleman Report presents examination results indicating significant academic differences among various groups of children in the nation's schools—and often within the same school—it gives no hint as to how these differences come to manifest themselves within the individual classrooms. What is left unexamined is the *process* by which there come to be winners and losers.

I would suggest that the process whereby there emerges a stratification system within the schools and within individual classrooms has its genesis with the teacher—his or her values, norms, and expectations as to what kinds of children can perform and what kinds cannot. W. I. Thomas many years ago set forth what has become a basic dictum of the social sciences when he observed, "If men define situations as real, they are real in their consequences." This is what I have observed happening in classrooms. The teachers reported upon in this study assumed a certain reality (middle-class children can learn and lower-class children cannot) and then acted upon this assumption in their classroom organization and behavior. In so doing they created that which they "knew" to be true before they began.

Robert Merton (1957) elaborated upon the work of Thomas and de-

veloped his theory of "the self-fulfilling prophecy." Merton posited
that most people act most of the time in accordance with what they
believe to be the expectations held for them by others. Thus the perception of what is expected is strong enough to evoke the behavior
that was anticipated. The influence of others can bring one to act almost in spite of oneself. Merton notes (1957, p. 421):

... Men respond not only to the objective features of a situation, but
also, and at times primarily, to the meaning this situation has for them.
And once they have assigned some meaning to the situation, their
consequent behavior and some of the consequences of that behavior
are determined by the ascribed meaning.

What is so pernicious about the self-fulfilling prophecy is that, once
meaning has been ascribed to a situation and both the person and
others begin to respond in terms of it, then whether there was any
truth in the original evaluation is beside the point. Merton suggests
(1957, p. 423), "The specious validity of the self-fulfilling prophecy
perpetuates a reign of error." Schools are organized in such a manner
as to perpetuate the "reign of error" Merton describes. The system
orients itself to the rewarding of the achievements of middle-class children and to the denial of the achievements of lower-class children.
Schools assume that middle-class students can learn, and they do.
Likewise, schools assume that lower-class students cannot learn, and
they don't.

How do such assumptions come to be? How do teachers come to
"know" that some children can do it and some cannot? The answer
may well lie in what can be termed the "culture of schooling." The
values, the ethos, the milieu of schools create for those within them a
reality shaped by cultural values predominant in the middle-class
strata of the society. Katz (1971, p. xvii), in his study of the development of public education in the United States, suggests that such
middle-class values have historically left schools estranged from the
working-class and poor communities. He writes:

... The schools are fortresses in function as well as form, protected
outposts of the city's educational establishment and the prosperous

citizens who sustain it. In their own way, they are imperial institutions designed to civilize the natives; they exist to do something to poor children, especially, now, children who are black or brown. Their main purpose is to make these children orderly, industrious, law-abiding, and respectful of authority. Their literature and their spokesmen proclaim the schools to be symbols of opportunity, but their slitted or windowless walls say clearly what their history would reveal as well: They were designed to reflect and confirm the social structure that erected them.

Given such conditions, can one assume that lower-class and working-class children will conform to what the schools require? There has been deep antagonism, often overtly hostile, between the schools and the nonaffluent for more than a century in the United States. School establishments perpetuate the myth of opportunity by a distortion of reality: schools cannot fail, only children fail. Teachers, trapped between the community and the brokers of power within the schools, have sided with the establishment and have come to accept the definition that the onus of failure should be placed squarely on the backs of those who fail. *Ironically, what the teachers create through their expectations for children is precisely what the schools were designed to make real—class inequality disguised as individual differences.*

Many, and especially those in the field of education, I suspect, will strongly disagree with the foregoing analysis. For them, culture deprivation and genetic differences will suffice as fairly accurate explanations for why winners and losers emerge within schools. I see adherence to such views as no more than another tactic by which those who have direct responsibility for children seek to ignore their own complicity in the perpetuation of an unjust system. Their refusal to acknowledge it is a denial of the profound importance of the institution of schooling for the life chances of children. The creation of winners and losers is ultimately a political statement by the schools as to whom they deem fit to partake in the benefits of American society. Denying political control does not make it go away. The class system in this society does not magically appear for the young person when he finishes his schooling. He has been socialized all through childhood and adolescence to "know" and "accept" his place as either a "have" or a "have-not," and the process inherent in compulsory education becomes the mechanism to insure that socialization.

Design of the Present Study

To observe the process by which schools create winners and losers, it is necessary to make oneself a part of the school and classroom milieu. The process of socialization within classrooms involves the development of attitudes, values, beliefs, notions about the world, and notions about self. One cannot discover the influences of the educational experience upon the child merely by relying upon abstracted measures of aptitude, attitude, grades, or IQ. Although these indexes may provide guidelines to the current performance of the child, they do not elucidate the complexities of the classroom by which "products" such as grades or test scores are generated. It is in the examination of classroom behavior that I believe one finds the clearest expression of what the educational experience means for the life chances of the child.

A teacher spends nearly one thousand hours with her students during the course of the school year. Such intensive and continual interaction within the confines of a single room results in the development of an internal order and logic that becomes apparent only to those who seek to make themselves a part of that classroom. Thus one must view the educational experience as it occurs *over time*. The plotting of grades and teacher reports as measures of a child's progress remain at best only an abstraction of actual behavior and performance.

In its broadest scope, the research in this study from September 1967 to January 1970 involved both participant and nonparticipant observation of school, home, and peer experiences of a group of black students.[1] I sat as a nonparticipant observer in the kindergarten class-

[1] An appendix describing in detail the methodology for this kind of study is available from the author on request.

room of these children at least twice weekly throughout the 1967–1968 school year and then again when they were in the first half of their second grade year (1969–1970). The length of the formal classroom observations varied by time of day, day of the week, and length of observation, the latter ranging from forty-five minutes to three and one-half hours. While the children were in their first grade year, I visited the class a number of times informally, but did not systematically observe. During all formal observations a continual handwritten account was kept of classroom interaction and activity. Smith and Geoffrey (1968) have termed this method of classroom observation "microethnography." During the informal observations notes were made immediately upon leaving the school. No mechanical devices were used to record classroom activities.

In addition to the classroom activities of teachers and students, I also observed conversations in the teachers' lounge, the monthly meetings of the Parent-Teacher Association (PTA), field trips with the students, special assemblies in the school, medical examinations of the students, library periods, sessions with the speech therapist, noon hour recreation on the playground, movement in the halls between classes, and teachers at lunch. Interviews were conducted periodically throughout the study with both teachers and administrators. I also visited several of the children in their homes, where I met their parents, participated with the children in softball games, walked with them in their neighborhoods, read to them, took them for rides in my car, and watched television with them. The circumstances of the particular observation dictated whether I was able to take notes during the activity. In the nonclassroom but school-related observations I was frequently unable to take notes (on field trips, for instance, I was usually given "responsibility" for the boys); but I could quite easily do so during PTA meetings. The only time notes were taken during any of the home observations was in interviews with parents.

It would perhaps be well to clarify what I believe to be the benefits derived from the long-term and detailed study of one group of children. The single most apparent weakness of the vast majority of studies on urban education is that they lack any longitudinal perspective. A number of studies on schooling have utilized a single episodic approach, more closely resembling the description of a still-life painting than an ongoing activity. Likewise, even where there have been attempts at the direct observation of classrooms, the time span allotted often has been quite short; Smith and Geoffrey (1968) completed their study in one semester, Leacock (1969) in four months, and Eddy (1967) in three months. Secondly, as I have suggested, the complexities of the classroom cannot be reduced to the mere evaluation of differences by a measurement technique over some specified time span. The abstraction of classroom activities to various scores and test results can only give indication of output, not of process. Finally, it is only with long-term participation in a social system such as the school that one becomes aware of the subtle nuances, the brief references that have meaning only within that system, of the gaps between word and deed, and of the official versus the unofficial notions of how the roles and tasks for various participants are defined. The privilege of sharing "inside" gossip and the personal feelings of the participants is not achieved by presenting a letter of introduction.

There is a legitimate concern about the degree to which one can generalize from data gathered in one school to other schools in the same city, to other urban schools in the nation, and to the process of schooling itself. The school reported upon in this study was one of five selected by the district superintendent as available to the research team. All five schools in the district were visited and extensive observations were conducted in four by various members of the staff. The district superintendent's selection of these schools was based, apparently, on the fact that relatively few researchers had visited them previously. The principal of the school I studied, however, suggested that I was fortunate in coming to his school since his staff, and the kindergarten teacher in particular, were "equal to any in the city." From other descriptions of urban black schools, both popular (Kohl, 1967; and

Kozol, 1967) and academic (Eddy, 1967; Fuchs, 1969; Leacock, 1969; and Moore, 1967) the school in this study does not appear atypical— except that the physical facilities were less than ten years old.

Admitted limitations of the use of participant and nonparticipant observation are that it makes the sample size small, the scope of the study narrow, replication difficult, and the basis for generalizations limited. The benefits, though, are derived from the development of an extensive case history and the accumulation of large amounts of data on few subjects; and what generalizations can be made are grounded in the similarity of that sample to others removed in both time and place. Ultimately, one must choose a methodology that best suits the particular problem at hand. Participant and nonparticipant observation seem best suited to describing the reality of schools and schooling.

In a funnel-like fashion the following chapters seek to describe the process by which one particular urban school generated successes and failures. Chapter 1 focuses on the city school system and the school itself, its social and cultural milieu as well as the training, attitudes, and values the teachers brought with them to the various classrooms. Chapter 2 and 3 describe the kindergarten experience of one group of children, from the first day of school to the last. Chapter 4 briefly follows the same group of children and outlines some of the patterns of organization in the first grade that were found to be influenced by the kindergarten year. Entering into second grade, Chapter 5 traces the interactions and activities of the same children until the first weeks after their Christmas vacation. This is followed in Chapter 6 by a summary of the study as well as a discussion of several alternatives for breaking the cycle of a perpetual creation of winners and losers.

The System and the School

1

Individual classrooms in any school do not exist in a social, cultural, or political vacuum. They are tied in innumerable ways to the teachers and activities of other classrooms, to administrators and their policies as well as to the larger school system of which they are one small unit. Though it has been in vogue for some time to tell "horror stories" of what children face in schools, particularly in urban schools, there has been scant attention paid to the nature of the school or to the system in which such abuse occurs. By ignoring these two additional levels of influence on the child and focusing exclusively on the classroom, some recent studies leave unexplicated the bureaucratic, cultural, and political properties of the schooling process. What follows in this chapter is an attempt first to elucidate important aspects of the school system which impinge on the classroom situation and then to focus somewhat more specifically on the social and cultural milieu of a single school. By this gradual funneling process, one can arrive at a study of individual classrooms within the context of larger system properties.

Part 1: The System

A New Majority

As has occurred in a number of other northern cities, St. Louis has experienced not only a decline in population, but a dramatic shift in the
composition of that population. In the twenty years between 1950 and
1970, for example, St. Louis lost more than 190,000 residents (from
approximately 850,000 to 660,000). What these gross figures do not
indicate is the profound change in the racial background of the residents during this same time. The white population dropped from
702,000 to 376,000 and the black population rose from 154,000 to
291,000. Whites left the city of St. Louis during these two decades at
the rate of 16,320 per year while the blacks moved in at the rate of
6,855.

These demographic shifts have been reflected in the schools. The
percentage of white students in the public schools declined during
these two decades from 78 percent to 36 percent, with a corresponding shift in black enrollments from 22 percent to 64 percent. By 1970,
St. Louis ranked fifth in the nation in percentage of black students.[1] In
1970, there were just over 117,000 students in the St. Louis public
schools, with a black-white distribution of approximately 75,000 to
42,000. Of the nearly 75,000 black students, over 33,000 came from
homes supported by the public welfare program of Aid to Dependent
Children (ADC).

Gittell and Hollander (1968) suggest that an important indicator of a
school system's willingness to innovate in the face of changes in the
composition of the student body, and, more fundamentally, changes
in the very character of the community, is whether the school system
will allow independent study and evaluation of its policies and practices. These authors aver that a willingness to allow studies of the sys-

---

[1]Washington, D.C. was first with 93.5 percent black enrollment; Newark second with
72.5 percent; New Orleans Parish was third with 67.1 percent; and Baltimore fourth
with 65.1 percent.

tem and the ways in which innovation can be introduced to meet changing school conditions is an important indicator of the openness and concern of those in decision-making positions. In a comparative study of six urban school systems, they conclude that New York City was the system most supportive of independent study and St. Louis the least.[2]

With almost complete lack of recognition of outside reports and studies, the St. Louis Board of Education has relied heavily on studies by individual Board members and staff studies internally commissioned. In the area of school integration, for example, Gittell and Hollander (1968, p. 10) note:

Staff studies led to the present integration policy, adopted in 1964, which, though it emphasizes the neighborhood schools, provides bussing from core schools to reduce overcrowding. A 1964 study by a community group has been largely ignored by the board. . . . The board in St. Louis has neither encouraged or sponsored independent researchers or community groups.

More recently a Community Study Conference, which was organized by citizens in 1969, submitted a study containing 107 recommendations for the Board to consider. In response to the report, the chairman of the Board commented (*St. Louis Post-Dispatch,* Jan. 18, 1970):

Why, there's absolutely no unanimity of opinion in this report. It contradicts itself. The recommendations are too short to be helpful. I just don't think there is an awful lot to it.

A second unidentified Board member noted:

I frankly don't think they're [the recommendations] worth a damn. And I sincerely doubt whether it will provide us with much guidance. I'm sick and tired of getting blasted by people who make it seem as if we've never considered any of these things before.

Another possible indicator of a school system's willingness to respond to its new majority would be the extent of programs specifically initiated for the recently arrived students. Of particular importance in

[2]Between these two polar positions, they ranked from more open to more closed Detroit, Baltimore, Philadelphia, and Chicago, in that order.

gauging the sensitivity of the school system would be those programs begun before the rise of black militancy in the mid-1960s. Since the advent of urban violence and protest, the bandwagon of school programs for black and low-income students, financed primarily by the Federal government, has traveled into every corner of the land. But what of the years before the mid-1960s? The census data clearly indicate that the shift from white to black was in full motion, but at the time school systems were facing less external pressure for innovation and response to these changes. Examples may be found again in the six urban districts studied by Gittell and Hollander (1968), who rated response (or lack of it) on a continuum from an attempt at continual innovation to a mere perpetuation of the status quo. Three school systems —Detroit, Philadelphia, and New York—all gave evidence of seeking to keep abreast at least in some degree with the changes in the schools. One might note, for example, that Detroit was the first of the Great City Schools in 1959, or that Detroit, Philadelphia, and New York all had more than 1,000 volunteers working in the schools before 1963. Baltimore, Chicago, and St. Louis had not established volunteer programs in any way comparable to these.

    Though St. Louis as a school system had not taken many definitive steps toward innovation and modification in the face of the change in pupil composition, there was one program initiated in the city schools which received considerable national publicity. This was the Banneker District Project, founded and directed by Dr. Samuel Shepard from its inception during the 1957–1958 academic year. As District Superintendent of the Banneker District, one of six districts in the city school system, Dr. Shepard initiated a program with the principle objective of raising the performance levels of students through increased teacher motivation, parental assistance, and student participation in learning activities. Shepard called for between-school competition within the district, both academic and athletic, as well as frequent meetings of teachers and administrators with parents and community leaders. The results of the program showed positive increases in the achievement scores of the children in reading, arithmetic, and language. Though recently some doubt has been expressed about the long-term effects of this program on student performance (Semmel, 1967; Doyle, 1969), it cannot be denied that when it was begun in 1957, it was one of the most innovative and creative projects for urban poor students in the nation. It is perhaps significant however, that none of the money necessary for this program was provided by the St. Louis school system, but instead, was granted by the Federal government.

Decision Making in the System
The urban school systems studied by Gittell and Hollander varied considerably in their responses to the vast influx of black students. The reason for this variability can be seen in two factors; the distribution of decision-making authority in the systems, and the pressure for participation by community, parents, and teachers. In St. Louis, as opposed to New York City, for example, the call for "community control" of public schools has been both faint and sporadic, because, it appears, the white community believes it already has control of the schools and the black community is not organized to challenge that white control. (In a school system with a black student population of 64 percent, three of the ten board of education members are black; the superintendent of schools is white.) Furthermore, such groups as the teachers, the local black organization supporting civil rights, the few vocal white liberals, and the organized business community have not actively sought to upset the status quo.

Since there is little pressure for more direct citizen participation in the affairs of the schools, the St. Louis system has been slow to respond to change. Although there is no prospect for effective community control of the schools, the school system itself has taken steps to decentralize its operations through the creation of six district superintendent positions. Until 1967 these district superintendents administered only grades kindergarten through eight, but the responsibility has now been expanded to include high schools as well. Though the creation of these six posts was touted as a means of bringing decision making in the schools closer to the needs of students, the vision has not been realized. Restricted in budgetary and policy considerations to the status of minor powers, the six district superintendents must also comply with curriculum dictates of the central administration. It is for this reason that all classrooms in the city at the same grade level are using the same curriculum. Likewise, the district superintendents lack authority to modify instructional procedures, for all teachers in the elementary schools are required to teach a specified number of minutes of each subject; for instance, 250 minutes a week of reading, 135 of science, and 75 of spelling at the fourth grade level. In the face of such rigidity, it is testimony in favor of Dr. Shepard's program that he has had the successes that he has. Though the district superintendents in St. Louis are organizationally in a position to have direct and significant influence on the classrooms of their districts, they appear in actuality to serve as a type of buffer zone between the central administration and the dissatisfactions of parents, teachers, and community leaders. Rather than possessing the necessary power to alter the conditions of their schools, they serve as an outer defense perimeter to guard the place where the real power in the school system lies—the center.

The center in St. Louis is the Board of Education. It is there that all major educational policy decisions are made and any changes in the system must originate. Thus the creation of a three-tier tracking system, the initiation of a proficiency and reading test which every student must pass to receive his high school diploma, the perpetuation of a racially separatist neighborhood school concept, and the resistance to alternative curriculum materials all result from decisions by the Board. In addition, the major administrative posts in the school system are filled by appointees of the Board. Such a situation effectively serves to dampen the enthusiasm of Board appointees for changes that do not have Board approval.

The major appointee of the Board is the Superintendent of Schools.

His $25,000-a-year position carries no significant policy-making authority independent of the Board. He essentially functions as the operations manager for the school system. It is indicative of the Board's determination to maintain control over decision making that it has chosen seven of the last eight superintendents from within the St. Louis system. By thus avoiding the uncertainty of dealing with outsiders, the Board insures that its appointees will be "safe."

As suggested earlier, the other determinant of a school system's response to a large influx of black students is the degree participation of parents, teachers, and community. In St. Louis the teachers have spent much energy fighting among themselves over such questions as who was to serve as the bargaining agent in contract negotiations, whether blacks or whites were to control the teacher organizations, and whether to define their activities as unionist or professional. When they have turned their attention to the Board, the paramount issues have been salaries and fringe benefits. Proposals for improving the teaching situation (other than occasional statements in favor of lower class size) have been noticeably absent. Sjoberg et al. (1966) have suggested that this movement away from an identification with or commitment to the clients in a service-centered bureaucracy comes from an attempt to create an appropriate "professional" image. Maintaining social distance from the client is protection against accusations of "overidentifying" with his desires and claims, overidentification being viewed as an unprofessional indulgence.

With teachers in a city directing few of their energies toward restructuring the school system to allow more flexibility in curriculum, classroom activities, and community participation, one might turn to the parents and community as sources of dialogue and change. But again, in St. Louis there has been little movement on the part of parents to seek an active role in the education of their children. Doyle (1969) suggests the following:

. . . One must recognize that militancy has never been strong in St. Louis. The St. Louis Negro is Southern in style—polite, acquiescent, and, until recently, knew his place. Furthermore, the city has a second-generation Negro elite which exercises its own control over less advantaged blacks while enjoying a comfortable niche with both the white elite and the politicians. The Negro elite—as well as the white community—has demonstrated that militancy doesn't pay.

Yet militancy and participation are not synonymous. The Banneker District program of Dr. Shepard indicated that parents did participate in the activities of the schools when they believed that the schools were working for the benefit of their children. Mass meetings of parents and school personnel frequently attracted standing-room-only crowds, and hundreds signed a "Parent's Pledge" indicating their willingness to follow the ten points suggested to aid the improvement of their children's education.

For St. Louis, however, this has been the exception rather than the rule. And even this participation may have been more illusory than real, given the resistance of the system to inputs from outside the center. Signing of pledges and attendance at mass meetings may have become placebos to be given when there were no means for adequate treatment. Parents, community leaders, and teachers neither were nor are part of the decision-making apparatus of the St. Louis system and there is little indication that they are likely to become so in the near future. The choice appears to be one of participating on the conditions established by the Board or not participating at all. In either event, the center of power remains undisturbed.

Content with the tried and true, and seemingly impervious to pressures for change from the outside, the Board remains committed to approaches and philosophies that ignore the realities of the classrooms. But ignoring such realities does not make them go away. New responses are imperative. The massive influx of tens of thousands of black people into the city has resulted in a black community within St. Louis of nearly one-third of a million persons. The word "within" is used advisedly, for the black community is very much separate from the white. Taeuber and Taeuber (1965) note that the residential segregation index for St. Louis at the time of the 1960 census was 90.5. [The

higher the index (100 is maximum) the greater the residential separation of whites and blacks.] What this figure implies is that 905 of every
1,000 black families would have to be moved to achieve an equal distribution of blacks throughout the city. Residentially, St. Louis is a city
of nearly complete apartheid.

Racial Isolation in the Schools

Since the St. Louis schools emphasize the neighborhood school concept, it is inevitable that schools will reflect the racial separation that is
found in the community. Until the landmark school desegregation decision of the United States Supreme Court in *Brown* v. *Board of Education of Topeka,* Missouri law formally sanctioned the segregation of
schools by race. St. Louis sought after this decision to desegregate its
schools in a three-step program, but with little effect, as the neighborhood school concept insured the continuation of de facto segregation
in the place of de jure segregation. In its directive to desegregate the
schools, the Board instructed school officials to proceed in such a
manner as to necessitate ". . . a minimum of boundary changes in order
to relocate the smallest possible number of pupils." In St. Louis it is not
possible to have it both ways; the alternatives are to desegregate with
major relocation of boundaries to cross segregated neighborhoods or
to perpetuate the segregated pattern of neighborhood schools with a
"minimum of boundary changes." The school system has opted for the
latter.

At the time of his report to the United States Commission on Civil
Rights in 1967, Semmel (1967) found that approximately 90 percent of
all black elementary school pupils attended racially segregated black
schools.[3] Only 30 of the 123 elementary schools in the city were integrated based on the figures Semmel analyzed, and of those 30, 19

[3]For Semmel, any school which had more than 90 percent enrollment of one race was
a segregated school. Reference to a "black school" denotes a school with a black
enrollment above 90 percent, and reference to a "white school" denotes a school
with a white enrollment above 90 percent.

were integrated by means of a bussing program designed to alleviate overcrowding in the black schools. Thus in a city system with 123 elementary schools, only 11 schools were integrated by residential integration. Semmel also notes that all 11 schools which were integrated at the time of his report were showing an increasing black enrollment, evidence of the black pressure on white residential areas. Of the 12 high schools in the city, three were integrated at the time.

As a result of the de jure system of segregation in the schools before 1954, there existed in the city a completely dual system of schools and faculties save for the upper positions of the school administration. Below the Board of Education and the Superintendent, all other professional staff were divided by race—each to deal with schools of his own color. When the de jure system was abolished, both a benefit and a handicap faced the black personnel in the schools. The benefit was a large cadre of experienced black professionals already established as both administrators and teachers; the handicap was the legacy of a segregated system which stressed the "separate" but never acknowledged the "equal" in black-white relations.

When the Board of Education and various school officials undertook to merge the two groups of teachers and administrators after the 1954 decision, they abolished the criterion of race as a factor in the hiring, promotion, or transfer of personnel. Though at this point the school system was in a position to create truly integrated faculties, it was decided that "whenever possible employees were to retain their present assignments, being transferred only to meet the needs of the service" (St. Louis Board of Education, 1956). The decision to keep teachers in assignments held at the time de jure segregation was abolished virtually guaranteed that segregated faculties would remain intact. When examining the school faculties ten years later, Semmel (1967) concluded: "The basic pattern of faculty segregation at the elementary school level has not changed." In 1966, 48 black elementary schools had no white faculty member and 37 white elementary schools had no

black faculty member. Seventy percent of all elementary school faculties were de facto segregated.

A second factor contributing to the maintenance of segregated
school faculties has been the position of the two teacher unions on the
issue of the seniority system as the basis for requesting transfers from
one school to another. Both the St. Louis Teachers Association, affiliated with the National Education Association, and the St. Louis Teachers Union, affiliated with the American Federation of Teachers, have
persistently endorsed the seniority system and resisted any attempts
at its abolishment. Being unwilling to exercise the authority to transfer
teachers to create integrated faculties, the Board of Education has
condoned the use of the seniority system, thus perpetuating segregated teaching staffs. Relying on teacher voluntarism as the basis for
integrated faculties is like waiting for Godot. As Semmel (1967) notes:

. . . School officials are sympathetic to white teachers who seek to
leave Negro schools. Many of the white teachers who transferred were
women of middle age or advanced years whose teaching experience
had been with whites, often middle-class whites. School authorities
believe that many of these teachers lack both knowledge of the cultural background of Negro children from poverty-level families in the
center-city ghetto and the ability to deal with discipline problems that
often occur in the Negro slum school. School authorities reported that
some of these teachers expressed fears, whether real or imagined, of
working in all-Negro neighborhoods.

A third factor in the segregation of faculties is the dual system of en-
forcing discipline in the schools. From observations by members of
our research team, corroborated by the findings of Semmel, there appear to be two standards for administering discipline. Corporal punishment is nearly completely absent from white schools; but its use in
black schools has been acknowledged by school officials, and I observed it myself with some frequency. It is not clear whether corporal
punishment follows the segregation of faculties or whether, since
white teachers feel powerless in black schools because they dare not
employ it, its use leads to a segregated teaching staff. Nevertheless,

the dual system of disciplining children based on their color remains.

The placement of both new teachers and those doing their practice teaching in the city schools is the fourth means by which segregated faculties have been maintained. During the 1960s the St. Louis school system, like many other urban systems, was faced with a severe shortage of qualified teachers. The lure of newer facilities, higher fringe benefits, smaller class size, and a middle-class student body sent many teachers to the suburban areas surrounding the city. As a result, there were simply not enough certified teachers for the city school classrooms. During the 1968–1969 school year, the St. Louis system relied on the daily services of 415 substitutes to fill the classroom vacancies (St. Louis Board of Education, 1969). Of the 6,878 full-time teachers in the system in 1968–1969, nearly a third (2,012) did not have their teaching certificates. At the beginning of the same school year, the schools were faced with filling 536 vacancies left by teachers at the end of the previous academic year.

A significant source of teachers for the city schools has been the city teachers' college, operated by the school system itself. In 1966–1967 the enrollment at Harris Teachers College was 987, and it had increased to 1250 in the 1969–1970 school year. The teachers' college had during the decade consistently supplied between one-third and one-fifth of all new teachers entering the school system. In 1969–1970, 158 of the 716 new teachers hired for the St. Louis system came from Harris.

All new teachers coming into the St. Louis schools are assigned their first positions by the school administrators, though a teacher may request a specific school or geographic region. This authority of the central administration could well be used to create integrated faculties. To date, however, it has not been done. The school officials have insisted that they could not afford to assign white teachers to black schools for fear that the white teachers would turn elsewhere for a position. Thus, in the attempt to secure the services of as many white teachers as possible, the officials have institutionalized a procedure whereby the newly hired white teachers are first assigned to white schools (if the teacher so chooses) in hopes of keeping them from leaving for suburban schools. It is only after the assignment of the white teachers that the newly hired black teachers receive their classrooms for the upcoming year. With white teachers filling the slots available in white schools, blacks are given the remaining positions in the black schools. School officials have been unwilling to run the risk of learning whether white teachers would teach in a system that positively promoted the racial integration of school faculties (cf. Crain, 1968, for a further elaboration of the resistance of officials to school faculty integration.)

The requests and subsequent placement of graduates of a recent class from Harris Teachers College would suggest that fears for whites teaching in black schools may not be entirely justified. Before the beginning of the 1965–1966 school year, 71 white graduates from Harris accepted the following positions: 28 in all-white schools, 33 in integrated schools, and 15 in all-black schools. The school administration appeared less than eager to learn whether black Harris graduates could successfully teach in white schools. In the same year, ninety black graduates from Harris received the following positions: 64 in all-black schools, 23 in integrated schools, and 2 in all-white schools. Semmel, commenting on this situation, notes (1967):

The failure to assign Negro Harris graduates to white schools probably results from the reluctance of school authorities to send more than a small number of highly qualified, experienced Negro teachers into the white schools. In part this attitude is a response to white community prejudices; in part it is an attempt to demonstrate to the white community that Negro teachers are equal to any by sending only the best to the white schools. This attitude either drains the best Negro teachers from the Negro schools or keeps the number of Negro teachers available for white schools at a perpetual minimum. It is inherently discriminatory because school authorities have no reluctance to assign or keep the less qualified teachers, white or Negro, in the Negro schools.

The meshing of the teachers' college into the larger pattern of racial segregation in St. Louis schools is further evidenced by the placement of the senior year students in practice-teaching settings. Here again, the administration bows to fears of white hostility toward black teachers; in 1966, 29 of the 107 white seniors (only 27 percent) spent their semesters in all-white schools while 53 of 99 black students (more than 53 percent) spent their semesters in all-black schools. A 1970 interview with one of the administrators at Harris involved in placement of practice teachers revealed that an attempt was being made to provide an experience for all senior students in both black and white schools. The administrator suggested that it was a beneficial learning situation for the students to "teach in both a good and a bad school." When queried as to what constituted a good or bad school, he replied that the good schools were on the "south side" and the bad schools were on the "north side." (Such a geographical division represents an accurate separation of the city into racial groups; whites live in the south half of the city below Lindell Boulevard and the blacks in the north half above Lindell.)

At the beginning of this chapter it was noted that classrooms do not exist in a social, cultural, or political vacuum. Consequently, to analyze the racial composition of the city, its influence on the schools and faculty, the locus of decision making in the system, and its participants, and to describe the pervasive racial separation of blacks and whites from one another is to give some context for the discussion of events inside individual schools and classes. There is one further system-wide property of the St. Louis schools which should be elucidated before turning to a study of a single school. Given the continued influx of Harris Teachers College graduates into the city schools, examination of the curriculum and training program of that college should provide some indication of the background with which a substantial number of teachers come into their classrooms. It is important to note that this background includes more than specifics of pedagogical techniques; it also carries with it an ideology of how children learn and what one can expect from the good and bad schools of the city. An analysis of the program by which Harris teachers are prepared offers another opportunity to study the impact of the macrosystem on the events inside the microcosm of the classroom.

Teacher Preparation at Harris

The first two years of the Harris training program are highly similar to the liberal arts curriculum at most universities and colleges, with an introduction to history, literature, the natural and social sciences, and physical education courses. During the freshman year the only course directly related to teacher training is a three-hour course entitled "Introduction to the Elementary School." No training-related courses are offered during the sophomore year.

Professional training begins in earnest with the junior year. Courses are required in educational psychology, literature for children, language arts teaching, learning disabilities, and modern mathematics for teachers. The second semester also involves the student in his or her first encounter with a city school classroom. The course is entitled "Observation-Participation Teaching." Its members spend at least the first half of the semester observing teachers in classrooms and then gradually become involved themselves, teaching and leading group activities supervised by one teacher.

However, in an evaluation of the observation-teaching course, Connor and Smith (1967) show that in a sizable number of instances (though not a majority) the students are not allowed actually to participate in the class but spend the semester simply observing. Their next opportunity for classroom contact in the city schools does not come until the last semester of their senior year. It is then that the students work in classrooms as "apprentice teachers."

At the beginning of the apprentice teaching semester, all students are provided with a bulletin entitled *Apprentice Teaching Program.* Connor and Smith (1967, p. 7) have developed a series of statements

which they believe summarize the general objectives of the apprentice
program as outlined in the bulletin.

1. Understanding the "development of skills in each subject-matter area from Kindergarten through Grade VIII"
2. Understanding the "importance and relation of learning in primary levels to middle and upper levels"
3. Understanding the nature of good classroom organization and management
4. Understanding good teaching techniques with individuals and groups
5. Knowing classroom techniques or devices that are helpful to the teacher
6. Knowing about the school services in the building
7. Becoming acquainted with and knowing how to fill out school records
8. Understanding differences in background and behavior of pupils from different socioeconomic areas
9. Knowing how to evaluate pupil learning
10. Understanding the necessity of continuing development of one's knowledge in all the subject areas taught
11. Understanding the importance of developing good working relationships with the principal, teachers, pupils, other members of the staff and parents
12. Developing an understanding of children
13. Developing enthusiasm for teaching.

In an attempt to summarize these objectives, it may be well to note that of the thirteen, four deal with teaching children (4, 8, 9, 12); three deal with how to "navigate the system" (6, 7, 11); personal development is the aim of three (10, 12, 13); two others define the interrelationships of teaching material through the various grades (1, 2); and finally, two objectives deal expressly with techniques to ensure classroom "management" (3, 5). It is evident from this listing that the process of preparing the apprentice teacher for the classroom moves beyond the transmission of necessary pedagogical information to inculcate "acceptable" interpersonal behavior within the organization, the techniques of paper shuffling, and the desirability of creating in oneself the "motivation" to teach.

Conspicuously absent, it seems to me, from the list of objectives is any indication to the new apprentice that the classroom experience will be exciting, innovative, rewarding, stimulating, creative, or, conversely, frustrating, depressing, confusing, and disheartening. The orientation appears to be one of extreme utilitarianism with an emphasis upon good worker relations, good client management, and a minimum of emotional involvement in the activity itself. The teaching experience is not defined as good in its own right, but is approached as a task which must be dealt with pragmatically. In addition, "enthusiasm" to undertake the task is something that must be *developed*.

Erving Goffman (1959) has noted that when persons come into situations of social interaction, they attempt to present themselves in such a manner as to create congruence between the expectations of others and their own self-conceptions. He has also written (1961) that when one is dependent upon others to a considerable degree for "survival" within a particular social system, one will go to further extremes to present a self that conforms with the expectations of the others of importance within that system. One might expect that the apprentice teacher, dependent on "survival"[4] within the program at Harris for accreditation as a certified teacher, would be quite conscious of the "self" he or she presents.

The emphasis upon "correct" presentation has been extensively institutionalized at Harris. That is, the apprentice teacher does not have to rely on intuition for clues to expectations about classroom behavior. Rather, the college has codified its expectations for apprentices in a

---

[4]The evaluation of the performance of the apprentice is done by three individuals: the classroom teacher, the principal, and the college supervisor. It is the college supervisor who ultimately grades the student on her apprentice teaching and more importantly, decides if she should have a position in the St. Louis public schools.

listing of twenty statements under the heading, "What Makes a Good Apprentice." The list from *Apprentice Teacher Program* (1967) is included to give further evidence of the formal ideology of the Teachers College and what it desires in the way of an adequately socialized "end product."

1. Observations of the teacher and pupils are keen.
2. Assignments and instructions are clearly stated and understood and anticipate pupil difficulty.
3. Motivating devices are economical of time.
4. Opportunities are provided for pupils to exercise judgment and apply common sense.
5. Chalkboards and bulletin boards are used to advantage.
6. Penmanship is good.
7. Apprentice-pupil relationship reveals a fine spirit of cooperation.
8. Community resources are utilized.
9. Visual aids are employed.
10. The term "sit-down apprentice" does not apply.
11. Concerns himself vitally with skill development.
12. Concerns himself with pupil behavior, use of materials, time, and equipment.
13. Writing on the chalkboard is visible to all while it is being used.
14. Feels no hesitance about writing on the chalkboard.
15. Plans in advance.
16. Uses the experiences of the class.
17. Enriches himself by reading and interviewing profusely in case his background courses and experiences have been limited.
18. Develops new material with the class before it is used.
19. Knows where to get supplementary materials and how to use them.
20. Avoids exclusive use of the lecture method of presentation.

This list again reflects the utilitarian approach of Harris toward training future teachers. There is a strong emphasis upon a mastery of technique—assignments, economical use of "motivating devices," use of bulletin boards, penmanship, visual aids, writing on the chalkboard, supplementary materials, and methods of material presentation. By what is omitted from the list, one might gather that a sensitivity to cultural diversity, stimulation of creativity, and the creation of a milieu in which the child can make and evaluate his own learning options are considered less vital than the twenty points listed. The teacher must be "technique conscious" in order to stay "on top" of the class.

It is not unreasonable to hope that in a city school system which has a majority of black students, the teacher training program especially designed for the system would be cognizant of the characteristics of the students. At Harris, however, this does not appear to be the case. The emphasis is a traditional one oriented toward the language, culture, and norms governing white middle-class society. The apprentice teacher leaving Harris for a new position has had little or no classroom sensitization at the Teachers College to various aspects of white-black social and cultural variations. From observations, there are three readily apparent areas in which lack of training hinders the effectiveness of the teacher in the classroom situation. They are black linguistics, black culture and history, and the use of classroom paraprofessionals. Each of these can be commented upon briefly.

The English dialect spoken by black people, particularly those who are low-income, is not the same dialect spoken by whites. Evolving from the realities of slavery, segregation, racism, and northern ghetto life, there has developed within the black community a speech pattern that has an order and logic of its own. Yet when black children come to the public schools, they face a teacher, curriculum, and cultural system that deprecates the language they speak as "ghetto English" or "street talk." As a consequence, the black children are forced to communicate in a dialect foreign to their own. The training of teachers reinforces the notion that there is really only one "correct" way to speak and that this is to use the "standard" dialect of the schools. Harris Teachers College provides the prospective teacher no training in the structure, content, or the means by which black linguistics could be used in the classroom. The inevitable result is not only communication gaps between teacher and child, but the refusal of many teachers to allow children to speak the only way they know how. In one class I observed, a continual refrain from the teacher was "Shut your mouth until you learn to talk right."

A second area in which the teachers of black children should have competence is that termed black studies, black history, or Afro-American history.[5] So long as the teachers of black students have little or no understanding of the social and historical backdrop that frames the current conditions of the black population in the United States, they will continue to present incomplete and erroneous material. Much of what I observed black teachers teaching about black people was little more than stereotypes, conventional folk wisdom or simple racism.

The lack of training in black studies has two serious consequences for the teacher in the black classroom. The first is that without factual material, there is a randomness to discussions which offers students an incomplete view of black people. The student gathers bits and pieces, incorrect or correct, but without a sense of coherence or historical progression. The African background of his ancestors, the struggles of his forefathers under slavery, and the realities of American racism are ignored or downplayed as the student instead learns the myths of American history. (In one classroom, the only observed reference to a black historical figure was to Harriet Tubman.)

The second consequence, which follows from the first, is that schools perpetuate what they like to term the "cultural deprivation" of black students. To give black students a white history is to deprive black students of their own history. Whether deliberate or not, such an omission also thwarts the black student's development of his consciousness as a black person, which is integral to his survival as a person in American society. It is hypocritical for schools on the one hand to negate the

[5]Courses in black studies are offered at Harris, but there is no guarantee that a prospective teacher will have taken such courses. Black studies are one of eighteen elective areas in the Harris curriculum, and the student needs a total of six courses between two of the eighteen areas

society of the black student and on the other to lament the "lack of
motivation" black students display in a white curriculum.

The third lack in teacher training evolves from arrangements which
require that teachers manage the behavior of those in their classrooms. In the case of students, teachers decide when it is permissible
to go to the bathroom, to the playground, to the library or to the office
of the principal. The influx of paraprofessionals into the classrooms
has placed teachers in the position of having to manage a new group.
The federal programs of the Office of Economic Opportunity and the
Office of Education and those of Manpower Training have all sought to
provide employment and training, especially for low-income persons,
in the classrooms of urban schools. Many of the teachers observed in
this study did not make effective use of the paraprofessionals, and employed them at janitorial tasks such as cleaning mirrors in the bath-
rooms or sweeping the floors. Other tasks assigned included distrib-
uting food to children in the lunchroom, serving as ushers at school
assemblies and PTA meetings, or working the Mimeograph machine.

It is no secret that teachers also find themselves doing similar trivial
tasks during the course of a school day; and if these tasks must be
done, they can at least be shared with assistants. The issue, though, is
whether this is all that paraprofessionals are capable of contributing to
the classroom. Riessman and Gartner (1969) have concluded after a
survey of the bulk of the literature on the utilization of paraprofessionals in teaching-related activities: ". . . The illustrations presented
here, representative of many others, indicate that aides can have an
impact upon pupil learning and that their continued use and further
training may have an even more powerful effect." The program at Harris does not give the teacher any instruction in the use of aides to create such an impact in the classroom. As an area for employment, the
training of paraprofessionals will be of increasing importance in urban
schools, especially if certain mandatory work regulations are enacted
with regard to federal welfare legislation. To leave teachers unprepared to use aides to best advantage, to restrict this new talent to the

washing of mirrors and sweeping of floors, works ultimately to the detriment of students, teachers, and paraprofessionals themselves.

The general picture which emerges from an examination of the program at Harris Teachers College is one of strong adherence to traditional practices and values. The normative as well as functional aspects of the program serve to preserve the status quo in St. Louis schools—whether it be with regard to racial separation, insensitivity to black values and cultural heritage, the continued use of well-worn pedagogical techniques, or restriction of options for experimental teaching situations. The schools are seen as fulfilling their function in their present form, and the students of Harris are socialized to fit that form. Moreover, as future teachers they are trained not only to accept the system, but also to expect students to fit into the institutional arrangements of schooling. The result is that the children are managed, the equipment is preserved, and the records are completed.

Part 2: The School

A block away from a major thoroughfare, by which many whites travel each morning from the suburban areas into downtown and return home in the evening, stands Attucks School.[6] The school is located on the north side of the city in the black community. It shares a city block with several small homes, two burned-out buildings, a liquor store, and a service station. In the immediate vicinity are two corner grocery stores, four storefront churches, and a used tire and battery shop. The residential units in the area are primarily small single-family dwellings and two-story apartment buildings. In 1965 the census tract including Attucks School was listed as being 98 percent black (Liu, 1967). The racial composition of the school quite clearly reflects the racial characteristics of the neighborhood. There are slightly more than 900 stu-

[6]The names of the school, all staff, administrators, and students are pseudonyms. Names are provided to indicate that the discussion relates to living persons, not to fictional characters.

dents in the school, all of whom are black. Likewise, all teachers, administrators, secretaries, special service personnel and janitors are black. Since Attucks School was built in the early 1960s, a white child has never attended the school.

Premises

The outside appearance of Attucks School varies, depending upon the rate at which litter accumulates and the janitors replace the broken windows, from that of a building under siege to that of any typical new two-story elementary school. At the beginning of the school year the building is most attractive, but its appearance steadily deteriorates as the year progresses. During the first weeks, flowers bloom around the base of the flagpole and along the sidewalk leading to the main entrance. The grass is mowed and the hedges along the front of the building are trimmed and free of weeds. The large playground surrounding the school on two sides is cleared of broken glass and trash. The five-foot chain-link fence encompassing the playground has no debris caught at its base. With the coming of winter, less is done to maintain the appearance of the building, and by spring, flowers must push their way up through layers of paper, glass, and leaves. The most consistent work done on the outside during the winter is the replacing of broken windows with large sheets of plywood. The long rows of windows on the front side of the building by spring have achieved a checkerboard effect of wood alternating with glass. Only with the advent of spring are broken bottles and litter cleared away, the plywood replaced with glass once again, and the playgrounds swept.

As one enters Attucks School through the main entrance, the offices of administrators and special service personnel are to the left, two gymnasiums and the library in a corridor ahead, and the classrooms along a corridor to the right. The following note records impressions of the building on my first visit:

All the walls on the first floor were soft colors—yellow, blue, green, and beige. The color scheme matched a darker tone of a color on the lower half of the wall with a lighter tone of the same color on the upper half. The floors, of green and white tile, were clean and waxed. There were no noticeable marks on the walls or the floors. The building gave the general appearance of being well kept. Walking down the corridor of classrooms reminded me of walking through a modern hospital; the doors leading into classrooms resembled doors into wards. The atmosphere was aseptic.

Social and Cultural Themes in Attucks School: The "Ideology of Failure"

Perhaps the single most pervasive and influential theme within the school which gave support to the winners-losers dichotomy was the idea that very few of the Attucks students would "make it" in American society and that large numbers would not.[7] For any number of reasons cited—the small number of two-parent families, the overwhelming presence of poverty, the lack of parental concern and of reading material in the home—the teachers and the administrators of Attucks School expressed the belief that the majority of students were failures. As a consequence, the role of teacher *as teacher* became minimized for large numbers of children because there was a fatalistic assumption that teaching really could make no impact or reverse the skid into failure.

   The basis for this assumption was what the teachers and principals saw around them every day—that very few black people in American society do make it and large numbers are left out. Acting on what they believed to be true, the teachers attempted to salvage some fulfillment from their jobs by concentrating on those few students who they be-

[7]This section will not attempt to elaborate on all the social or cultural themes discernable in the school, but will focus on those that appear directly to reinforce notions of the inevitability that some children will become winners and others losers. Thus the themes, for example, of emphasizing the Christian religion; of school participation in holiday related events—Halloween, Valentine's Day, Thanksgiving, Christmas, Easter, and so on; and of American nationalism will not be analyzed.

lieved had some opportunity to escape "the streets." Overwhelmingly
in the classes observed, those few students designated by the teachers as possessing the necessary traits for mobility were the children of
middle-class black families trapped in the inner city by suburban racial
segregation.

The pervasive view that black schools are warehouses full of failures
permeated the attitudes of both administrators and teachers. One of
the principals at Attucks School suggested, when asked, what he believed would become of the children:

"Well, many of these children will go on. Most will finish elementary
school and most of them, I believe, will start in high school. Some
will drop out, though. A few of them will finish high school and start
college. I am trying to say that I don't think that the school is going
to make that much difference. If it does, you won't really be able to
say. I feel some will be successful, but most will be at the same level
as their parents. Some will be on relief. Now I would say that when
this generation grows up the percentage on relief [55% in the
school currently] should decrease, and that will be an accomplishment in itself."

One teacher who had stratified her children on perceived ability levels
noted:

"I guess the best way to describe it is to say that very few children
in my class are exceptional. I guess you could notice this just from
the way the children were seated this year. Those at Table 1 gave
consistently the most responses throughout the year and seemed
most interested and aware of what was going on in the classroom."

Of those children whom she placed at the remaining two tables, she
commented:

"It seems to me that some of the children at Table 2 and most all the
children at Table 3 at times seem to have no idea of what is going on
in the classroom and are off in another world all by themselves. It

just appears that some can make it and some cannot. I don't think that it is the teaching that affects those that cannot do it, but some are just basically low achievers."

A second grade teacher when interviewed expressed many of the same attitudes as the teacher quoted above. This teacher also tracked her students by table, although she did not use numbers for table designation. Instead she gave the three tables, ranked in descending order of perceived ability, the names "Tigers," "Cardinals," and "Clowns." Of the Tigers she noted:

"Well, they are my fastest group. They are all very smart. They all feel an education is important and most of them have goals in life as to what they want to be. They mostly want to go to college."

On the Cardinals:

"They are slow to finish their work, but they do get finished. You know, a lot of them, though, don't care to come to school too much."

Finally, the Clowns, whom she seated at the last table:

"Well, they are really slow. You know most of them are still doing first grade work.
    "They are very playful. They like to talk a lot. They are not very neat. . . . They always want to stand up. . . . All these children, too, are very aggressive.
    "I don't think education means much to them at this age. I know it doesn't mean much to Lou and Nick. To most of these kids, I don't think it matters very much.
    "This is just the way it goes for a lot of the kids in the class. They are not going to go anywhere."

The presence of such attitudes at all levels of the city public school system provided a constant reiteration of the causes for the failure of so many of the students. So long as the source of the failure of the students was held to be outside the structural and bureaucratic domain of the school itself, then the school and its practices were not called into question. In such a perspective, teachers were encouraged to "do the best they could" and be realistic in their assessment that they really could not do much for the majority of their students. As a consequence, since students were not to be taught yet had to remain within the school for many hours each day, the task for the teachers became one of maintaining control—insuring that the students did not disrupt the smooth functioning of their own confinement.

Violence and Control
Though the appearance of the school and the silence in the halls during class periods gave the impression of tranquility, there was an undercurrent of violence that was never far below the surface. Corporal punishment was administered by the teachers as well as by the principal in disregard of the rules. According to school regulations, no child was to be struck by anyone but the principal and then only in the presence of the classroom teacher. There appeared to be an informal agreement among the teachers that nothing be openly said about their use of corporal punishment—primarily, it seemed, because most of them relied on it. The teachers frequently stressed in interviews that they believed the children lacked the self-control necessary to maintain proper conduct in the halls and that the threat or use of violence was necessary to keep them "on the line."

During the periods of the day when there were large numbers of children in the hallways at one time, the teachers would come out of their rooms and stand by their doorways. They would carry long rattans four or five feet in length, wrapped in white adhesive tape. There appeared to be a general assumption shared by all the teachers as well as by the principal that the implicit threat of violence was necessary to insure that the children would move in an orderly fashion in the halls. Though I did not observe frequent use of rattans, there were occasions when the implicit threat was transferred into explicit violence.

As I left the kindergarten classroom at 2:05 p.m., the bell had just rung to begin recess. As I entered the hall, two boys were fighting with one another while the teacher was hitting them both on the back of the neck with a long rattan. There was a great deal of shouting. The halls appeared to be in complete chaos. A number of the teachers were out of their rooms and using their rattans. It was evident that, even though the teachers were hitting the children, they were not in control of the situation.

On another occasion, though I did not observe the actual use of rattans, their presence suggested the final resolution of any teacher-pupil conflict.

As I walked from the kindergarten classroom toward the principal's office during the recess period, I saw several teachers gathered around a group of students. One teacher called out in a loud voice, "Okay, now stay on that line. Boy, get yourself back on that line." This she said in a rather firm and harsh voice. The four teachers with this group of students all carried their rattans and one teacher kept hitting the side of her leg with her rattan.

Control of the children was a concern not only during recess but also during regular class sessions.

As I walked with several of the children from the kindergarten room to the nurse's office, we passed the room of one of the fourth grade teachers. She was standing by her desk, and we could quite easily hear her shout at one of the children: "You shut your big fat mouth and keep your head on the table or I'll keep it there for you."

The teachers' periodic discussions of methods of controlling the children and the necessity for doing so reinforced their belief that the children were extermely violence-prone. Within the classroom, they suggested, it was only the continual and persistent use of control-oriented behavior that inhibited the emergence of violence and the disruption of the teaching process. At least some of the teachers had chosen the grade levels at which they taught on the basis of how much discipline they thought necessary to control the children.

On the way to the teacher's lounge, Mrs. Benson introduced me to one of the special education teachers on the second floor, Mrs. Warner. The three of us began discussing the special education class in the school, and Mrs. Warner said that she had received a minor in special education, but that she would not mind going back to teaching children in a regular class. She stated that she would especially like to teach kindergarten because they "were all such cute little dolls. They will do anything you want." Mrs. Benson then commented that she didn't really like to teach the second grade, "because you have to spend so much time with them individually." She said, though, that she did like the children because they were "so lovable." "They will come up and love me and hug me and want to kiss me. You know, I'm afraid to shout at them because they are so small and so cute that I'm afraid that I will make one of them cry." Mrs. Warner then commented that the warmth of the children was one of the reasons that she liked kindergarten. She then noted, "You know, girl, you will never get me teaching some of those older kids. They would just as soon hit you as look at you." Mrs. Benson agreed and stated that that was the reason that she would never teach above the third grade level. She stated that children beyond third grade were so "tough and hard" that one could "not do anything with them."

Likewise, the seventh grade teacher said that she decided to teach seventh grade only after she knew she could "control them." She stated that since she could handle the older students, she would rather teach them instead of the younger "crybabies."

Mrs. Crawford said that she didn't worry too much about any of the students "jumping her" because they were all so "puny." She stated that she did have one boy who gave her a lot of trouble, but she smiled and said, "He chooses to stay home a lot so I don't have to worry." One of the other teachers said, "You mean David" and Mrs. Crawford responded, "Who else" Then several of the other teachers began to speak about David and his brothers and sisters in the school. They also commented about his mother coming to the school and "nagging" about the grades given to her children. Several of the teachers said that they would be glad when the children had all left the school, for then they would not have to deal with the mother.

With the very young children, a different technique was occasionally used—that of the threat of extreme punishment beyond the experience of the child.

As I walked past the door to the first grade classroom, I heard the teacher, Mrs. Logan, say to the children that she did not like to eat little boys and little girls. She stated that she was not a "mean animal." She said that she was their very best friend in the school and that anytime they ever had anything to tell her or ask her, they should do so because she was their friend. She then said, "I've never eaten a little boy or girl in my whole life." Her voice then became quite harsh, and she continued, "But when you want to go to the bathroom, you have to ask me; you cannot simply get up and walk out of the room."

Though the teacher said that she had never eaten a child and that she would not enjoy doing so, she implied that it might happen should the children fail to ask permission to go to the restroom. On another occasion during a field trip with the second grade class to a large building downtown, the teacher warned the children that they would have to stay away from the edge of the stairs or she would "throw them over the railing" to the floor two stories below. The children appeared to have no reason to doubt her word, and they all moved down the stairs staying very close to the wall. An adult would dismiss such threats as hollow, but perhaps they sound quite plausible to a five-year-old who hears them from a teacher.

When a teacher was out of her room for any length of time, it was an accepted practice in the school for a student from one of the eighth grade classes to come into the room and supervise the children. The older child was allowed to use whatever methods he or she deemed necessary to maintain control in the class. One such situation resulted in serious consequences:

As I was about to leave the nurse's office with Brad, four young girls walked into the office, one of them crying very loudly, almost hysterically. The nurse calmly walked over to them and asked what was the matter. One of the girls not crying explained that this girl had just come back to school after an eye operation and that a big girl in the classroom had hit her with a stick. The child that had been hit was in the first grade. The child was bent over and I could not tell what damage had been done to her eye. As I shortly walked back to the kindergarten classroom, I passed the first grade room. I looked in through the door window and observed a large eighth grade girl walking around the room indiscriminately striking the children with the rattan. Almost all of the children were out of their seats and making attempts to keep out of the reach of this girl. Several of the children were crying, one boy was holding the back of his neck and a girl was holding her arm. The older girl continued to stalk around the room attempting to reach the children to strike them. She was shouting to them to "shut up," "sit down," and "git back in your seats." I entered the room, and as I did, the teacher from the room across the hall followed me. She dismissed the eighth grade student and told the first grade students to get ready for recess. Several of the children were sobbing.

When the teacher dismissed the eighth grade girl, she did so without rebuke, merely indicating that the girl could leave as it was time for recess and that she would now take the children out to recess with her own class. Apparently the situation did not seem to her to warrant any admonition to the older girl.

Older children were used to control younger children in other ways. The eighth grade boys were the school patrol, who had responsibility not only for helping children to cross the streets safely before and after school, but also for maintaining quiet and order in the halls and assisting the two teachers assigned to the playground during lunch period. The four boys assigned to the inside corridors were observed pushing smaller children in the halls as well as forcing them out of the halls onto the playground. The four patrol boys on the playground, who shared with the teachers the responsibility of lining up the children by grade before they could reenter the school after a recess or lunch period, would push and shove the children into lines on the playground and then shove them as they began to walk inside. (All the children marched double file into the school with the younger grades first, girls before boys.) Children in the upper grades were also used as lunchroom monitors to supervise the younger children as they ate. No teachers were assigned to lunchroom duty. Supervision was assumed by the cooks, occasionally by a teacher's aide, by the older children, and by the physical education instructors. The principal was seldom present. *The violence system of the school was hierarchical, all teachers and the principal free to exercise violence against any children and the older children free to do so against the younger.* At least some of the students recognized this; several fourth graders told me that they wished they were eighth grade patrol boys so they could "beat up" children they did not like.

The violence within the school appeared to reflect the presence of violence in the larger cultural milieu. On one occasion when I went to the school, the children were very excited and related that there had just been a murder in front of the school. A man walking on the sidewalk had been shot from a passing car. During another visit, I witnessed the police chasing several fugitives in front of the school, and a number of shots were fired. I once observed a very real threat to the kindergarten teacher, as two men came off the street and intruded into the classroom.

Two men, appearing to be in their early twenties, walked into the classroom and stood by the door. The kindergarten teacher walked over to them and asked what they were doing. They replied that they were watching. She became very firm and told them that they would have to leave the school. At first they refused to move and she said again, "I'm asking you to leave or I will call the principal." They then left the classroom and stood in the hallway. She asked them if either had a pass to be in the building and they stated that they did. She asked to see it and they told her that they weren't going to show it to her. She then went to the first grade classroom, saying that she would call the office. The men left the building and she soon returned to the class. She commented to me that the teachers on the first floor were often bothered by intruders off the street. She stated that they were "roughhousers" who were no longer in school and wanted to cause trouble for the teachers and the students. The kindergarten teacher appeared quite disturbed and upset. Before she went back in front of the class, she stated, "It's awfully hard to teach when you have to be a policeman too."

With no other means at her disposal, the kindergarten teacher attempted to bluff her way out of the situation and make the men leave without incident. It was a bluff because there was no phone in the first grade classroom by which the teacher could contact the office. There was a two-way communications system in the building but the switch was in the principal's office. The teachers spoke of this type of incursion on several occasions and expressed anxiety over the lack of security in the school during class hours. They pointed out that, with each teacher isolated in her room, there was little chance anyone would know if another was in danger.

Patterns of Reciprocity

Attucks School is one subunit of a larger organized and structured bureaucratic organization, the city public school system. There is a series of regulations which all schools in the city must follow, and the authority to insure compliance lies with the central administration. The individual schools also have their own rules, and on this level it is the principal who insures that regulations and goals are not disregarded. As Gouldner (1954) and many others have noted, within a bureaucracy and its series of formal rules there develop informal norms and patterns of behavior. An example I observed of the impact of failure to adhere to established norms involved the two principals who were at Attucks School during the course of my study. The first, Mr. Miller, was in the school during the 1967–1968 and 1968–1969 school years. The second, Mr. Elder, took over the position on September 1, 1969.

The principal's job entailed responsibility for the school and its functions, but not the authority commensurate with such responsibility. This was especially true of the principal's relationship with the teaching staff. He was dependent upon their performance in their roles as teachers and their acceptance of his leadership in order for the school to function. Yet he did not have the formal power to dismiss teachers who would not comply with his "requests." (The principal was not in a position to make demands, for they might be ignored or challenged, thus creating a direct confrontation in which the exact extent of his authority was at question.) The teachers, on the other hand, were dependent upon the principal in at least one very crucial area—the disciplining of disruptive students in their classrooms. Regulations stipulated that teachers must request the principal to use physical punishment against a child. It was to be the prerogative of the principal to strike children. In Attucks School an informal norm of reciprocity developed whereby the teachers granted legitimacy and leadership to the principal in return for his discipline of difficult students.

During the 1967–1968 school year, the pattern of reciprocity between principal and teachers became seriously strained and was nearly broken by the end of the year. The conflict arose from the teachers' complaint that the principal, Mr. Miller, was failing to handle the disruptive students sent from the classroom to his office to sit for a period of time in the "bull pen." Occasionally, the teachers claimed, Mr. Miller would ask a student who had been thus detained as punishment to do special errands for him in the building. One teacher said that when a student whom she had sent to the office for disciplining came back in twenty minutes with a message from the principal, she decided that she would no longer send any of her students to the office. This was also the case with a number of the other teachers, most notably those from upper grades. An informal boycott of the principal's authority developed among many of the teachers as a response to his failure to take what they considered adequate measures against difficult students. The teachers said that Mr. Miller was not providing them with the necessary support to insure that they could teach without disruptions. Thus, a number of the teachers ignored the informal norm of reciprocity, and they began disciplining children within their individual rooms, seemingly without the knowledge or permission of the principal. Additional tactics employed by the teachers to negate the authority of the principal during that school year included either avoiding or leaving early from staff meetings, failing to participate on committees established by the principal, and not submitting reports on time to the office.

The formal bureaucratic structure of the city public school system provided a mechanism that enabled teachers to bypass the principal in the hierarchy and deal directly with the supervisor at the district level. As the displeasure of the teachers with Mr. Miller increased, several of them told me that they had expressed their views to the district office through the district supervisors. Mr. Miller was transferred to another school within the district at the end of the 1968–1969 school year. Subsequently, when I returned for formal observations in the 1969–1970 school year, different teachers related how they had urged the district office to remove Mr. Miller as principal. It is not possible to

state conclusively that the discontent of the teachers was the major
reason for the transfer, but it may have served as a significant catalyst.

After the arrival of the new principal, Mr. Elder, at the school for the
1969–1970 school year, I did not witness the same high incidence of
physical punishment among the teachers as in previous years when
Mr. Miller was principal. The frequency with which teachers used their
rattans during recess periods was also noticeably less. The continual
presence of the principal with children in the halls and his willingness,
in the words of one teacher, to "get down with the children instead of
always trying to be above them" were used to explain the decrease in
student disruption.

From the informal conversations of the teachers, I believe the amount
of classroom violence had also decreased. They commented repeatedly how well they liked the new principal and said that he handled
discipline problems to their satisfaction. The degree to which he would
"back them up" when discipline problems arose especially pleased
them. The informal norms of reciprocity reemerged. The teachers actively complied with the requests of the principal, and he, in turn, dealt
with disruptive behavior in the classrooms. All appeared to recognize
the necessity for this mutual support as movement toward the establishment of the exchange began. Several teachers sent students to the
office on the first full day of school, and, there was perfect attendance
at the first staff meetings the principal called. But even though Mr.
Elder supported his staff in discipline matters, the threat of violence
and punishment continued to be present in the school. While acts of
violence in the halls decreased considerably, the teachers still occasionally exercised the use of corporal punishment within their individual classrooms. I observed both the second and fourth grade teachers
strike children.

Exchange of Information
The teachers at Attucks School also developed among themselves a
series of informal norms governing the exchange of information consid-

ered important either to individuals or to the group. The most important of these obliged a teacher to share with others pertinent information on classroom organization or control. Though there was occasional trading of suggestions on methods of discipline, teachers primarily shared information regarding persons believed to be disruptive to the classroom routine, whether parents or students. When a teacher had trouble with a certain student or parent, she would pass this information on to the others, most often at either the recess or lunch period. On several occasions, I noted teachers making a special effort to inform another teacher about a student entering her class who was labeled disruptive.

One student and his family who had acquired an undesirable reputation among the teachers were David and his mother (mentioned earlier in the comments of the seventh grade teacher, Mrs. Crawford). At one time, David had been transferred to another school because of "classroom overcrowding," according to the teacher.

As the gossip about Miss Stern drew to a close, a teacher from the fifth grade came into the room momentarily and told Mrs. Crawford that she had better "be careful" because she had heard that David was being transferred back to Attucks School. Mrs. Crawford commented, "That boy better not come back over here, because if he comes, I go. I've already got Jim and Terry, and if I have David besides, it's all over." The teacher who had come into the room responded, "I'm not sure, but I heard the principal talking about it on the phone." "Girl, I sure hope not," was the reply of Mrs. Crawford.

Being thus forewarned, the teacher then had the options of requesting the principal that David be placed in a different room or attempting to arrange an exchange with another of the seventh grade teachers for one of their difficult students. A third possibility would, of course, have been to argue that continued "classroom overcrowding" made it unfeasible to bring David back into the room. Regardless of personal relations, the teachers were expected to share information with others directly affected. At no time did I hear of a teacher deliberately with-holding information from another teacher because of either personal animosity or belief that the other teacher had failed on a previous oc-casion to reciprocate information.

An Atmosphere for Failure?

It is a premise of this study that to understand the phenomenon of aca-demic success or failure among black children in urban schools, one must look beyond the boundaries of the individual classroom and ex-amine the social and cultural milieu of the school itself. *In Attucks School both the milieu of the classroom and the milieu of the school appeared to sustain one another in a pattern of reinforcement of ac-cepted values and modes of behavior.* The ideology of failure, the presence of violence and control-oriented behavior, patterns of teacher-principal reciprocity, and exchange of information among the teachers all helped to establish the atmosphere within the school and within individual classrooms. There was a cycle in which the milieu of the school influenced the learning experience of the children, which in turn helped to define the behavior and responses of the teachers and principal who had major responsibility for the social themes set by the school.

Such conditions as negative expectations for the children, the utiliza-tion of violence, and the exchange of deprecatory information among teachers are destructive of a humane and supportive learning milieu. They may in fact sustain the very forms of behavior and academic per-formance which the teachers decry. The principal and the teachers conform to patterns of behavior they claim to be necessary because of the performance of the students and thus place themselves in the posi-tion of instigating and reinforcing the failure and withdrawal of stu-dents.

Furthermore, so long as the structure and orientation of a school like Attucks retain the form described, one can expect these social and cultural conditions to continue. For example, the organizational arrangements of the school sustain the presence of violence by causing it to be sanctioned as punishment and accepted as legitimate by school officials. The debate within Attucks School was not about whether violence should be used, but about when it was appropriate. This suggests that if there is serious intention of treating black children in a more humane manner within the school palliative measures of "restraining" the use of violence will not be sufficient. Rather, there will have to be a fundamental shift in how black children within the school are viewed. They must no longer be viewed as people to be "controlled," but rather as individuals to be taught and, most importantly, respected. The use of coercion and violence on children as young as four or five to insure institutional conformity reflects on the nature of the institution as well as the regard in which the children are held by those who know them incapable of defending themselves.

Kindergarten: Beginning of the Journey

2

Kindergarten in American society is not considered to be "real" school. It is instead a year of orientation for children four, five, or six years old that prepares them socially and emotionally to participate in an institution which will consume the major portion of their lives for the next twelve years or more. The goal of kindergarten is to lay the foundation of acceptable behaviors and attitudes that make a "good" student. Kindergarten might be called an academic "boot camp," entrusted with the task of transforming compulsory draftees into willing participants. Its success is an important consideration in the life chances of any child.

The St. Louis school system traditionally provided three days before the beginning of the school year in which parents could come to the school to register their children. When a child was registered for kindergarten, parents were given a green brochure outlining the kindergarten experience. It described activities designed to prepare the child for reading, arithmetic, and "school adjustment." The brochure also offered the parents a series of suggestions on how they could aid in preparing their children for kindergarten. Each of the pages listing an activity the parent could share with the child illustrated the same thing taking place in a classroom. Each of the parent-child activities was labeled with a large red "DO." For example:

DO give your child a chance to play with children his own age.

Do show interest in the work your child brings home from school.

DO take your child to interesting places like the zoo and the riverfront.

DO activities with your child to help him learn of his world.

1. Put water outside to freeze, bring it inside to melt.

2. Mark important days on the calendar for your child.

3. Look at picture books with your child.

4. Read to your child as much as possible.

The classroom in the illustrations contained twenty-five white students, four black students, and a white teacher.

When registering, the parents were also asked to complete a number of forms requesting information on any preschool experience and medical information about immunizations, allergies, or special physical conditions. There was also a standard form requesting name and address of parents, occupations, phone numbers, other individuals to contact in case of an emergency, and name of family doctor. The last form to be completed by the parents was entitled "Behavioral Questionnaire" and listed twenty-eight items. At the top of this questionnaire are the following directions in capital letters: "ARE YOU CONCERNED ABOUT YOUR CHILD IN ANY OF THE FOLLOWING AREAS? CIRCLE YES OR NO." The twenty-eight items included, for example, bed-wetting; wetting during the day; thumb sucking; restless, shy, gloomy, sulky, disobedient, or selfish behavior, lying, or bowel problems. One can only guess at the reputation which would precede a child listed as thumb-sucking, bed-wetting, gloomy, disobedient, selfish, lying, and loose-boweled.

The information supplied by the parents at the time of registration was only a portion of the information the kindergarten teacher possessed about the children when they first entered her room. Two days before the school year began, the teacher also received from the school social worker a list of children in the class who were receiving public welfare funds. (If a child came from a welfare home, this fact was made a part of his permanent record; the letters "ADC" were printed in red at the top of his transcript.) The final major source of information available to the teacher concerning her new students was her own experience and that of other teachers with older siblings from the same family. Many families who had children in Attucks School during my study had acquired among the teaching staff a reputation which fell into one of three categories: "good people," "never see them," or "troublemakers." There was a strong informal agreement among the teachers that they would share information about any of the families in the last category and especially about children moving from one grade to another. Frequently, on the first few days of school, discussions in the teachers' lounge turned to various families and which teacher now had which children. There were admonitions like "watch out," "don't get his old lady upset" or "just keep him colorin'."

It should be noted that not one of these various sources of information on the child available to the kindergarten teacher was directly related to academic potential. Rather, they were social facts about the occupational status of the home, medical care for the child, attitudes of other teachers, the child's behavior as seen by his parents, and the structure of his family—number of siblings, whether the child lived with one, both, or neither of his natural parents.

Day 1

Public school in St. Louis begins on the first Thursday after Labor Day. For this first day, Mrs. Samuels, a teacher's aide, was assigned to work with Mrs. Caplow, the regular kindergarten teacher. Before the children came into the room, both teachers busied themselves with preparations—the making of name tags, the organizing of necessary forms for those who would be late registrants, and arrangement of chairs around the tables. Mrs. Caplow brought three dolls from her storage closet which she said she had just completed sewing the night before.

All three dolls were made of white cloth with brown, yellow, and green dresses. Black yarn had been used for the hair. Earlier preparations also included the taping of pictures and posters on the walls.

On one of the walls is a large drawing of the "three little pigs." On another wall is a drawing of a red schoolhouse. Five labeled pictures are on one of the bulletin boards. The first is entitled "Summer Fun" and shows two white males in swim trunks on a high dive. The second is called "Summer Play" and shows six white children playing on a jungle gym. "Autumn" is a picture of a squirrel. "We Sing" shows thirteen white children and a white teacher gathered around a piano. The last picture is entitled "We Work," representing six white children engaged in handicraft activities on a picnic table. There is not a picture of a black person anywhere in the room.
     The first child, Laura, and her mother enter the room at 8:20. Laura's mother greets Mrs. Samuels, "Good morning." Mrs. Samuels responds, "Good morning, how are you?" Mrs. Caplow also replies, "Good morning. Haven't seen you since we worked together on the Headstart project." Again Mrs. Samuels: "So glad to see you, girl." Mother: "Have you met Laura?" Mrs. Samuels: "No, I haven't. Hello, Laura." Laura makes no answer and stands quietly looking around the room. The mother and Mrs. Samuels then walk to one corner of the room and begin talking. Laura is left standing in the middle of the room by herself.

   Laura, however, was not the only child left alone during the morning. Other parents also left their children as they spoke with a teacher or another parent. In addition, those children who were brought to the class by older brothers or sisters found themselves left to wander the room.

A boy, approximately twelve years old, brings his younger sister to the kindergarten. Mrs. Samuels asks the youth, "This child is not registered. Why didn't your mother register her?" The twelve-year-old responds that he doesn't know anything about registration and that his mother told him to bring his sister. Mrs. Caplow and Mrs. Samuels begin to discuss the situation and the decision is to register the child on the basis of information supplied by the older brother. Mrs. Caplow then asks the boy several questions about his younger sister. When finished with the questions, he leaves the room without a word to his younger sister, who stands by herself looking at the other children.

While Mrs. Caplow sat at her desk registering children as they came to the room, Mrs. Samuels was to spend her time with the children. However, the distracting power of Laura's mother kept Mrs. Samuels with her for the first full forty minutes of the class. During this interval Mrs. Samuels called to the children a few times to go and pick another toy from the toy chest or to try the same puzzle again. Laura was the only child who came to Mrs. Samuels to show her that she had completed her task. At another point, Mrs. Samuels passed by where the children were seated in order to speak to Mrs. Caplow. One of the children showed her completed pegboard to Mrs. Samuels, but she did not respond in any manner.

Of the nine children in the room at 8:50 none had cried or tried to leave the room when they had been left by a parent or older sibling. Shortly after 9:00, however, one child attempted to leave while his mother was still present.

A mother and boy come into the room and go to the teacher's desk. Mrs. Samuels walks over to the desk and says to Mrs. Caplow, "This boy I know from church." The boy begins to run for the outside door. Mrs. Samuels says in a rather firm voice to the child, "Stop. Don't go outside; come in here and sit down." On his way back to teacher's desk this child picks up one of the dolls Mrs. Caplow made and says to Mrs. Samuels, "What color this?" Mrs. Samuels responds, "What?" The boy says, "Green." Mrs. Samuels says, "Yes, you are right."

A sense of randomness pervaded many of the classroom activities throughout the early part of the morning. This is perhaps best characterized by the continued and unexplained presence of a twelve-year-old boy in the kindergarten class.

One mother who has brought a child to register for the class also brings along several older children. One of the older children immediately goes to the toy chest and begins to carry a number of toys to the table for the younger children to play with. One boy immediately begins to hoard all the toys as they are placed on the table. Mrs. Samuels comes to the table from the group of adults and asks the boy, "What if someone else wants to play with the toys?" The boy responds, "I want all." He has at this point accumulated nineteen toys while the rest of the children at the table have none. The mother who had brought along the older youth has left, but he remains in the kindergarten room.

Also, one child sat by herself at a table for 50 minutes without any comment from one of the teachers. This was the child who was brought by her older brother and left standing alone in the center of the room. Her name, it was later learned, was Lilly.

At 9:30 there were no longer any parents in the room registering children, and Mrs. Samuels made her first motion toward the establishment of organization in the class.

Mrs. Samuels says to the children, "All right, boys and girls, let's put our toys away very, very neatly. Let's walk, not run. Put your toys away very neatly. Who would like to help put the toys away? Put them in this box very neatly." The boy who had been hoarding the toys says, "No, they mine." The teacher takes the toys out of his hands and carries them to the box. Lilly continues to sit alone, no one having spoken to her for more than an hour. She has a pegboard, but she does not go to put it away at the teacher's general request to the class. Mrs. Samuels continues, "This table looks so very neat, but what about the other side?" (where Lilly sits). She turns to Lilly and says, "Oh, we should all put our toys away very quietly." Mrs. Samuels then takes the board from Lilly and puts it on a supply table nearby. After doing this, she comments, "Now, doesn't this all look so nice? All the chairs are under the table. Isn't it pretty, boys and girls? Now let's all of us go out to the center of the room and make a circle. Who knows what a circle is? We all hold hands. We are going to play 'Simon Says.'" (Note: She did not allow time for any child to make a response to her question.)

Though the class was to play the game "Simon Says" numerous times during the school year, it is worth documenting this very first instance for it gives not only an example of good teacher-student communication which eventually broke down, but also of the teacher's reactions.

Mrs. Samuels asks, "Does anyone know how to play Simon Says?" A boy responds, "We all do what Simon Says." Mrs. Samuels: "Yes, do only what Simon Says. Do not do anything when someone says 'I say.' Let me give you an example. Whenever Simon Says to raise your hands, you all raise your hands. But when I say, 'I say raise your hands,' keep your hands down. I think I would like to be Simon Says first." Mrs. Samuels begins the game with "Simon Says, raise your hand." All the children except Randall raise their hands. Then she says, "Simon Says to touch your toes." Again all the children but Randall touch their toes. He stands with hands on hips. She continues with "I say to put your hands on your hips." All but two of the children do not follow. Randall remains with his hands on his hips and one girl does the same. "Now who would like to be Simon Says?" A girl answers, "I would." "All right, go ahead." The girl comes into the center of the circle and says, "Simon Says to raise your hands." All of the children do it. Mrs. Samuels asks who would like to be next and Laura says she would. Laura comes into the circle and says, "Simon Says to raise your hands." All the children do.

"Now who would like to do it?" Another girl raises her hand, is chosen and comes into the circle. She says, "Simon Says to raise your hands." All the children do. After the third repetition of the command, Mrs. Samuels says, with some noticeable irritation in her voice, "Okay, that is all of that. I will be Simon Says again. Simon Says to line up to go back to the other side of the room, girls in front."

Mrs. Samuels led the children back to the chairs, where she asked them to be seated. She announced that they were going to talk about themselves. In the short interchange given here, there occurred what I have termed the "unprogrammed response," a response completely out of the context of what the teacher was trying to elicit from the children. This was to happen again and again during the course of the year.

Mrs. Samuels says to the children, "When I ask you a question, you can raise your hand to let me know you did it. If you do not want to raise your hands, you can nod your head. How do we all raise our hands?" A child responds, "Touch me toe." Another child says, "I have a pocketbook." A third says, "I have Cheerios for breakfast." Mrs. Samuels says in a brisk fashion, "No, listen to me. Do what I ask you to do." She then drops any further questioning and begins to read a poem about parts of the body. "This is the circle which is my head, this is my mouth where words are said," and so on.

At 10:10 the five-minutes-to-recess bell rings and Mrs. Caplow asks the boys to come with her to the boys' restroom and asks Mrs. Samuels to take the girls to the girls' restroom. There ensues a good amount of talking, some laughing, and the sound of water running, and the boys begin taking turns flushing the toilet when Mrs. Caplow steps out of the restroom. She goes back in for them and has them come to "the line" to prepare to go on the playground. Mrs. Samuels escorts the girls out and they take their places in front of the boys. The bell rings for recess; Mrs. Caplow opens the door and the children leave. At the same time, a mother and son enter the room to register.

Day 2

Returning to the school the next morning, I noted that a large pane of glass was broken in the principal's office. The shattered glass was still in the frame as well as on the sidewalk. The reception awaiting the children on their entrance into the kindergarten class was considerably more structured and organized than the previous day. Mrs. Caplow (who now had sole charge of the class) greeted each of the children at the door, instructed them to take a seat, and followed the last child to where they were all sitting. She asked them to come over to the piano and sit on the floor around the piano bench. This the children did. The first recorded instance of Mrs. Caplow's accepting the spontaneous comments of a child then occurred:

Frank says to Mrs. Caplow, "I goin' have a birthday." Mrs. Caplow responds, "Good, Frank. When is it?" Frank replies, "Next July."

It appeared that Mrs. Caplow was most willing to accept the spontaneity of the children when they were not involved in a structured activity. Several minutes later when she was calling the names of the children and handing them their name tags, Frank again called out, "Mrs. Caplow, I saw a elephant at Grant's Farm. I saw a horsey too." Mrs. Caplow ignored this comment and went on with the roll call. And again a bit later, when she was telling the children about the pet turtle in the room:

Mrs. Caplow asks the class, "Do any of you have a pet at home?" Joe replies, "I have a big dog. He a big dog and he bite you if you hit him in the mouth." Mrs. Caplow responds, "But you can play with him, can't you?" Joe says, "Yeah." Other children at this point begin to talk of their pets, but the teacher ignores their comments and tells them that they are not to touch the pets in the classroom.

Another pattern of communication between the teacher and the children that was to occur frequently was one in which the teacher introduced an element of mystification into an explanation given in answer to a question or comment from one of the children.

Mrs. Caplow is explaining to the children that it is important not to touch the pets in the class for yesterday in the afternoon section one of the pupils took a goldfish from the bowl and it died. She then points to the turtle bowl and says that the children are not to touch the turtle. One of the boys calls out, "You got a play turtle in the jar." Mrs. Caplow responds, "Yes, that turtle is there to keep the turtle shell hard. It is a naturalizer to keep the water just right for the turtle." (The boy was referring to an imitation chemical turtle placed on one of the rocks in the bowl.) The boy who made the comment gives no reply.

When Mrs. Caplow had completed the discussion on pets, she instructed the children:

"All right, stand up in a nice circle. Each of you is going to have a chance to count the number of children in the class." She begins with LeRoy. LeRoy walks around the room touching each child on the shoulder, counting as he goes: "One, two, three, four, five, six, thirteen, twenty-seven, ninety-five." "All right, LeRoy. Now it is your turn, Mary."

The acceptance of an incorrect performance without comment was frequent during the remainder of the year. In this instance, other children also counted incorrectly, but not in the same pattern as LeRoy, and Mrs. Caplow accepted all their attempts with an "Okay," "Thank you," or "All right." At no point during the morning was there ever a correct counting of the children. A corollary to the teacher's accepting incorrect information from the students occurred when she herself gave them incorrect information.

After the children have counted the other students, Mrs. Caplow leads them over to the turtle bowl, where she shows the class how she feeds the turtle. After the feeding, she asks the class to go to their chairs because she is going to read a story to them. When the children are seated, she brings out a small book entitled *Today I Go To School.* After reading several pages about a girl leaving home and walking to school, Mrs. Caplow turns the book around to show a picture of the girl in her new class. Mrs. Caplow says, "This class looks just like ours." All the children in the picture are white and the teacher in the picture has blond hair and blue eyes.

While Mrs. Caplow was reading to the students, Susan sat by herself in a far part of the room looking at the rest of the class. Mrs. Caplow had tried repeatedly earlier in the morning to get Susan to join the activities of the class, but Susan consistently withdrew from the other students. Shortly after Susan arrived that morning and came to the semicircle where Mrs. Caplow was calling the roll, she had left the group. Mrs. Caplow asked her to come back and she did. This occurred, however, three times in the space of ten minutes. The fourth time Susan left the group she hid behind the outside door.

Mrs. Caplow sees Susan leave the group and go outside. Susan is crouching behind the door. Mrs. Caplow goes after Susan and says, "Susan, come here right now." The tone of her voice is one of irritation and impatience. Susan starts back into the room and Mrs. Caplow grabs her by the arm and brings her back to where the rest of the students are seated. When Mrs. Caplow and Susan reach the group, Mrs. Caplow pushes Susan down to the floor. Susan begins to cry.

Mrs. Caplow's use of physical restraint was not effective in hindering Susan from again attempting to leave the group. She did so again in a few minutes. From that instance, Mrs. Caplow simply ignored the child and only occasionally asked if she would like to return to the rest of the group. Several times she did return, but more frequently she would only shake her head "no." Until recess at 10:15, Susan spent most of her time alone at the other end of the room. She did line up with the girls to go outside when the 10:10 "recess ready" bell rang.

Day 4

During the time of my visit, 8:25 to 10:15 a.m., Mrs. Caplow did not appear. Likewise, no substitute or replacement appeared. The children were left entirely on their own. There was a good deal of movement among the children and a noise level above that of my previous two visits, but the movement and noise came from children engaged in activities of their own choosing.

One boy is looking at the bird in the birdcage. Two other boys are at the toy chest. Two girls are at the play stove and the rest of the children are seated at the tables. Several of the children at the tables are either working with the pegboards or stringing beads on a long cord. A spontaneous differentiation of the group by sex begins to emerge as the boys all gravitate to the toy chest while all the girls go to the tables and work with either the pegs or beads. Shortly one girl enters the room eating a bag of potato chips. A boy picks up an airplane and begins to sing the national anthem. One girl puts her head on her desk and is about to fall asleep.

At 8:40 a mother came into the room to register her daughter. Her expression was one of surprise as she looked into the room. The boys by that time had become more active, and they were running through the room with trucks, hitting the girls on the backs of their heads. The girls remained very passive and did not attempt either to defend themselves or strike back at the boys. Two of the boys began fighting among themselves on the floor with a third boy on top of both of them. The mother and her daughter went and sat by the piano. At this point the first grade teacher walked into the room and asked if Mrs. Caplow was in the room. The children and I all said that she was not.

Upon hearing that Mrs. Caplow is absent, the teacher shrugs her shoulders, picks one of the boys, and begins to leave. On her way out, she asks the children if they have something to do. She tells them in a commanding manner to "Get quiet." She continues, "All the girls are so quiet and beautiful. The boys get quiet and busy also. Everybody stay nice and quiet as you wait for Mrs. Caplow." She then leaves with the boy.

Upon the teacher's direction that everyone was to "stay nice and quiet," the children who were out of their seats either went to the toy chest or to the play area. Lilly and one other girl continued to sit immobile at their desks and did not move for more than an hour. They simply sat and watched the other children. There was no observed verbal exchange between them, though they sat next to each other.

For the next twenty minutes the classroom was a place of activity and enjoyment. The boys were no longer hitting the girls or each other. Several of the girls got water from the sink and placed it in pots on top of the play stove. They acted out an elaborate scene of playing house and cooking for a meal, setting out some dishes for the meal. Then the boys began to take the dishes from the girls, and one of the girls began to struggle to keep them. At this point the same first grade teacher reentered the room.

She asks, in a rather harsh manner, "Is everybody busy?" The girl who was struggling with the boys tells the teacher, "The boys keep snatchin' my things." In a rather sarcastic fashion the teacher says to the boys, "Don't we know that boys play with boys' things and that girls play with girls' things?" She then turns to Joe and says in a loud, harsh voice, "Hey, little fellow, get quiet. Find something to do. Not so loud, little boy." She then turns to the girls at the table and asks, "Do all you ladies have something to do?" When I question the teacher as to the whereabouts of Mrs. Caplow, she says, "Guess she might be at a meeting."

When the teacher left the room, the children immediately returned to their previous level of noise and activity. Several childern also began to take on the job of classroom management. Laura, on two occasions, told other students they were not to play with the piano. She also said to the entire class that they should clean the room before Mrs. Caplow came. The children continued their pursuits, either individually or collectively in small groups. They asked neither me nor the first grade teacher where Mrs. Caplow was.

At 9:50 a.m. the woman who had sat with her daughter on the piano bench for an hour and ten minutes stood up and said to me, "I got to go. If she ain't gonna come, I got things to do. Can't sit here all day." With that she gave me the registration material for her child and left the room. Almost simultaneously another mother and her child entered the room. This mother also gave her registration material to me, though I said that I was not the teacher and in no position to register her child. She replied that the principal had said I would take the material. She handed them to me and left the room. As soon as she left, her son came sobbing to me. I had to hold the boy for more than five minutes to quiet him. Finally I asked if he would like to work on a pegboard and he said that he would. I found a pegboard for him and he immediately became absorbed. Many of the other students continued to keep themselves occupied:

Five of the girls have gotten paper and taken it to the painting easel. They all begin to paint. The boy who was crying is actively engaged with the pegs, and since I showed him the technique, three other boys have gotten pegs and pegboards and joined him at one of the tables. A fifth boy sits and watches while the sixth boy in the room plays with trucks by the toy chest. A jar of red paint falls from one of the easels and I ask the girls if they will help clean up the paint. They say that they will and go to the restroom for paper towels.

When it was time for the recess, the first grade teacher came into the room and had the children form a line. I left the room at this point and went to the principal's office to speak with Mr. Miller. He said, when I told him that the kindergarten room had no teacher, that he was aware of the situation and that he was certain another teacher would voluntarily take the class. Perhaps he was reluctant to ask a teacher directly to supervise the room; if so, his waiting for a volunteer had not succeeded.

Day 5

On my arrival at the school, I noted two more broken windows in the principal's office. Glass was scattered on his desk. In the kindergarten room, the children were beginning their opening exercises, which opened with the singing of "My Country, 'Tis of Thee," followed by the Pledge of Allegiance and finally closing with a prayer. The teacher would say each line in the three parts for the students, who were expected to repeat it. The prayer the children were saying was as follows: "Now before we work today/ Let us bow our heads and pray/ To God who kept us through the night/ And woke us to the morning light./ Help us, Lord, to love Thee more than we ever loved before./ In our work and in our play, be Thou with us every day."

   Apparently Mrs. Caplow had returned to the class the previous day shortly after the recess period, for she had had time to take the children on a tour of the school building to meet the "school helpers."

Mrs. Caplow asks, "Now, boys and girls, who remembers what we did yesterday on our tour of the school?" She then proceeds to call on several of the children as they raise their hands. One child says, "We saw principal." Another says "We saw room wit' lot book." Mrs. Caplow responds, "Yes, boys and girls, we saw and met our school helpers." She then takes pictures of a principal, a doctor, a custodian, a nurse, a teacher, and a secretary and shows them to the children one at a time, and says that these are pictures of their school helpers. All the pictures are of whites and most have blond hair. One child comments that the picture of the principal doesn't look like the principal and the teacher says with emphasis that it is a picture of the principal. The child again says the picture does not look like the principal.

The discussion of the trip through the school the previous morning was a lead into a plan for the children to take a trip around the outside of the building.

Mrs. Caplow says, "Now we are going to take a tour of the outside of our school." Joe says, "I saw a big grouchy bear out there this mornin'." Mrs. Caplow does not respond to Joe's comment.

The teacher and the children then proceeded to walk around the outside of the school, the children displaying the most interest in the ashes that were coming from the chimney of the school. Several of the children remarked that they had never seen such large mosquitoes as were coming from the chimney. Another child, Frank, commented on the large number of parrots on the playground, and Laura corrected him that they were pigeons. When the children returned from the trip, the teacher suggested that the class write on the blackboard a story of their tour. This suggestion produced a certain degree of anxiety in the children.

Mrs. Caplow says, "Let's write a story about our school tour." One child says, "I write no story." Another, "I no want to." A third, "I want to paint." Mrs. Caplow responds, "I know you do not want to, but we must learn how to read and write." Joe says, "I want to make horseshoe." Mrs. Caplow says, "Not now, Joe." Mrs. Caplow now writes on the top of the blackboard, "Our School Tour." She then says, "Okay, boys and girls, what did we do on our school tour?" "Went outside," was the response from one child. Mrs. Caplow: "Did we take a tour?" No response from the children, and she continues, "What is a tour?" Laura says, "A trip." Mrs. Caplow: "Okay, let's write, 'We took a trip and we met our school helpers.' " (Actually they met no one.) She then says, "That is a short story."

Situations such as this, in which the children did not participate with the teacher as she attempted to elicit responses from them, began to occur frequently, resulting in a "phantom performance" by the teacher. She would ask questions and the children would make no reply. The teacher would, however, proceed as if the children had answered her.

When Mrs. Caplow finished the "short story," she told the children that they would now have an opportunity to draw a picture of the school.

Susan calls out, "I ain't got no paper." Mrs. Caplow responds: "Oh, no, Susan, let's not say 'ain't.' Let's say, "I haven't any paper.' " Susan says, "I haven't no paper."

This short exchange between Susan and Mrs. Caplow underscores what was increasingly evident in the class—that some of the children were speaking in a manner acceptable to Mrs. Caplow and others were not. In short, there was one group who used standard American English with the teacher, while another group used black American English. Mrs. Caplow would accept comments from the children in the former but not in the latter. Throughout the year she corrected the pronunciation and grammar of those who used black American English, which she termed "street talk" and said had no place in the classroom. She frequently told several students that they should "not open their mouths until they learn to talk right." As a result, the verbal interaction between the teacher and these children gradually deteriorated to a low level of interchange.

Mrs. Caplow noted that she was using a prayer in the opening exercises and stated that the principal, Mr. Miller, had given the teachers no directive. He simply stated that if they wished to pray, they could. I asked about the recent Supreme Court ruling banning prayers from the school and she responded, "The Supreme Court said that you cannot force a child to pray."

She said she wanted to hold a tea for the parents the coming week and that later in the same week she would like to take the children on a field trip. I asked where the children would go on the trip and she said that they would go to the city park to "look at the leaves change colors."

She continued, "You notice, right now, I am spending a lot of time trying to orient the children to the school. The next part of the program will be a safety program when I discuss red, yellow, and green lights and stop signs. I try to have one new idea for the children each day. I asked what the new idea for today would be and she stated that it was the school prayer. She stated that yesterday the idea was the calendar and Monday it had been the Pledge of Allegiance to the Flag. She commented that she had to "go slow with the children because they have such short attention spans" and that they are so "physical in all their actions."

In a rather random fashion she then discussed future field trips to the city museum and the use of audiovisual materials in the class— especially several programs on television. She spoke of how the children would develop through the year as they learned to play together, how their skill in coloring and printing and their speaking ability would also improve. She stated that it makes her feel very good when the first grade teacher comes and tells her how nicely her ex-kindergarten children are progressing. Finally, she commented, "You know, the social development of these children is just as important as what they learn. We must teach them how to play together."

A number of clues about the assumptions that Mrs. Caplow brought to her teaching can be deduced from this short chat. At least a part of her "Teaching Credo" might be stated as follows:

1. Religion is important to children and should be taught, even if it means misinterpreting the law.
2. A teacher should have "ideas" to pass on to her students.

3. Electronic equipment is helpful to the teaching process.

Relating to children specifically:

4. Children should be aware of nature.
5. Children should be aware of safety procedures and the school sur- roundings.
6. The attention span of the kindergarten child is short.
7. Kindergarten children are "physical in their actions."
8. Social development is crucial at this age; in fact, is equal in impor- tance to the teaching of academic materials.
9. Children must be taught "groupness," that is, "to play together."
10. As the children grow older, social and academic skills will both improve.

From observations so far in the class, several others could be added:

11. Standard American English is acceptable in the classroom, black American English is not.
12. Girls are orderly and neat, boys are rowdy and messy.
13. In order for a lesson to be successful, the teacher must have the attention of all the students at one time.
14. When children leave the classroom, they should do so in silence and lined up, girls before boys.
15. An important component of schooling is learning a patterned rou- tine of activities. As a corollary, once the routine is set, teachers should not deviate from it.

Day 8

The children and the teacher had evolved a pattern of organization and a routine for the day that simply began repeating itself day after day. However, special note should be made of two events that occurred on the eighth day. One was the first and only trip of the entire year for the children to the school library, and the second was Mrs. Caplow's es- tablishment of a permanent seating arrangement that was to continue throughout the remaining eight and one-half months of school. These two events will be discussed in turn.

As a further way of acquainting the children with the facilities and staff of Attucks School, Mrs. Caplow arranged for a tour of the library room. It was a policy of Attucks School that the kindergarten classes were not to have library privileges. Instead, Mrs. Caplow was to come to the library and select whatever books she wished the children to have. What follows are sequential excerpts of the children's single visit to the library room.

As the children enter the library room, walking two by two with the girls in front, they say to the librarian, "Good morning, Mrs. Spring." This they were instructed to say by Mrs. Caplow. Mrs. Spring responds, "Good morning, little children. Good morning, little people." Mrs. Caplow directs the children to their seats around small tables. As Laura begins to take her seat, Mrs. Spring says in a harsh tone, "No, I will give you the chair." She pushes Laura down in the chair and then pushes both Laura and the chair up to the table.

Mrs. Spring comes in front of the group and says, "Do you little people know what room this is?" Joe responds, "Pictures." Mrs. Spring turns to Joe and says firmly, "Did you want to say something, sweets?" Joe responds, "I see pictures." Mrs. Spring asks, "What else do you see?" Anne says, "I see flowers." "Yes, and what else?" Art answers, "Record player. We got one them at home." Mrs. Spring: "When you come to the library, you will be interested in getting books." (Note: Her original question was not answered and she drops it.) She picks up a book and says, "See how pretty the colors are in this book? I am sure Mrs. Caplow will take some back to your room and read them to you if she has time. When we read a book, do we wet our fingers? (No response from the children.) No, we use dry fingers. As we read, we do not eat, especially we do not eat candy." Several of the boys at the far table are not listening but instead are looking at the pictures around the room. Mrs. Spring walks up to this table and says, "You little boys in front will not know where to get books when you come here by yourself. If you do not listen, you will not know how to get books." (Note: They won't be back for a year and she hasn't said anything to anyone else about getting books.)

"Now, boys and girls, face the screen and watch the film. When it is all over, I want you to tell me how much you have enjoyed it." (Note: Enforcement of the "school is fun" concept.) The film is about a cap salesman who wears his caps on his head and has to get them back from a group of monkeys who take them while he is asleep. Throughout the film, the children are quiet and attentive. When it ends, Mrs. Spring turns on the lights, walks to the front of the group and says, "Did you like that? What did you like best about it? Did you like the way the monkeys tricked the man or the way the man tricked the monkeys?" (Note: Questions come rapid fire with no time for answers.) Joe gets up from his seat to go to the bookshelf. Mrs. Spring firmly snaps her fingers at him and says in a harsh tone, "Little boy, get back in that seat."

A number of books are displayed on one table. Of the several dozen books there, only one has a picture of a black person on the cover. There are many with pictures of white people.

Mrs. Spring is reading to the class from a book about manners entitled *What Do We Say?* She interrupts in the middle of one passage and says, "I'm disappointed. I'm disappointed." She then takes Joe and Frank by the back of their necks, marches them over to a wastebasket, forces them to bend over the basket, and has them spit out their gum.

Mrs. Spring says, "All right, boys and girls, it is time to go back to your room." The children begin to rise out of their chairs. Mrs. Spring snaps in a harsh voice, "Not yet. No one told you to move.

Now, sit still. I want the six little girls at this table to come with me. Now, I want the rest of the girls to come. Okay, now, my friends the boys can come and stand behind the girls." Joe begins to tell Mrs. Spring about the earthworms he brought to class that morning. Mrs. Spring grasps Joe by the cheeks, pinches his mouth closed and says in an angry and frustrated way, "Joe, we are not having free talk period. You will have to keep your mouth shut." She gives a little extra pinch and lets go. Mrs. Caplow then says, "Okay, boys and girls, let's tiptoe back to our room." The children file out two by two.

The other important event for the children on the eighth day of school was permanent assignment to a seat at one of the three tables for the remainder of the school year. For the first seven days of school the children were free to choose any seat at any of the three tables they wished. But Mrs. Caplow announced that "it was time to get going with the work" and so assigned seats. The seating order, however, was not random. Mrs. Caplow assigned the students to the various tables on the basis of her intuitive perception of their attributes and capabilities. When she made the seating arrangement permanent, she did so without the benefit of any testing or formal evaluation.

The assignments, though, were not made in a vacuum. Mrs. Caplow possessed the four sources of information about the children discussed earlier: the preregistration form, the list of children from families receiving public welfare payments, the responses of the parents to the "Behavioral Questionnaire," and finally, both her experiences and those of other teachers with older siblings and parents of the children now in the kindergarten class. In addition, Mrs. Caplow had had seven school days in which to observe the children in the class. Thus classroom behavior, degree and type of verbalization, dress, mannerisms, physical appearance, and performance on the assigned early tasks were known to her as she began to form opinions.

There can be little doubt, I think, that her evaluation had already begun. Within a few days, only a certain group of children were continually being called on to lead the class in the Pledge of Allegiance, read the weather calendar each day, come to the front for "show and tell" periods, take messages to the office, count the number of children present in the class, pass out materials for class projects, be in charge of equipment on the playground, and lead the class to the bathroom, library, or on a school tour. This one group of children, who were always physically close to the teacher and had a high degree of verbal interaction with her, she placed at Table 1.

As one progressed from Table 1 to Table 2 and Table 3, there was an increasing dissimilarity from group to group on at least four major criteria. The first appeared to be physical appearance. While the children at Table 1 were all dressed in clean clothes that were relatively new and pressed, most of the children at Table 2, and with only one exception those at Table 3, were all quite poorly dressed. Their clothes were old and in many cases quite dirty. As time went on, it also became apparent that the children at Tables 2 and 3 had a noticeably different quality and quantity of clothes to wear, especially during the winter months. Whereas the children at Table 1 would come on cold days with heavy coats and sweaters, the children at the other two tables often wore very thin spring coats and summer clothes. The single child at Table 3 who came to school quite nicely dressed came from a home in which the mother was receiving welfare funds, but was supplied with clothing for the children by the families of her brother and sister.

An aspect related to the physical appearance of the children was their body odor. There were two children at Table 2 and five children at Table 3 who frequently had an odor of urine about them. There was not a clear distinction among the children at the various tables as to the degree of "blackness" of their skin, but there were more children at the third table with very dark skin (five in all) than there were at the first table (three). There was also a noticeable distinction among the various groups of children as to the condition of their hair. While the three boys at Table 1 all had short haircuts and the six girls at the same table had their hair "processed" and combed, the number of children with either matted or unprocessed hair increased at Table 2 (two boys and three girls) and eight of the children at Table 3 (four boys and four girls). None of the children in the kindergarten class wore their hair in the style of a "natural."

A second major criterion which appeared to differentiate the children at the various tables was their interactional behavior, both among themselves and with the teacher. The several children who began to develop as leaders within the class by giving directions to other members, initiating the division of the class into teams on the playground, and seeking to speak for the class to the teacher ("We want to color now"), all were placed at Table 1. This same group of children displayed considerable ease in approaching her. Whereas the children at Tables 2 and 3 would often linger on the periphery of groups surrounding the teacher, the children at Table 1 most often crowded close to her.

The use of language within the classroom appeared to be the third major differentiation among the children. While the children placed at the first table were quite talkative with the teacher, the children placed at the remaining two tables spoke much less frequently with her. The children placed at the first table also displayed a greater familiarity with standard American English within the classroom. The children placed at the last two tables often responded to the teacher in the black dialect, but the children at the first table did so very infrequently. In other words, the children at the first table were much more adept at the use of "school language" than were those at the other tables. The teacher used standard American English in the classroom, and one group of children were able to respond in a like manner. The frequency of a "no response" to a question from the teacher was recorded at a ratio of nearly three to one for the children at the last two tables as opposed to Table 1. When questions were asked, the children who were placed at the first table were those who most often gave a response.

The final criterion by which the children at the first table were quite noticeably different from those at the other tables consisted of a series of facts about social background which were known to the teacher before she seated the children. Though I have no way of knowing how this knowledge figured in her decisions when she assigned seats, it does contribute to developing a clear profile of the children at the various tables. Table I gives a summary of the distribution of the children at the three tables on a series of variables related to social and family conditions. Such variables may be considered to give indication of the relative status of the children within the room, based on income, education, and size of the family.

Some hypothesis is necessary to explain my belief that the teacher

Table I. Distribution of Socioeconomic Status Factors by Seating Arrangement at the Three Tables in the Kindergarten Classroom

	Seating Arrangement[a]		
Factors	Table 1	Table 2	Table 3
Income			
Families on welfare	0	2	4
Families with father employed	6	3	2
Families with mother employed	5	5	5
Families with both parents employed	5	3	2
Total family income below $3,000/year[b]	0	4	7
Total family income above $12,000/year[b]	4	0	0
Education			
Father ever grade school	6	3	2
Father ever high school	5	2	1
Father ever college	1	0	0
Mother ever grade school	9	10	8
Mother ever high school	7	6	5
Mother ever college	4	0	0
Children with preschool experience	1	1	0
Family Size			
Families with one child	3	1	0
Families with six or more children	2	6	7
Average number of siblings in family	3–4	5–6	6–7
Families with both parents present	6	3	2

[a]There are nine children at Table 1, eleven at Table 2, and ten children at Table 3.
[b]Estimated from stated occupation.

did not assign the children to the various tables randomly. I would contend that she developed, through some combination of the four criteria outlined above, a series of expectations about the potential performance of each child and then grouped the children according to perceived similarities in expected performance. The teacher herself informed me that the first table consisted of her "fast learners" while those at the last two tables "had no idea of what was going on in the classroom." What becomes crucial in this discussion is to ascertain the basis upon which the teacher developed her criteria, since there had been no formal testing of the children's academic potential or capacity for cognitive development. She made evaluative judgments of their abilities after seven days of school.

Certain criteria became indicative of expected success and others became indicative of expected failure. Those children who closely fit the teacher's "ideal type" of the successful child were chosen for seats at Table 1. Those who fell farthest from it were placed at the third table. To understand what the teacher considered "success," one would have to examine her perception of it within the larger society. Thus, in the terms of Merton (1957), one might try to determine Mrs. Caplow's "normative reference group." In her case it was, I believe, a mixed black-white, well-educated middle class, and the attributes considered most desirable in such a group became the basis for her evaluation of the children. Those who possessed these particular characteristics were expected to succeed, while those who did not could be expected not to succeed. A child could attain highly prized middle-class status in the classroom by getting along easily with adults; by demonstrating facility in standard American English, leadership ability, and a neat and clean appearance; by coming from a family that was educated, employed, living together, and interested in the child; and by the ability to participate well as a member of a group.

The kindergarten teacher appeared to have been raised in a home where these values were emphasized as important. Her mother was a college graduate, as were her brother and sisters. The family lived in

the same neighborhood for many years, and the father held a responsible position with a public utility company. The family was devoutly
religious and those of the family still in the city attend the same church.
She and other members of her family were active in a number of civil
rights organizations in the city. Thus, it appears that the kindergarten
teacher's "normative reference group" coincided quite closely with
those groups in which she did participate and belong. There was little
discrepancy between the normative values of a mixed black-white
educated middle class and the values of the community from which
she came, and she had attained attributes indicative of "success"
among the educated middle class. She was a college graduate, held
positions of respect and responsibility in the black community, lived in
a comfortable middle-class section of the city in a well-furnished and
spacious home, together with her husband earned over $20,000 per
year, was active in a number of community organizations, and had
parents, brother, and sisters with similar educations, incomes, and occupational positions.

The teacher ascribed high status to a certain group of children by
placing them among the "fast learners" at Table 1. Having defined, on
the basis of her reference group, the qualities essential for achievement, she responded favorably to those children who possessed them.
Her resultant preferential treatment of a select group of children appeared to be derived from her belief that certain behavioral and cultural characteristics are more conducive to learning than are others.
In a similar manner, those children who appeared not to possess the
criteria essential for success were ascribed low status and described
as "failures." They were relegated to positions at Tables 2 and 3.

The organization of the kindergarten classroom after the eighth day
of school according to the teacher's expectation of success or failure
became the basis for differential treatment of the children for the remainder of the school year. From the day that the class was assigned
permanent seats, what went on in the classroom was perceptibly dif-

ferent. The fundamental division of the class into those expected to learn and those expected not to permeated the teacher's work with the class.

I have argued that the development of the kindergarten teacher's expectations of differential academic potential was significantly determined by her subjective interpretation of a series of characteristics. These characteristics appeared in large part to be related to social class. On the basis of her evaluation, the class was divided into groups: those expected to succeed ("fast learners") and those expected to fail ("slow learners"). In subsequent chapters it will be argued that this categorization had the following results:

(1) Differential treatment was accorded the two groups in the classroom, the group designated as "fast learners" receiving the most teaching time, rewards, and attention from the teacher. Those designated as "slow learners" were taught infrequently, subjected to more control, and received little if any support from the teacher.

(2) The interactional patterns between the teacher and the various groups in her class became increasingly rigidified, taking on castelike characteristics, during the course of the school year. As a result, the gap in completion of academic material between the two groups widened as the school year progressed. In short, what the teacher expected by the eighth day of school did in fact come to pass.

(3) The consequence of the differential experiences of the children within the same kindergarten classroom was that they were differentially prepared for the first grade. The first grade teacher grouped the children according to the amount of "readiness" material they had completed in kindergarten. The group separation that began in kindergarten based on subjective criteria was carried on in the later grades, but was based on objective measures of past performance. Empirical verification replaced teacher intuition as the basis for classroom grouping. By either measure, the winners stayed winners and the losers stayed losers.

Further Aspects of Classroom Organization: Time and Control

Charles Silberman (1970, p. 122) states, "The most important characteristic schools share in common is a preoccupation with order and
control." He is correct. Order and control are perceived as necessary
for the smooth functioning of any organization concerned with production, crisp bureaucratic efficiency, and the meeting of schedules.
School is a collective organizational experience; it requires the child
to subordinate his desires or wants to those of the institution. Were
children allowed to pursue ideas, interests, or explorations until they
tired of them, there would have to be a drastic restructuring of the curriculum in American education. But in the absence of any modification
that would allow individual interests to emerge, there has to be social
control to assure the achievement of the collective goals which are
school goals. As Waller reflected in an important book long neglected
(1937, republished 1965; p. 355):

It is only because teachers wish to force students to learn that any un-
pleasantness ever arises to mar their relationship. We have defined the
school as the place where people meet for the purpose of giving and
receiving instruction. If this process were unforced, if students could
be allowed to learn only what interested them, to learn in their own
way, and to learn no more and no better than it pleased them to do, if
good order were not considered a prerequisite to learning, if teachers
did not have to be taskmasters, but merely helpers and friends, then
life would be sweet in the school room. These, however, are all conditions contrary to fact. The conditions of mass instruction and of book
instruction make it necessary that learning be forced.

American schools would be in chaos without clocks. Time is of the
essence in a production schedule, and any divergence from that
schedule disrupts future events during the day as well as the immediate situation. In such circumstances, it is imperative for the teacher to
maintain control over the class so that unprogrammed and spontaneous events do not halt the assembly line geared to manufacturing units
of learning. As Philip Jackson has noted (1968, pp. 12–13):

It is he [the teacher] who sees to it that things begin and end on time, more or less. He determines the proper moment for switching from discussion to workbooks, or from spelling to arithmetic. He decides whether a student has spent too long in the washroom, or whether those who take the bus may be dismissed. In many schools he is assisted in this job by elaborate systems of bells and buzzers. But even when the school day is mechanically punctuated by clangs and hums, the teacher is not entirely relieved of his responsibility for watching the clock. The implications of the teacher's clockwatching behavior for determining what life in school is like are indeed profound. This behavior reminds us, above all, that school is a place where things often happen not because students want them to, but because it is time for them to occur.

Though kindergarten may not be considered real school it does not escape the routine of schooling. Mrs. Caplow had invited the parents of the kindergarten students to a tea on the ninth day of school from 9:00 to 10:00 a.m. She had decorated the room with some fresh flowers as well as pictures drawn by the children. But, more important to this discussion, she also prepared for the parents two charts on large poster board. The first of these was entitled "Your Child's Day in Kindergarten." The top half of the chart gave the schedule for the morning section of the kindergarten and the bottom half outlined the afternoon session schedule. The chart for the morning section is found in Table II.

Based on a 210-minute class session each morning, the following figures suggest the division of time within the kindergarten for a period of one week.

Music	100 minutes
Creative activities	200 minutes
Language arts	300 minutes
Physical activity:	
Games—rhythms	100 minutes
Rest	75 minutes
Recess	75 minutes
Organization	200 minutes
	1,050 minutes

Table II. Time Allotment for Daily Curriculum Activity in A.M. Kindergarten Classroom

"Your Child's Day in Kindergarten"

Time of Day	Length of Period (Minutes)	Activity (Mon.–Fri.)
8:30–8:40	10	Organization
8:40–8:58	18	Creative arts
8:58–9:28	30	Language arts
9:28–9:35	7	Rhythms
9:35–10:05	30	Language arts
10:05–10:15	10	Organization
10:15–10:30	15	Recess
10:30–10:40	10	Organization
10:40–10:55	15	Rest
10:55–11:17	22	Creative arts
11:17–11:30	13	Games
11:30–11:50	20	Music
11:50–12:00	10	Organization

The figures imply that theoretically a full forty percent of the child's time in the school had no relation to academic endeavors. In reality, the likelihood is that the nonacademic activities took even more time than was allocated. For example, Table II suggests that the first organization period should have been no more than ten minutes. Yet on day 8, the organizational time was twenty-eight minutes. One of the shortcomings of this type of time schedule is that when one event runs beyond its alloted minutes, something else must be foregone in order to keep the schedule. Thus on day 8, the eighteen minutes that should have been spent in creative arts, but were instead given over to organization, were not caught up later. Creative arts were passed over altogether, and the teacher went on to language arts.

Another shortcoming of Mrs. Caplow's timetable is that the interests of the children will not always coincide with the hands of the clock. Attention may lag behind the initiation of an activity, and the children may not begin to build enthusiasm until it is time to go on to something else. This is one of the most detrimental effects of this type of classroom organization, for the rigidity of a time schedule thwarts the capacity of children to concentrate for periods of time on a subject of interest to them. One of the continual refrains of the teachers at Attucks School was that their students lacked an "attention span." Their solution was a fragmented and chopped-up curriculum in which children were intellectually shuffled about during the course of the morning in seven, ten, thirteen, fifteen, eighteen, twenty, twenty-two and thirty minute segments, on the claim that this was necessary to hold their attention.

There is an alternative interpretation. Children come to schools able to concentrate from very short periods of time to quite long periods of time, depending upon their moods, their interests, and how frequent or infrequent their interruptions. What the school curriculum does is reinforce the patterns of short attention and attempt to extinguish the long attention patterns. Thus the school fulfills its own prophecy; it brings about what it erroneously thought to be true in the first place. There is no place in the schedule for a child to have the freedom or opportunity to carry on his interest in a particular matter beyond the slotted time. Herbert Kohl (1967) adds a further dimension when he writes:

The tightness with time that exists in the elementary school has nothing to do with the quantity that must be learned or the children's needs. It represents the teacher's fear of loss of control and is nothing but a weapon used to weaken the solidarity and opposition of the children that too many teachers unconsciously fear.

The assault on learning coupled with the control-to-the-minute of children makes kindergarten very real indeed. Schools provide no respite from schooling.

The second chart Mrs. Caplow had in the room during the tea with the parents was entitled "Developmental Areas of Kindergarten Program." It listed without elaboration the following five areas:
1. Emotional and social development
2. Orientation to school life
3. Physical development

4. Intellectual development
5. Aesthetic appreciation development.
One might infer from Mrs. Caplow's "Teacher's Credo" (discussed earlier in this chapter) how she would interpret the content of each of these areas.

A Special Service

In addition to such special service personnel at Attucks School as the librarian and the social worker, there was also a speech teacher who worked both with individual students and entire classrooms. It was a policy of Attucks School to assign the speech teacher to each of the kindergarten sessions for one-half hour per week. Thus, as one further aspect of the classroom routine, Miss Allen would spend one-half hour each Thursday morning with the children in Mrs. Caplow's class. The following sequential excerpts taken during Miss Allen's first visit give an indication of a fairly typical speech lesson.

   In preparation for Miss Allen's visit, Mrs. Caplow begins putting name tags on each of the children. Miss Allen at this time enters the room, says nothing, and goes to the piano bench, where she sits. Mrs. Caplow instructs the children to go over to Miss Allen. Miss Allen says nothing to the children. She simply puts her hand on the shoulder of each child and tells him or her where to sit. Tom is one of the last children to receive his name tag from Mrs. Caplow, and as he walks toward Miss Allen, he appears uncertain where to sit. Miss Allen's first words in the class are a sharp directive to Tom: "Tom, come over here and sit by the edge of the row." After she has seated the remaining two students, her next words are: "Now, all of you cross your legs." This the children do. "First, my name is Miss Allen. I am the speech teacher. Say 'Good morning, Miss Allen.' " The children respond. Miss Allen repeats the same instructions and asks the children to respond. They do. "I will come to see you every Thursday morning and when I come we will talk about speech. Does anyone know what speech is?" Joe calls out, "Talk." "Yes, it's all about talking. Now, today we are not going to talk about your speech, but about animal speech."

To begin the lesson, the teacher asked the children if any of them had a dog. Several said that they did, and Miss Allen then gave the dog sound (woof, woof) and asked the children to repeat it. They did, and this exchange was repeated twice. The same was then done for the cat (meow, meow). Mrs. Allen then announced that they would talk about animals on the farm and the sounds that farm animals make. She asked how many of the children in the class had been to a farm, and four children from Table 1 raised their hands. She questioned those who held up their hands.

"What do you see on the farm?" David responds, "Tigers." Miss Allen says, "No, you don't see a tiger on the farm. You see a tiger in the zoo. Now, who else knows an animal on the farm?" Laura says, "Cow." "Yes. Now, let's all say moo, moo." The children repeat "moo, moo." Frank then suggests a horse and after Miss Allen first gives the sound, the children repeat, "whinnie, whinnie." Anne says, "I seen chickens." "Yes, what do you call a lady chicken?" Tom: "Turkey." "No, they are called hens. Now, all of you say cluck, cluck, cluck." The children do so. The same is then repeated for the rooster and baby chicken (cock-a-doodle-do and peep, peep).

When finished with the animal sounds, Miss Allen began to show individual pictures of farm animals to the children. Each time a picture was shown, she asked, "What sound does this animal make?"

The children respond with a conglomeration of answers for each animal. Horses are said to go "oink, oink" or "quack, quack" while the ducks go "moo, moo." Some of the children do give the right sound for the animals, but many more do not. When Miss Allen shows a picture and elicits the response, she does not comment on the correctness or incorrectness of the answer. She merely proceeds to the next picture. I note that one child continues to say "moo, moo" for every picture that is shown. Miss Allen's only comment to him is that he should pull his legs together. The same set of pictures is repeated, and there is the same mixture of answers. Again no comment from Miss Allen on the responses. (Note: Throughout this exercise, she has been brisk and mechanical. It is as if she were late for another appointment and wanted to get out of the class as fast as possible.)

As the final portion of the speech lesson, Miss Allen told the children that they were going to perform a "barnyard symphony." She asked them to stand and began to group them in twos and threes. For each of the eight groups she designated a farm animal sound. After the eight groups were formed and each had a sound, she went from one group to another asking the children to repeat the sound after her. When this brief rehearsal of each of the sections was completed, she stood in front of the children and explained that when she pointed at a group, they were to begin repeating their sound over and over again. She also told them that while they were making their sounds they were to twirl around in circles. The notes capture the scene as the music begins.

Miss Allen first points to the cows and this group begins to "moo, moo" and also twirl. Then come the pigs, the chickens, the ducks, the cats, the dogs, the horses, and finally the roosters. All the children are now saying their sounds, and spinning around, bumping into each other, occasionally falling down and quite evidently growing dizzy. Miss Allen stands at the front pantomiming a conductor with grand sweeping gestures. It is almost as if she were oblivious to the falling children, the incoherent mumble of the barnyard, and the look of disbelief on the face of Mrs. Caplow sitting at her desk. When a number of the children are on the floor from dizziness, Miss Allen says, "Okay, you all did very well. Isn't it fun to be in a symphony?" Miss Allen moves to collect her materials, and as she does so, she says, "Next week we will talk some more. But I hope that the frisky people will be able to sit quietly next time. Susan, you must have ants in your pants. You are so frisky today." Without another word Miss Allen leaves the room.

Kindergarten had begun for real!

Kindergarten: Through Three Seasons

3

St. Louis has a beautiful autumn. The warm days may linger into the first weeks of November. It is during this Indian summer that one finds a respite between the heat and humidity of the summer and the coming of cold and slush in winter. But like many others, teachers and students miss a good deal of this, for they spend most of the day inside a building. Writing about St. Louis, Smith and Geoffrey (1968, p. 129) note that the teachers miss:

> . . . the pastoral quality of other people's Indian summer. [Instead] . . . the teacher finds satisfaction in the stabilization of his group into a working unit. Expectations have been clarified, roles have been settled, and movement towards generally accepted goals is well begun.

This description is apt for Mrs. Caplow and her kindergarten class. From fall to winter to spring, the routine, the pattern, the predictability of the class activities would remain stable with only a few exceptions.

This chapter contains three major sections, one for each of the three seasons the children spent in the kindergarten classroom. The division of the activities of the children by seasons most closely reflects the manner in which Mrs. Caplow herself saw the various segments of the school year. Such divisions as individual months or report card dates had very little if any effect on her plans for the class. One of her major considerations was to insure that two important dates fell in each segment, the events for fall being Halloween and Thanksgiving; for winter, Christmas and Valentine's Day; and for spring, Easter and May Day.

During the year, an important shift in my focus of analysis occurred. Until Christmas, I concentrated on the activities of the teacher and the entire class, studying general patterns of organization, routine, and teacher-student and student-student interaction. After Christmas, however, I concerned myself more closely with four children—two selected by Mrs. Caplow as "doing well" and seated at Table 1 and two others selected as "doing poorly" and seated at Table 3. Her selection was in response to my request to her to select two children in each of the two categories so that I might observe them more specifically. I shifted my focus in anticipation of learning more about how individual children cope and adapt to the contingencies of their position in the class hierarchy. In such a manner, I hoped more fully to "get inside" what it meant to be at Table 1 or at Table 3. This final narrowing of the analysis was intended to reach the ultimate output from the funnel—individual children from within a single classroom within one school in the entire city school system.

This chaper will detail, in an essentially ethnographic manner, the patterns of social organization and the processes of socialization the children experienced during the course of their kindergarten year. After reading the account of the school year, the reader may object that some repetitious material has been included. Such, indeed, is the case. It is included deliberately to give a small indication of the repetitiousness to which the students themselves were subjected. Much of the day-to-day predictable routine has been omitted in this chapter, though, for to include it would necessitate a much expanded book. What follow are segments of life in the classroom, admittedly chosen selectively but with the hope of providing an accurate reconstruction of how one teacher and her students made it through the year.

Fall

Allport (1954), Goodman (1964), and Proshansky (1966), among others, have all noted that the preschool and first years of elementary school (ages three to approximately seven) are generally recognized as the crucial period in the child's development of feelings about himself and others who are ethnically different. As Proshansky and Newton indicate (1968):

During this period the child becomes increasingly aware of racial differences and learns labels and affective responses associated with various ethnic groups including his own. The research indicates that the Negro child and his white counterpart become aware of color or racial differences as early as age three or four and that within this awareness lies an inchoate understanding of the valuations placed on this color by the larger society.

Within the kindergarten classroom the child is actively involved in two simultaneous processes: first, determining his identity and second, ascertaining the *value* related to it. Though analytically the conception and evaluation of identity must be kept separate, they are inextricably interwoven. The child in Attucks School learned that he was black within a context that defined "black" in clearly affective terms.

"Whiteness" was the norm when the children first came to the kindergarten classroom. For the first days the teacher had put on the bulletin boards several pictures of whites engaged in "Summer Fun" and "Summer Play." These pictures were replaced in three weeks with several of a fall motif. Two of the new pictures showed large trees with beautiful golden foliage. The third, entitled "Autumn is Here," showed two white women and a white man walking through a forest area where the leaves had changed. From the first days of school, the children were surrounded with pictures of white people. There was not a picture of a black adult or child in the classroom. When pictures of whites were labeled as "Our Principal," "Our Nurse," or "Our Librarian," the children were presented with a clear contradiction. They were told those whom they knew to be black were actually white.

September 26

A subject that periodically arose in informal discussion with Mrs. Caplow was what she believed to be a lack of parental interest and involvement in the children and their school activities. She commented on
several occasions that if the home were more concerned about the
school, the school situation would vastly improve and teachers "could
really begin to teach." In cases where there was parental participation
she believed it, for the most part, to be tenuous at best, that, with the
least discouragement, the parents would lose all interest in the activities of the school. Such participation was evaluated not only in terms of
presence at PTA meetings or volunteering food for the class bake sale,
but supplying the child with two cents each day for a half-pint of milk.

Mrs. Caplow introduced me to Mrs. Ennis, the school aide. Mrs. Caplow explained that Mrs. Ennis came to each of the rooms and took
count of how many children would be having milk after the recess.
She then told Mrs. Ennis to bring milk for all but those who did not
have their two cents. I volunteered to buy the milk for the children,
but she responded, "Oh no, if we started doing that, it would encourage the parents not send their money. If the child goes a few
days without milk, they will let the parents know—and besides, it is
only two cents. Those children who did not bring their money will be
able to rest while the other children drink their milk. I guess those
who forgot their money did not tell their parents to give them any."

All five of those children who did not have money for milk were seated
at Table 3 and four of the five came from homes supported by public
welfare funds. Denial of nutrition was but one example of the penalty
paid by the poor for their "nonparticipation" in Mrs. Caplow's classroom.

September 28

The teacher began a series of lessons to teach the children the notion
of "equal." She would have two or three children come to the front of

the room and each hold, for example, a cup. She would then call two or three other children to the front and give them a saucer. She would then ask the class whether there was an equal number of cups and saucers. Or she would call two groups of children to the front, asking the class whether there was an equal or unequal number in the groups. At times, the discussion of the concept "equal" became quite elaborate. One such lesson used the motif of a birthday party.

Mrs. Caplow tacks on the flannel board a picture of a white mother and five white children looking at a birthday cake. She says to the children when the picture is in place, "Okay, now every day when we come to school we want to learn something new. Let's look at this picture." Several of the children are not looking at the picture, and Mrs. Caplow says, "Oh, let's all look here." The children do. Joe, in anticipation of the teacher, asks, "Do you want us to tell you about the picture?" Before Mrs. Caplow can respond, he continues, "I see a birthday cake." Mrs. Caplow: "That's good. What else do you see?" Laura: "They are having a birthday party." Mrs. Caplow: "Yes, what else?" Anne: "They are goin' drink milk." Mrs. Caplow: "Yes they are."

In the picture there are party favors beside each plate. Mrs. Caplow points to these and explains that a favor is a "prize" one might receive at a party. Beyond this, there is no explanation of either "favor" or "prize." With this prelude to the lesson on equals, Mrs. Caplow asks four children to come to the front of the room, two to stand on each side of her. She hands each child a rolled piece of paper tied with a red ribbon and says, "Isn't it fun to receive favors at a party. Aren't all of you children having fun?" All the children raise their hands. Mrs. Caplow then asks if the two groups of children with her have the same number of favors. Laura responds, "Yes," and Mrs. Caplow asks the four children to take their seats.

Later in the morning the children again provided the teacher with the unanimous response she desired. The entire class appeared to have learned the clues quite well.

Mrs. Caplow says, "How many of you can be quiet workers? Raise your hand." All the children raise their hands. She continues, "How many of you can be good workers today?" The children still have their hands raised and she looks at them, smiles, and says, "That's nice. Now put your hands down."

Within this incident there is an additional example of a "phantom performance" by the teacher. The children did not have an opportunity to make a response to her second question, yet the teacher spoke to them as if they had.

After the lesson on "equals" and before the speech teacher's arrival, Joe asked Mrs. Caplow if Miss Allen was going to teach the class. Mrs. Caplow responded that she would but that it would be later in the morning. The children began immediately to talk among themselves about Miss Allen, and Mrs. Caplow asked, "Why are some of you so excited today?"

The children continue to whisper among themselves and Mrs. Caplow then says, "Okay, let's see who can be real quiet today. The people that are very smart are those that are very quiet. Now I am going to ask you what day it is and only the smart people will raise their hand. They will not talk out." Frank says, "It's Sunday." Mrs. Caplow replies, "Frank, I thought you were smart, and besides today is not Sunday. Smart people do not talk out." Mrs. Caplow continues, "Okay, if you know what day it is, raise your hand." Several children raise their hand, and there is no talking. She calls on Fred. "Fred, do you know what day it is?" Fred responds, "It Monday." Mrs. Caplow asks Fred to give his answer in a complete sentence. "Fred, say, 'Today is Monday.' " He does. Mrs. Caplow then asks the entire class, "Is that right, boys and girls?" Several of the children answer that it is not. She says, "Yes, it is not Monday. What day is it, Virginia?" Virginia responds, "Saturday." Mrs. Caplow does not ask Virginia to repeat her incorrect answer in a complete sentence and merely tells her that it is not Saturday. She then turns to Laura and says, "I guess I will have to call on Laura. Laura, what day is today?" Laura: "Thursday." Mrs. Caplow says, "Yes, that is very good." Laura also is not asked to repeat her answer in a complete sentence.

There are several aspects of this interchange between Mrs. Caplow and the students that bear comment. To Fred, Mrs. Caplow made it clear that even if he gave an incorrect answer, there was a "correct" manner in which to do it. All answers were to be in complete sentences. Yet this same instruction was not enforced with Virginia, the next child called to give the name of the day. When Mrs. Caplow came to call on Laura, she did it in such a manner as to humiliate the other children. Laura was held up as the example of a student who could be depended upon after other children had displayed their failure. (Laura sat at Table 1, Virginia at Table 2, and Fred at Table 3.)

When Miss Allen entered the room, Mrs. Caplow again put name tags on each of the children and instructed them to go sit by the piano. Miss Allen's first words were directed toward Susan. "Susan, are you going to be quiet and still today?" Susan made no response. While the children continued to come to the piano, Laura called Fred an "almond head." Fred, in turn, responded, "Girl, you the almond head." Miss Allen then began the lesson:

In a very loud voice she asks the children, "What speech helpers do we have when we talk?" David answers, "Our mouth." Miss Allen says, "No. What parts of the mouth do we use?" She now points to parts of her mouth—tongue, lips, and so on, and the children name them. She continues, "Now, when we are going to use our mouth, what do we use?" Frank says, "Tongue." Her response: "No." Joe: "Our lips." "No." Tom: "Our chin." "No." She now points to her jaw and one of the girls says, "Jaw." Miss Allen responds, "Yes, now all of you say jaw." The children do.

Miss Allen told the children she was going to teach them a poem. She did not tell them either what a "poem" was or what the title of the poem was.

"I want to see everyone's eyes right here. Look at me. Everyone's eyes look right here." She is pointing to her mouth. She rises from her seat, goes to Marcia and lifts her by both arms from the floor, and brings her next to the piano bench. She tells Marcia, "Now I can keep you from looking out of the window." She then recites the poem.

Lips together, me, me, me;
Teeth together, see, see, see;
Tongue peeks out, three, three, three;
that's the way for you and me.

Tip of tongue, two, two, two;
Tip again, do, do, do;
Lips again, lu, lu, lu;
That's what our speech helpers do.

She asks the children to repeat the poem, and no child makes a sound. She asks the children to repeat the poem line by line after her, first with the words and then a second time through simply saying "lu, lu, lu" in place of the words. The children are completely baffled and say nothing. At the end of the second repetition she comments, "Okay, that was good. We will have to do that again next week." (Note: A phantom performance par excellence!)

Until this time, her only physical contact with any of the children occurred when she picked Marcia up from the floor and carried her to the piano bench. However, when she asked the children to repeat the poem for the third time she rose from her seat and began to move around the room pinching the children, turning their heads, pinching ears, and shouting into their faces, "I want to see your eyes." After completing the poem she sat down and then had the children repeat it for the fourth time. She attempted a short review with the children on what they had covered in the lesson and then gave instructions on how to say "goodbye" to her.

"Okay, that is all for today, boys and girls. But before I leave, what are our speech helpers?" She sticks out her tongue, puckers her lips, and points to her jaw. She continues, "Now, I am going to say 'goodbye' just once to you and you can just once tell me 'goodbye, Miss Allen.' You are not to make any other sound to me. 'Goodbye, boys and girls'." The children respond, "Goodbye, Miss Allen." The room is now very quiet and the speech teacher moves towards the door. As she is about to leave, one of the girls says softly, "Goodbye, Miss Allen." Miss Allen turns to the child and says in a loud and harsh voice, "I told you not to say anything else to me." She then walks out of the room.

In an attempt to soothe the children, Mrs. Caplow spoke to them in a soft voice and told them that they could now either sit at their tables or color any picture they wished. Ten of the children put their heads down on their tables, and the remaining twenty began to color.

During this period, I had a chance to speak informally with Mrs. Caplow. I asked her what she thought was the greatest difficulty she encountered in teaching kindergarten. She said that without a doubt her major problem was to "get the children to begin to work together." She defined working together as "being quiet, being polite, learning manners, not to look on the paper of anyone else, and to always ask permission when they want to do something in the room." She said that she had to "start from scratch" with the majority of the children in the class because the parents "did nothing for the children," and that she wanted to remain a kindergarten teacher because she could "get to the children early before it is too late." She again urged that I observe the children closely throughout the year, and she predicted that I would not know by the coming June that "they were the same group of children." They would be less "fidgety," more able to concentrate because of "longer attention spans," and "able to do their own work"; and there would be an end to the "trouble" in the room caused by boys rolling on the floor. She noted that she enjoyed teaching kindergarten because "it is such a rewarding and wonderful thing to work with these children and see them grow."

October 3

During the month of October, Mrs. Caplow spent many hours involving the children in various Halloween activities. Again the bulletin boards were changed, and pictures of bats, witches, pumpkins, and ghosts replaced those of autumn. Next to the piano Mrs. Caplow constructed a five-foot witch with a broom, tall pointed hat, and blond hair, and surrounded on the floor by pumpkins. The witch was the subject of her first discussion with the children concerning Halloween:

Mrs. Caplow is standing by the piano and asks the children to look around the room and tell her what they see that is new. Frank answers, "A witch." Mrs. Caplow: "Yes, but why do we have a witch in the room now?" Laura: "Because it's October and in October we have Halloween." Mrs. Caplow: "Yes, that is right, Laura. Okay, now can any of you boys and girls tell me what the witch is doing?" Mike answers, "She moppin'." Mrs. Caplow then asks Joe what he believes the witch is doing and he suggests the witch is "cookin'." Mrs. Caplow asks what Joe thinks she is cooking and Joe replies that the witch is cooking pumpkin sauce. When Laura is asked, she responds that the witch is cooking a pumpkin pie. Tom is asked and says also that the witch is cooking a pumpkin pie. Marcia gives a similar answer. When Virginia is asked, she responds that the witch is cooking carrots. Frank calls out that the witch is sweeping the floor.

Mrs. Caplow did not offer her own interpretation of what the witch was doing and simply accepted all the answers of the children without indicating that any one was more or less plausible than another. The four children who followed Joe answered as he did that the witch was cooking, whether it be pumpkins or carrots. This continual repetition of what has already been said Henry (1963) has termed "perseverating." The children were asked to respond to a question that had no real meaning in relation to their experience; they were asked to respond from their world of fantasy. There is a papier-mâché figure dressed in black with a broom leaning against a piano in a kindergarten classroom. The teacher asks the class what they believe "the witch is doing." The teacher, by asking what the witch is doing, implies that the figure labeled "witch" is engaged in some activity. The children appear to have resolved their anxiety about handling such a situation by giving a routinized response.

She continues, "Why do we have a witch in the room?" Frank responds, " 'Cause Halloween is comin'." Mrs. Caplow: "Yes, and at Halloween all sorts of strange things happen. At Halloween witches and goblins come out. Bats and bugs fly around the city. Ghosts float up and down the street. It is indeed a strange night." She asks the children, "Is the witch real?" Many of the children say, "No, no." She answers, "You are right. She is not real. I made her. She will not fly away on her broom because she is just a pretend witch."

There is no way of knowing what impact Mrs. Caplow's description of Halloween had upon the children. They may very well have believed her (for who is a five-year-old to dispute the word of an adult and a teacher?).

American culture includes a wide variety of fantasy figures which are taught in a standardized way to children. There are Santa Claus, the Easter bunny, the good fairy who puts a coin under the pillow when a tooth falls out, and all the characters from fairy tales and nursery rhymes. The middle-class child is familiar with these characters from the fantasy world long before he enters public school. From a young age, he has also heard stories about Mother Goose, Snow White and the Seven Dwarfs, Alice in Wonderland, Mickey Mouse and many others. From this exposure to fantasy and the stories that are its vehicle, the child "gets to have a certain public phantasy capability, which enables him to deal easily with whimsy" (Henry, 1963, p. 291). The assumption of the kindergarten teacher at Attucks School that the black child from the urban ghetto shares these make-believe figures or in fact understands fantasy as does the white child is questionable at best.

There are at least two factors that might inhibit the sharing of this aspect of culture. The first is the reality of class differentials between the poor and the middle class, and the second is differences between the cultural milieu of urban blacks and that of white suburbanites. One might ask to what degree these two classes share fantasy beliefs. There are no data on the significance of make-believe for the black child. The kindergarten teacher, however, assumed that the black and white child could work from the same fantasy context, regardless of cultural and class differences.

Later the same morning, Mrs. Caplow began to teach the children their first Halloween song, "Tis Halloween Night." The lyrics of the song are as follows: "Witches and goblins, jack-o'-lanterns and funny faces, black cats and flying bats, all come on Halloween night." When the children had spoken the lyrics twice, Mrs. Caplow asked them to sing the song. She gave them special directions as to how they were to sing it.

"Okay, let's make it sound real spooky." This she tells the children in a soft and hushed voice. "Let's make it like witches and goblins are really flying around the room." The children sing the song, though they are weak and off key. When they finish Mrs. Caplow says in a hushed voice, "Okay, now say boo!" The children all say "Boo." She asks, "Will that scare anyone?" The children respond with a much louder "Boo." She comments, "Okay, that's good. That would really scare somebody. Now you should tiptoe back to your seats just like little ghosts." The children walk on their tiptoes back to their seats.

The Halloween motif was carried further when the teacher had the children make jack-o'-lanterns from colored construction paper. She informed the children that they were going to make jack-o'-lanterns, though she never explained the meaning of the term.

She asks the children what shapes there are for a jack-o'-lantern and Frank replies, "Round." Marcia says they are square. Mrs. Caplow says, "Yes, they are all shapes. Some are round, some oval, some thin, and some are even short."

Her reply confused two different attributes of an object. Shape is not the same as dimension, though she included "thin" and "short." Her explanation included mutually exclusive descriptions. Such is the basis for what Henry (1963) terms "anticognition" or the process of "antilearning."

October 5

I observed that the children did not pray after the opening morning exercises. I questioned the teacher about the omission, and she related that one of the parents had come to the school and asked to have her child excused from the morning opening activities. The mother explained that the family were Jehovah's Witnesses. Mrs. Caplow said that rather than have the child either leave the room or feel uncomfortable if he stayed, she thought it easier simply to omit praying.

There occurred during the class period a clear example of the way in which children from Table 1 continued to develop close rapport with the teacher. Laura said to Mrs. Caplow, "I love you, Mrs. Caplow." The teacher responded in a very pleasant voice, "Well, I love you too, Laura. In fact, I love all the boys and girls." Laura's comment appeared to make the teacher quite happy, and she was supportive and soft-spoken with the children during the remainder of the morning period.

The especially close relationship which was developing between Laura and the teacher had one unfortunate aspect. Laura became a means through which Mrs. Caplow expressed her belittlement of those children who could not participate as Laura did.

Mrs. Caplow asks the children, "Do you boys and girls know what week this is?" Jim raises his hand, as do a large number of children. Mrs. Caplow asks Jim if he knows the answer, and he responds "Tuesday." Mrs. Caplow says, "No, not the name of the day. Joe, do you know what week it is?" Joe responds, "October." Mrs. Caplow: "No, that is the name of the month. Anne, do you know the name of the week?" Anne: "It cold outside." Mrs. Caplow is becoming noticeably irritated and says, "No, that is not it either. I guess I will have to call on Laura. Laura, come up here and stand by me. Then you can tell the other boys and girls what special week this is." Laura comes to the front, stands by Mrs. Caplow and faces the class. Mrs. Caplow has her arm around Laura. Laura says, "It fire week." Mrs. Caplow responds, "Well, Laura, that is close. Actually it is Fire Prevention Week."

In the course of this interchange, Mrs. Caplow gave an additional hint about the answer that she sought only to Laura. While the rest of the children were merely asked what week it was, Laura was asked what "special" week it was. This was the kind of added assistance that insured that Laura would be the one that Mrs. Caplow "could always rely on." Secondly, Mrs. Caplow's obvious favoritism could not have gone unnoticed by the rest of the class. Not only did she single out a child to come to the front of the room to give the answer, but she also, in putting her arm around Laura, gave supportive contact that was seldom experienced by any child in the class. Third, the message in the question posed to the children was, again, unclear. That is, they appeared not to understand the word "week" and gave what seemed to be logical answers to an unfamiliar question. There may indeed have been an element of mystification in the question; for although I had previously observed discussions of the concepts of "day" and "month," I had seen no discussion of "week." In fact, there is nothing in my notes from the first weeks of school about any mention of the word "week" before the teacher asked this question.

October 10

As one lesson to familiarize the children with their "community helpers," Mrs. Caplow took the children on a short walk to a nearby fire station. Her instructions to the children before they left the room were as follows:

"Now, boys and girls, when we go to the fire station, let's use our very best manners and be polite. Let's show the firemen what smart people we are and how we can all mind our manners. The firemen are kind men. They help to save our houses when they start to burn, so we should be very nice to them and also be polite to them. Now, don't forget. We will want to use our very best manners. Does anyone know another name for the firemen?" None of the children make any response. She continues, "They are known as fire fighters. That's a new term that they like to be called. Say fire fighters." The children repeat the phrase. Mrs. Caplow: "That's good. So when we get there we can say, 'Good morning, Mr. Fire Fighter.' Now say 'good morning, Mr. Fire Fighter.' " The children repeat the sentence.

On the way to the fire station the children passed a fire alarm box and Mrs. Caplow explained to them that it was a place where one could "come and tell the firemen that there is a fire nearby." During the walk, many of the children expressed noticeable enjoyment in being able to shuffle their feet through the leaves. They also made comments on the condition of the trees:

Laura looks up at the trees and says, "Oh, look at the naked trees."

The children near Laura begin to giggle and Art comments, "Yeah, they sure naked, ain't they." Frank says, "They don't look like naked trees to me." Laura retorts, "Boy, don't you know naked tree when you see one?" Mrs. Caplow has overheard this conversation and says to the children, "Boys and girls, those trees are not naked, they are bare. Those are bare trees. All the leaves have fallen off so now the trees are bare."

October 17

This date was particularly important, both for the social organization of the children in the class and also for my future relation to several of the children. First, Mrs. Caplow discontinued teaching the class as an entire unit and divided it into two sections. The first section consisted of the children at Table 1 and the other section was the children from Tables 2 and 3. From this day forward, reading readiness, arithmetic readiness, and phonics were taught separately to the two groups. As was to become apparent very quickly, the amount of time spent teaching the Table 1 group was two to three times greater than for Table 2 and Table 3 children. Children from the last two tables were also used frequently as "stand-ins" for the first table. That is, when Mrs. Caplow wished to demonstrate a concept such as "addition" to the Table 1 students, she would have children from the last two tables come to the front, where she would use them as "numbers" to be added together. The children in front would be shuffled to create new addition problems for the children at Table 1 to solve. A typical problem was: "If I have two children on one side and one child on the other, how many would I have if I brought them all in front of me?" The children would then be moved through the various parts of the problem.

More and more frequently I had observed the children at Table 1 directing belittlement and ridicule at the children from Tables 2 and 3. Two incidents occurred during this morning.

David came to where I was seated and told me to look at the shoes that Lilly was wearing to school. I asked him why I should look at the shoes and he responded, " 'Cause they so ragged and dirty." (David sits at Table 1 and Lilly at Table 3.)

Susan has brought two magazines from home. She is at her table looking through one of them. Mrs. Caplow comes to Susan and asks if she would like to share the magazine she is not reading with another child. Before Susan can reply, Frank comes and takes a magazine from Susan, commenting, "She don't need a magazine." (Frank is from Table 1, Susan from Table 3.)

During the entire school year, no incident was recorded in which a child from either Table 2 or 3 initiated a derogatory remark to a child at the first table.

Mrs. Caplow told me that she had selected, at my request, two children in the class who she thought were "doing well" and two who were "doing poorly." I had asked her to do this so that I could begin more intensive observation of these four children within the classroom and also learn more about them and their parents outside the classroom. I asked her to select the children rather than doing so myself, because it is the teacher's perception of who does well and who does poorly in the class that is crucial. The two children selected as doing well, Laura and Frank, both sat at Table 1. Lilly and LeRoy, the two children selected as doing poorly, both sat at Table 3. On her own initiative, Mrs. Caplow also called the families of three of the children (Lilly's home did not have a phone) and explained who I was and that I wished to meet the parents. None of the three parents whom she contacted objected. In fact, during my first visit Laura's mother, especially, was quite vocal in her disappointment that I had postponed coming to their home until three weeks after Mrs. Caplow's phone call.

October 19
Miss Allen was to teach her fifth speech lesson to the class. The children, when they were told to form a semicircle around her, did so, but

at a good distance away, and they huddled very close together. A number of the children displayed noticeable anxiety, trying to leave the group either for the bathroom or for a drink of water, facing directly away from the group, or not responding to any of the questions Miss Allen asked. As Miss Allen described the "gray goose sound," Joe, one child from Table 1, asked whether the gray goose could drink water, but the teacher ignored the question. This was the only verbalization that any child in the class initiated with Miss Allen until she was ready to leave the room. Several of the children, notably, Susan, Art, and Mike, requested permission to leave the group. Susan did so three times.

Until the fifth speech lesson, there had not been a single recorded instance where a child sitting at the periphery of the group had attempted, within the context of the lesson, to establish contact with the speech teacher. This large group of students from Tables 2 and 3 sat passively throughout the lessons and would respond, most often, only when called upon. The first attempt of one of this group to establish interaction with the teacher and attempt to participate in the lesson took this form:

John, who has sat passively and quietly throughout the lesson, stands up all of a sudden at the rear of the group and calls to Miss Allen, "Call on me." The tone of his voice is somewhat desperate as he seeks to have the teacher select him for the question. Miss Allen, however, replies, "John, sit down. I cannot call on anyone who shouts out in class." John slumps back to the floor and turns his back to the speech teacher. He does not say a word for the rest of the lesson.

This was the first time I saw John attempt to gain the attention of either of the teachers, Mrs. Caplow or Miss Allen.

As John sat with his back to the teacher, Fred came and joined him. The two then sat in the same manner until Miss Allen had left the room. As she was about to leave, she went to Mrs. Caplow and spelled out,

"I-s F-r-e-d s-l-o-w?" Mrs. Caplow replied, "Oh, I don't think so. I believe that he is just shy." Miss Allen responded, "I thought maybe he was having problems." She was then about to leave, having said goodbye to the children and having them say a single goodbye to her, when two of the children at Table 1 at the last moment called out, "Goodbye, Miss Allen." She turned back to the children with a harsh rebuke: "You have already said goodbye to me. Now be quiet." She then left the room.

October 24

In each of the grade levels through the elementary school years, the teachers are provided with a curriculum guide. The St. Louis *Social Studies Curriculum Guide* (1967) stated the purpose of social studies within the kindergarten class as follows:

The aim of the social studies curriculum is to develop in the individual the attitudes, values, understanding, and skills necessary for the perpetuation and improvement of our democratic society and for the promotion of peaceful human relations throughout the world.

One of the guide's suggestions to the teacher for furthering the child's knowledge of "other people and other lands" was to plan activities for United Nations Day. Such observances were encouraged in order that the child gain "knowledge of the contributions of ethnic groups and nations to the world culture." For the 24th of October, Mrs. Caplow planned a celebration of United Nations Day, for which each child was to construct a flag representative of any member nation.

As was the case with the introduction of Fire Prevention Week to the class, Mrs. Caplow again made Laura her "showcase" child.

"If anyone knows what special day today is, raise their hand." Mary raises her hand and Mrs. Caplow calls on her. Mary says, "It cloudy." Mrs. Caplow responds, "Well, yes, it is cloudy today, but that is not what I asked for. Why is today a special day?" Joe raises his hand and he is called upon. He says, "It windy." Mrs. Caplow responds, "No, that does not make it a special day." Marcia is called on next. She says, "It cloudy." Mrs. Caplow replies, "No, that doesn't make it a special day." Virginia is selected and she states it is a "hot day." Mrs. Caplow repeats her statement, "No, that does not make it a special day. Laura, will you come and tell the children what special day it is today? Come and stand by me and tell the children what day today is. Susan, will you please be quiet so all the class can hear Laura. Laura, come here and face the class." Laura stands beside Mrs. Caplow, faces the class and says, "Today is United Nations Day."

Mary was then asked why the class should celebrate United Nations Day and she replied, " 'Cause they work for peace." Mrs. Caplow responded, "Yes, we will make flags to celebrate United Nations Day." Shortly thereafter, while the children were busy with a ditto sheet "number readiness" exercise, Mrs. Caplow came to where I was seated and explained she wanted the children to make the flags in order to "let them work with shapes." During the number readiness exercises, she prepared the materials that the children would use to make their flags.

When the children had finished their lesson and Mrs. Caplow had the materials ready, she demonstrated how to cut out various shapes for the flags, including stripes, stars, and rectangles. She also explained how to attach a handle to the flag and then told them to begin. There was no further discussion of various flags or pictures provided by which the children might gain ideas for their own flags. Though the children at Table 1 began work immediately, several of the children at the remaining two tables were quite hesitant. Two children, John and Lilly, did not begin until nearly half of the other students in the class were finished. As the children finished their flags, they went to show them to Mrs. Caplow. They then showed their flags to me, and as each child came up, I asked the name of his particular flag.

The uncertainty of the children at all three tables about what they were supposed to do is shown by a listing of some of the names given to the flags. Table 1: Our Country Flag; Star Spangled Flag; Right Flag; United American Flag; United Nations Day. Table 2: United Streak in American Flag; Our Flag; Airplane Flag; United States Flag. Table 3: American Flag; "H" Flag; United Story in American Flag; State Spangled Banner Flag; a Girl Flag; Knighted Nation Flag; United Station Flag; My Flag. The children were probably confused because the teacher never stated where or what the United Nations was. The only definition of the United Nations was given by Mary when she said that "they work for peace." The only flag with which the children were familiar was the American flag, and for the most part they resorted to their experience when asked to make a flag for an undefined organization.

As was to be done on several other occasions during the school year (Holloween, "Indian" day, and May Day), Mrs. Caplow had the children parade through several of the other rooms on the first floor. This was done ostensibly to allow the older children to see what the kindergarten children had made. Some of the children, however, were not able to carry their flags, as Mrs. Caplow had passed out two drums, a tambourine, three sets of musical sticks, and one set of cymbals.

Mrs. Caplow has the children line up in pairs. Those with the musical instruments are at the front. After all the children are in line, she puts "My Country, 'Tis of Thee" on the record player. Frank exclaims that it is a church song, but Mrs. Caplow says it is not. Three other children, when they hear the song, put down their flags and put their left hands over their hearts. After "My Country, 'Tis of Thee," Mrs. Caplow plays the national anthem. She has the children hold their flags above their head. Mrs. Caplow says to Laura, "Laura, suppose that you be the leader of our class to the different rooms." Frank calls out, "But I want to be the leader." Laura responds, "You not gonna be the leader, boy, I am."

When the national anthem ended Mrs. Caplow put on a long-playing album of military marching songs and had the children march through three of the rooms on the first floor. In each of the rooms that the class visited, Laura gave a short talk explaining why they were visting other classes in the school. She stated "Today is United Nations Day. It is a special day." As the children returned to the class, the marching music was still playing. Mrs. Caplow instructed the children to march by their desks, lay down their flags, and then march to the rest room. She stood by the record player clapping her hands to keep time with the music.

October 26

Mrs. Caplow often concentrated her teaching attention exclusively on the children at Table 1. Only occasionally did she ask questions during general class discussion of children at the other two tables. Once when she did ask a direct question of a Table 2 student the discussion reverted to the teacher and a student at Table 1.

Mrs. Caplow asks Mike, "Mike, you put up the weather symbol this morning. Can you tell us what it means?" (She is referring to a piece of gray construction paper cut in the shape of a cloud which Mike had tacked on the calendar under today's date.) Mike answers, "It cloudy outside." Laura then calls out, "It chilly outside too." Mrs. Caplow responds, "Well, it is not really that cold outside today, Laura." She then has the children count the number of days in the month. No further comment is made to Mike.

Additional evidence of the division between the Table 1 students and the remainder of the class was the continued closeness of the Table 1 group to the teacher during the morning opening exercises. Frank was noted as having "scooted up so close to Mrs. Caplow that he is practically sitting in her lap." Laura and Mary were also very close by. At the other extreme, Fred, Karen, John, Susan, Lilly, and LeRoy (all Table 3) were noted as being at the very periphery of the group, six to eight feet from the teacher. Later in the morning when Mrs. Caplow gave each of the children a name tag in preparation for the arrival of

Miss Allen, five children from the first table whose names had been called began to congregate at the piano. They had received no direction from Mrs. Caplow to do so and apparently simply moved to the piano on their own.

Susan, from Table 3, is called by Mrs. Caplow to come to the desk for her name tag. After she has her tag, she begins to walk toward the piano to join the five children already standing there. Mrs. Caplow calls to Susan in a harsh voice, "Susan, sit down. Sit down, Susan. Do not go over there." Susan then goes back to her seat and sits down. No comment is made to the five children at the piano that they also should go to their seats and sit down. They continue to stand by the piano.

In a very literal sense, the teacher was informing a child from Table 3 that she was not to infringe on the prerogatives of the Table 1 children.

October 27
The major substantive area that the teacher sought to introduce to the children after the long unit on the school was the family. I did not observe the initial lesson in this unit, but hints of what was discussed were evident during the second lesson.

Mrs. Caplow begins, "Now, children, yesterday we began to talk about the family. Mike, can you tell us who we said were the members of the family?" Mike replies, "My mother and my sisters." Mrs. Caplow responds, "Yes, the mother, father, brothers, sisters, and even pets make up our family."

In this instance, the child's response was distorted by the teacher's desire to inform the children that the family is not merely the mother and the children (though such is the case for nineteen of the children), but that it also includes the father, brother, and pets.

Within this same discussion of family size and members, I observed the single instance during the entire school year when the children were able to ask personal questions of the teacher and receive replies. The probing was begun by a boy from Table 1 and continued by others from the same table.

Joe asks Mrs. Caplow, "Mrs. Caplow, do you have any kids?" Mrs. Caplow responds, "No, I don't, Joe." "Why not?" Mrs. Caplow: "I just don't." "Well, do you love kids?" Mrs. Caplow: "Oh, yes, I love children." Joe: "Well, do you love us?" Mrs. Caplow: "Yes, Joe, I love all of you." "Would you like to have some children?" Mrs. Caplow, "Yes, I would, Joe." Mary calls out, "Take me, my mother don't want me anyway." Laura says, "Take me, too." Joe and Marcia also ask to be taken to Mrs. Caplow's house. She answers the children in a pleasant manner: "No, boys and girls, if I did that, what would your mothers think?" This ends the conversation and Mrs. Caplow introduces a movie.

Though Mrs. Caplow had said earlier to the children that the family consisted of both parents, children, and pets, she then showed a movie which featured only a mother bear and two cubs. The continual emphasis throughout the movie was on the loving care that the mother gave the cubs and how it was the duty of the mother to protect the cubs from the gruff and dangerous father. The last frame of the movie stated, "The mother bear has done a good job. Now her two cubs are on their own." The only male in the film was the father, who at one point said that he wanted to eat the children. The mother bear then had to fight to keep the father away from the cubs.

As one aspect of the discussion of the family, Mrs. Caplow talked with the children about the different kinds of foods that a family eats ("baby food," "children food," and "grown-up food"). The children were asked to give examples of each of the three types of foods and all of their responses were of a similar nature. Mentioned repeatedly were greens, Jell-O, candy, Kool-ade, cornbread, beans, grits, and potato chips. Mrs. Caplow then called attention to new posters that she had put on the bulletin board for the children to see. There were

five pictures listed under the heading "The Good Breakfast Foods."
All five pictures showed a white mother and her child. The first picture
showed the mother feeding the child a large platter of sliced ham and
fried eggs. The second showed both drinking a tall glass of orange
juice. The third was of the mother serving the child a ham casserole.
The child was eating a bowl of breakfast food that was smothered in
strawberries in the fourth picture, and the last showed both mother and
child drinking milk. If the children's answers can be taken as even
partly reliable, one would suspect that the posters showed foods that
were seldom if ever tasted by the majority of children in the class. The
irony of such nutrition lessons never did seem to occur to Mrs. Caplow.

October 31
Today the class had a Halloween party. Mrs. Caplow asked two
mothers, both of whose children sat at Table 1, to assist her with the
party. In the time period before the morning recess, the two mothers
arranged one half of the room for the party while Mrs. Caplow taught
the children in the other.

During the teaching lesson, there occurred an interactional pattern
between the teacher and several of the children that I had not previously observed. Mrs. Caplow issued contradictory commands to the
children, resulting in confusion of response.

Art walks up to the blackboard to look at the calendar. Mrs. Caplow
says to Art, "Art, you are spoiling our room. Go and sit down." He
does. She then instructs Marcia to "stand straight." She turns back
to Art and says, "Art, why are you sitting down, you are supposed
to be standing with the rest of the children. Now get up." He hesi-
tates at first and then slowly rises out of the chair.

There were occasions when the teacher's actions prompted the
children en masse to give contradictory responses.

Mrs. Caplow has just begun to carve a pumpkin into a jack-o'-lantern, and she asks the children if they have ever had pumpkin pie. All the children raise their hands, indicating that they have had pumpkin pie. She then instructs them to put their hands down and asks all the children who have never had pumpkin pie to raise their hands. Again all the hands go up. Mrs. Caplow comments, "Okay, I guess I will have to make it sometime." She then tells the children to put their hands back down.

Mrs. Caplow had told the children that she would like them to come to class on Halloween in costume, and eleven of the thirty children did so. Of these, six sat at Table 1, three at Table 2, and two at Table 3. Three of the costumes were store-bought, all worn by children from Table 1. Laura and Mary wore Cinderella costumes. Each carried a wand, wore a ballerina-type dress, and had a face mask that was white with golden hair. Frank wore a Superman costume but did not have a mask. Five other children wore masks but no costumes. Counting the five children with face masks plus the eleven who wore costumes, sixteen of the thirty children had some type of disguise. After recess the children were served hot dogs, potato chips, milk, ice cream and cookies. They then paraded through all of the classrooms on the first floor of the building and three more on the second floor.

November 6
The class was well into the unit on the family and family-related activities. Discussion continued:

Mrs. Caplow is seated by the flannel board. She has placed a picture of a young, blond white girl washing dishes on it. She speaks to the class, "Now, boys and girls, you see the picture of this little girl. She is helping her mother do the dishes. I think that all of us boys and girls should help our parents by doing chores around the house. All people in the family need to help and work together." Laura says, "I have to clean my own room." Mrs. Caplow responds, "That's nice, Laura." She goes on to explain that she bought two white mice to do a study on the effect of food. She tells the class that one mouse will be fed each day while the other will be fed only once every third day. Then the children will be able to watch the two mice play in their cage and see how the mouse that has no food does not play as much as does the mouse with food. She tells the children "healthy food makes for a healthy body."

Elaborating further on this discussion of nutrition, Mrs. Caplow holds in front of the children a picture of a black family of four at a large cloth-covered table eating a meal. They are using fine china and glassware. They have heaping salads, bowls of potatoes, and vegetables as well as a roast or steak on a platter in the middle of the table.

Mrs. Caplow puts the picture on the flannel board. She states, "Now, this family is eating a meal. Say 'meal,' class." The class repeats, "meal." She continues, "Who do you think this man is here in the picture?" One of the boys responds, "Daddy." She says, "Yes, but we call him father. This is the father, this is the mother, this is the sister, and this is the brother. Marcia, what do you believe they are having for dinner?" Marcia answers, "Syrup, Jell-O and greens." Mrs. Caplow ignores this response and asks Joe, "What is this little girl going to do?" (She is lifting a napkin to her face.) Joe responds, "She gonna blow her nose." Mrs. Caplow becomes quite irritated with Joe and says, "No, Joe, she is going to place the napkin in her lap so that does not soil her nice clothes if she happens to drop food in her lap." The children sit completely still and look quite confused. The room is totally quiet. Mrs. Caplow changes the subject.

Concurrent with the unit on the family, Mrs. Caplow began to introduce the children to activities and ideas related to Thanksgiving. For the witch beside the piano, she substituted a Pilgrim woman made from papier-mâché and painted with a white face and blond hair. There were also several posters on the boards in the room and a large picture of a turkey above the blackboard. After discussing the meal of the family in the picture, she drew a Pilgrim head on the blackboard. It had the face of a small boy.

She asks the class, "Who is this boy?" Art says, "A cowboy." She responds, "Well, who wears black hats?" Frank says, "Cowboys." Another boy, Mike, says "Indians." Joe says, "Old people." Marcia offers, "Farmers." Mrs. Caplow replies, "No, no, boys and girls, this boy's name begins with the Peter Puffer sound." Frank suggests, "Peter." Mrs. Caplow: "No, they are Pilgrims. Now all of you say Pilgrims." The children do. She then ends the lesson and passes out crayons and a ditto sheet with a turkey on it.

Mrs. Caplow quite frequently introduced the element of religion into the activities of the class. Though the morning prayer had been canceled, a prayer was said before food was served at class parties, and she often made mention of Christian beliefs. When asked in an interview session about the role that religion had played in her life and what influence religion had on the lives of the children in her class she responded:

"I believe that religion played a strong part—a very fundamental part in our family. My mother is a devout person. She kept us in Sunday school and church. Those of us in the city still attend the same church. Religion has played a big part in our upbringing. It seems to be lacking in children today. They don't seem to have the same spiritual values anymore. Now they have more things to take their interest. The church used to be the center of activities. Now there is a thousand and one things to do, I guess."

The religious origins and connotations of major school holidays had a central role in Mrs. Caplow's discussions. Three particularly important holidays were Thanksgiving, Christmas, and Easter.

Mrs. Caplow is seated on the piano bench next to the Pilgrim woman. She asks the class, "Boys and girls, what does the Pilgrim woman seem to be doing?" Laura says, "She prayin'." Mrs. Caplow responds, "Yes, she is giving thanks for all that she has been blessed with. Okay, now all of you fold your hands and we will pray just like the Pilgrim for all the blessings that we received." Mrs. Caplow also folds her hands and then recites, "Thank you for the food we eat, thank you for the world so sweet, thank you for the birds that sing, thank you Lord, for everything." After saying this verse, she sings it for the children. She then asks the children to say each line after her, which they do.

November 9
Mrs. Caplow introduced today what she termed "creative dramatics." The lesson was to focus on what the family members did at mealtime and the types of foods that the family should eat. The lesson began as Mrs. Caplow again showed the children the picture of the black family seated at a table with mounds of food and fine china, glassware, and linens.

Mrs. Caplow calls on Marcia to describe what the family in the picture is doing. Marcia replies, "They eatin'." Mrs. Caplow: "Yes, they are eating. What do you think they are eating?" Frank: "Breakfast." Mrs. Caplow: "Oh, do you think so, Frank?" Joe calls out, "Supper." Mrs. Caplow: "Yes, they are eating dinner. Dinner is the same as supper. How did the food come to the house? Where did they get their food to eat?" Rich says, "From the ground." Mrs. Caplow: "Yes, it grows in the ground, but then where does it go?" Frank: "To the store." Mrs. Caplow: "Yes, who usually goes to the store and buys the food for your house?" Marcia says, "My mama." Mrs. Caplow: "Well, who does the cooking in your house?" Marcia replies, "My mama." Frank interrupts, "But my daddy always does the barbecuin'." Mrs. Caplow: "Oh, does he? That is very nice." Mike calls out, "My daddy works so he can't be a cook." Mrs. Caplow: "That is a very good point, Mike. Father has to work so he can bring home the money that the family needs for food."

Again it was evident that Mrs. Caplow assumed that the family unit consisted of both parents plus children. This was also true of some members of the class who had both a father and mother in their homes. For nineteen of the thirty children, however, there was no father to bring home money for food.

Mrs. Caplow brought a small white table and four small white chairs into the center of the room. She also brought a piece of red burlap and laid it, still folded, on the table. She asked who could "be a good mother." All of the girls raised their hands in response to this question, and Mrs. Caplow said, "We will try Laura for the mother and David for the father." The boys were not asked who wished to be the father. Mary asked to be the grandmother, but Mrs. Caplow said that this family did not have a grandmother. She did select Mary to be the daughter and LeRoy as the son. She asked this group of four students to come into the center of the room.

She hands Laura the red burlap and asks, "What do we call this, Laura?" Laura responds, "A tablecloth." Mrs. Caplow: "Yes, we should *always* use a tablecloth when we eat. Okay, now the rest of you boys and girls sit down and be quiet and watch Laura begin to prepare the supper." Laura asks, "What am I supposed to do?" Mrs. Caplow: "I want you to do what your mother does at home. What would the son, daughter, and father do while you were fixing supper?" Laura: "I don't know." Mrs. Caplow: "Well, what will you serve for supper?" Laura: "I don't know." Mrs. Caplow: "What does your mother serve for supper?" Laura: "Greens and Jell-O." Mrs. Caplow: "Oh, well, I suppose that's all right." (Note: Mrs. Caplow seems taken aback by Laura's answer. She seems to be looking for a response more in keeping with the picture of the family eating mashed potatoes, green beans, and steak.)

Mrs. Caplow at this point turned her attention to David and LeRoy, who were to be the father and son.

Mrs. Caplow asks David, "David, what should the father do before

he reads the paper?" David: "He should ask if supper is ready."
Mrs. Caplow: "Well, ask her." David does and Laura responds,
"No." Mike calls from where he is seated, "When my daddy comes
home from work, he kiss my mama." Mrs. Caplow: "Yes, Mike.
When most fathers do come home from work, they kiss their wives.
Okay, now, Laura, call your family to the dinner table." Laura:
"Dinner ready." Susan, from where she is seated, asks, "If they
gonna eat, ain't they suppose to wash their hands?" Mrs. Caplow:
"Well, since we are only pretending and not really eating, we won't
wash our hands." Mrs. Caplow then instructs the four seated at the
small table that they are to "talk as a family talks at the dinner
table." LeRoy, who has said very little, is told by Mrs. Caplow to go
back to his seat. "I think we will have Joe as the new son. LeRoy,
you go and sit down. Joe, you seem to know what a son is supposed
to do. You come and take LeRoy's place." Joe then comes to the
table and immediately says to David, "Hey, ol' man, what you do at
work today?" David says, "I ain't do nothin'." Mrs. Caplow looks in
amazement at the two boys and says, "What are you two talking
about? Dinner time is time for the family to enjoy each other and
also enjoy their meal. Now talk in a pleasant manner to each other."
While the four in the center of the room sit silent, Mrs. Caplow turns
to the children seated at their desks and asks, "How many of you
eat your meals with your mother and father?" All the children raise
their hands. Susan calls out, "I got no daddy, but I eat with him anyway." Mrs. Caplow then instructs all the children to line up for the
restroom.

During this lesson on the family, Mrs. Caplow demonstrated such a
strong orientation to the concept of a middle-class family with proper
manners and "table talk" that any deviation from this norm simply was
unacceptable. To Laura, she could have shown real acceptance of
what her family ate for supper by referring to it as part of the make-
believe meal. Instead, there was only a vacant acceptance which ap-

peared to carry a second and opposite meaning to the child: that what she ate at home really was not acceptable, but it "would do." As a second example, when Mrs. Caplow replaced LeRoy with Joe, she substituted a boy from Table 1 who came from a home with both a mother and father for a welfare child who had no father in the home with whom he could talk. LeRoy was being penalized not only for being unable to engage in table talk with an imaginary father, but, more fundamentally, because he did not have the experience which could have made him acceptable in the role. The mere fact of being asked to sit and converse with David, an imaginary father, was an incongruity for the child.

As a final indication of Mrs. Caplow's strong emphasis upon middle-class mannerisms of speech and behavior during the skit, she did not allow Joe and David to continue the single creative and realistic exchange which occurred during the entire time the children were at the table, because the language was not standard American English and did not deal with an exciting job, but with the boredom of doing "nothin'." This was not an acceptable way to teach children about family life and appropriate table talk.

November 21
In Chapter 2 on the St. Louis School system, it was noted that the training of the apprentice teachers from Harris Teachers College takes place in the public schools. In Mrs. Caplow's kindergarten class there was an apprentice, Miss Phillips, during the last two weeks of November. The next to the last day of Miss Phillip's visit was also to be the last day of the unit on the family. Mrs. Caplow had scheduled a film as part of the final discussion. She suggested that Miss Phillips conduct the part of the family lesson dealing with the film and the discussion afterwards with the children.

Miss Phillips comes to the front of the class and speaks in a very soft and hushed voice. "Now, boys and girls, you have been talking about your family. You have been talking about your parents. Sometimes your parents tell us things for our own good, even though we don't understand them. Today we are going to have a film about a mother goat who told her little boys and girls things to do. They did not obey her so we will watch the film and see what happens to baby goats when they do not listen to what their mother tells them to do." Joe calls out, "If they don't listen, they get a whuppin'." Miss Phillips responds, "Yes, that is right. We have to obey our parents. The name of the film is 'The Wolf and the Seven Little Kids.' Now all of you will have to be quiet or you will not be able to hear the film. Kids are really baby goats so we could call this film 'The Wolf and Seven Baby Goats'." Susan at this point leaves the group and goes into the bathroom. Mrs. Caplow stands at the back of the room by the projector while Miss Phillips stands near the front of the group to the right side.

The film of the "Wolf and the Seven Baby Kids" was taken directly from the nursery tale. The film and the tale concern a mother goat who told her seven kids to be very careful of a wolf who lurked in the woods waiting to eat baby goats. The mother, who has to leave the home, warns the children not to open the door for anyone. The wolf, after trying a number of disguises, was finally admitted to the home. The frame of the film that showed the wolf entering the home had a caption at the bottom: "The wicked wolf rushed in. Look how all the babies ran to hide." Several frames later the wolf was shown with a bloated stomach from having eaten all the baby goats but one. The mother returned to find only one of her babies left and suggested that they go into the woods for a walk to "forget their sadness." In the woods they found the sleeping wolf. The mother goat performed a caesarian operation on the wolf and the six baby goats jumped out alive. The mother and the babies then filled the wolf's stomach with rocks. When the wolf woke, he went for a drink at the well, was pushed in by the mother goat, and drowned. When the film ended, Miss Phillips came to the front of the class:

"Now, that is all of the story, boys and girls. Do you see what will happen to you when you don't listen to what your mother and father tell you?" The children appear frightened by what Miss Phillips has said and are very quiet. Mrs. Caplow informs the class that they are now finished with their study of the family and they can color a picture of their own family until it is time for recess.

Winter

With Halloween and Thanksgiving past, the teacher and children turned their attention to Christmas. There was the expected change in posters and bulletin board displays, and the children colored Christmas trees instead of jack-o'-lanterns or turkeys. At Attucks School, the early excitement and quick pace of the first weeks was replaced by the tension of fatigue. The kindergartners' weariness with the routine was evident in the penultimate rehearsal of *A Christmas Carol* for the PTA meeting the following night.

December 12

As I walked into the kindergarten classroom, several of the children were trying to sing "God Rest Ye Merry, Gentlemen." When the group was approximately halfway through the first verse, Mike stood up and called to the class, "Stop all that noise. Now everyone be quiet." Mrs. Caplow turned to Mike and said, "That was very good, Mike. Be sure that you say it that way tomorrow night." Art, playing the role of Bob Cratchit, walked to Mike, playing Scrooge, and said, "Good morning, Uncle." Mike replies, "Bah, humbug." These two boys then exchanged several other lines. They seemed to know their parts quite well.

The play continued as two of the children, portraying poor persons, came to Scrooge and asked for money to buy Christmas presents. Scrooge answered, "I have no money for the poor. There are places for such people. Be gone with you." As the two poor persons were about to leave, the "angels of Christmas Past" were to come into the center of the circle of children. The following notes catch some of the scene as the children who were to be angels assembled for the entrance.

Mrs. Caplow calls for the angels in a very brusque voice with a hint of irritation. She appears very impatient with the children. The children on their part seem either confused or disinterested in the activity, because they move with neither enthusiasm nor energy. They have not lined up to enter; in fact, several are still at their seats. After Mrs. Caplow calls for the second time and in a firm voice for the angels, they begin to assemble. After they have gotten into the circle and given their short talk to Scrooge, they merely stand in the circle. Mrs. Caplow quickly tells the children to move out and briskly instructs the actors who are to come on. She appears irritated and seems to tolerate little hesitancy on the part of the children. Those children who are not involved, twenty of the thirty students in the class, sit in their seats displaying only sporadic interest in the rehearsal. Mrs. Caplow senses the confusion and lack of attention in the room and suggests that the class "line up for a drink of water." They do, the boys in one line and the girls in another. After all have had a chance for a drink, Mrs. Caplow asks them to come back to their seats. During the time that the children are at the drinking fountain, Mrs. Caplow brings into the center of the circle a small white table and six small white chairs.

When the children return to their seats, Laura is told to go to the table, as is Frank. (Laura is playing mother of the Cratchit family, and Frank is the oldest son.) Mary, who has the part of the daughter, is also told to go to the table. As she instructs these children to take their places in the circle, LeRoy, Joe, and Tom come from the boys' restroom. They are the last to come to their seats. As they near their seats, Mrs. Caplow tells them in a firm voice to sit down and puts her hand on the shoulders of LeRoy and Tom and pushes them into the chairs. She then returns to the children in the center of the circle. When Scrooge comes to the Cratchit home to eat Christmas dinner with the family, he enters and says, "Here I am, Mr. Scrooge." When Mike says this, Mrs. Caplow turns him around and instructs him to say his lines so that he faces the "audience." The play continues as the family and Scrooge are seated and ready to eat. At this moment, Mrs. Caplow calls to the remainder of the class, "Okay, now let's everyone be quiet. Here is the line. David, what do you say now as Tiny Tim?" David responds, "God, bless us, every one." Mrs. Caplow tells him, "Yes, David, but say it louder tomorrow night. We will want everyone to hear you."

Later in the morning as the children were resting, Mrs. Caplow and I were able to chat informally. She asked if I would be able to attend the program the following evening and I said yes. She commented that she hoped the children would be able to "do much better by then." (For the past eight school days, the class had been practicing this program for at least one hour per day.) She also asked when I planned to make another visit to Lilly's home. I said that I would be going later that same afternoon. She responded, "If there's any way that you can approach the subject with the mother, see if you can find out why it is that Lilly smells so strongly from urine. I wonder if she has to sleep in it or whether or not her bed is changed." She was seriously thinking, she said, of asking the school social worker to make a home visit to determine the conditions and what might be done for the child. (In a later conversation with the school social worker, I learned that she had not received such a request from the kindergarten teacher.) As she went back to check on the work of the children, Mrs. Caplow closed the conversation: "It is just pitiful that the child has to come to school literally stinking."

Laura and Frank, Lilly and LeRoy
When the teacher was asked to select "two children doing well and two doing poorly," she chose Laura and Frank as doing well and Lilly

and LeRoy as doing poorly. As I stated earlier, I deliberately left the selection to her because it was her perceptions of success and failure that determined the classroom experience of the children. After the return of the children from Christmas vacation, observation within the classroom focused specifically on the behavior and activities of these four children, rather than on the teacher, as had been the case previously. Thus I observed the children even when not in interaction with the teacher.

From the time that the teacher selected the four children, I began to visit periodically in their homes. The major concern of these visits was better to understand the home as one of the crucial learning centers for the child. I hoped that through observation in an alternative milieu I could make an attempt to state more clearly the interrelationship of the school and home as they influenced the child's learning situation. As a backdrop to the analysis of the education experience of the four children, a brief descriptive profile of the respective homes and families is offered.

Laura

Laura was an only child in a home where both the mother and father were employed. Both parents were high school graduates and the mother had some college experience. They lived in a four-room apartment that was small but always clean. The furnishings were new and protected by plastic covers. The parents spoke continually of their desire to move away from their inner city neighborhood to a suburban home. The plastic on the furniture was explained as necessary to keep it "looking new for the new house." During the nearly three years of the study, they did not move.

Laura's bed was in her parents' bedroom. Above it was a bulletin board reserved for her school papers. In the living room was a small desk with a supply of paper, pencils, and several boxes of crayons specifically for her use. She had been bought a number of educational toys and materials including a globe, a small typewriter, several alphabet books, and a variety of children's general reading books.

Frank

Frank was also an only child in a home where both the mother and father were employed. Both parents were high school graduates, and the mother also had a college degree. Frank's grandmother, who, like her daughter, was a college graduate, lived with the family in a seven-room home that was extremely well furnished, with wall-to-wall carpeting and expensive-looking furniture. The home was always neat and orderly. The grandmother kept house since both parents were working. Like Laura's family, Frank's parents spoke of moving to the suburbs away from the neighborhood where the grandmother had lived since childhood. Frank and his family did move to a spacious suburban home at the end of the kindergarten school year.

In their city home, Frank had a room of his own that was cluttered with model planes, trucks, a portable television, a record player, numerous books, an encyclopedia set, and a large chest of toys. On the walls were posted many of his papers from school as well as pictures of racing cars, jet airplanes, and a large bus. There was a small shelf that was well supplied with pencils, paper, crayons, felt-tip pens, and colored construction paper.

Lilly

One of eleven children, Lilly, her brothers and sisters, and her mother were supported by public welfare funds. The mother was not employed and had completed four grades of school in the rural South. At the age of eight, she quit school and went to work in the cotton fields which she did not leave until she moved north to St. Louis ten years later. The home consisted of both apartments in a duplex, dirty and in extremely poor repair. During the winter there was no heat other than from a gas stove in the living room and another in the kitchen. The home was owned by a Missouri state public welfare worker who also happened to be the family caseworker. From Lilly's mother's monthly welfare payment of $330, $150 was paid back to the welfare worker for rent.

Lilly slept upstairs in a converted kitchen. She shared a bed with three of her sisters. Her clothes were piled in one corner of the room on the floor as there were no chests or closets for any of the children. None of Lilly's schoolwork or that of any of her seven brothers and sisters in school was evident in the home. The only visible reading material was *TV Guide.* The children did not have a single book or toy among them. Their lack of possessions reflected conditions in the remainder of the apartment, which was sparsely furnished with old, dilapidated furniture. In many places on the walls there were large gaping holes where the plaster had fallen. The window of the front door was broken and covered with plastic and plywood.

LeRoy

Like Lilly, LeRoy came from a home supported by public welfare funds. There were six children in the family, including a baby born shortly before Christmas. LeRoy's mother completed eighth grade in the St. Louis school system and then quit to work to help support her family. She was married when she was nineteen. The family lived in a five-room apartment. LeRoy shared a bed with his only brother in a bedroom they had to themselves. The mother and baby slept in another, while his three sisters shared the third bedroom. The home was neat and well heated. The furnishings were in good repair though not new. LeRoy's uncle lived nearby and appeared to serve as a substitute father to the children, taking them riding in his car, fishing, and to sports events, and providing the mother with money to supplement her welfare payment of $205 per month.

In the bedroom shared by LeRoy and his older brother were a number of pictures of baseball players and cars. Several of his school papers lay in one corner. The room was clean though sparsely furnished with a bed and one chest. LeRoy had several toy trucks as well as a fishing reel, which he valued quite highly. He once told me that the reel was given to him by his grandfather. There were a few children's reading books in the home and the family subscribed to the city black newspaper.

The Classroom Experience of Winners and Losers

January 4
One of the routines that Mrs. Caplow repeated daily with the children was the opening exercise. Once the prayer had been deleted, the basic observances were the Pledge of Allegiance and the singing of the "My'Country, 'Tis of Thee." After these were completed, the children were given time to come to the front of the class and "show and tell." They could bring an item from home, tell of an experience, or describe something that they had made. The show-and-tell period quickly became an activity reserved for those from Table 1. On the first day back to school from the Christmas vacation, a number of children from all three tables had brought Christmas toys to school for show-and-tell, but most of these went unnoticed. Only children from Table 1 participated, save one girl from Table 3 who brought a pretty, dark-skinned doll for the class to see.

  A description of the period follows:

  The second child called to the front is Laura. Mrs. Caplow says to Laura, "Laura, what do you have to tell the boys and girls today?" Laura comes to the front of the group and says, "My mama made me this dress." Mrs. Caplow comments that the dress is beautiful and suggests to Laura that she take off her sweater so that the children can see the whole dress. The dress is a shift made from green corduroy. Mrs. Caplow asks Laura how her mother made the dress and Laura responds that she went to the home of a friend, where she sewed it. Mrs. Caplow again praises Laura's dress. "That's a very pretty dress, Laura. Now you may sit down."

The fifth child asked to come to the front is Frank. Mrs. Caplow says to him, "Frank, you come to the front of the room and tell the boys and girls something. What did you bring to show them today?" Frank comes to the front and says, "I brought two racehorses, see." He then reaches in his pocket and takes out two small plastic horses. Mrs. Caplow asks Frank if he plays with these two horses by himself and Frank replies, "No, friends come over to my house and we all play together." Mrs. Caplow asks the color of the two horses and Frank responds correctly that one is white and one is black. She then asks, "Frank, what is on the side of the horses?" Frank says, "Numbers." Mrs. Caplow continues, "Frank, do you know what those numerals are?" Frank responds "four and five." Mrs. Caplow concludes with Frank by saying, "That's right, Frank. Now thank you. You may go and sit down." Frank returns to his seat.

Lilly and LeRoy both sit at their tables. Lilly appears quite tired and has her head on her desk. LeRoy speaks briefly with Fred but otherwise has been quiet. Neither child has brought anything for the show and tell.

The interchange between Frank and the teacher is indicative of the manner in which Mrs. Caplow often sought to utilize verbal exchanges with the Table 1 students not only to encourage the students to speak to the class, but also to press them for academic performance. Thus not only did Frank discuss who besides himself played with the horses, but was also asked questions of color and number recognition.

Later in the morning when the speech lesson had ended and Miss Allen had left the room, Mrs. Caplow asked the class to listen to her directions.

"Now, boys and girls"—but before she continues, she notes that Lilly is attempting to remove her elephant name tag from around her neck. Mrs. Caplow says to Lilly in a firm voice, "Lilly, do not bother that name tag. I will take it from you later. No wonder that our name tags do not last very long when you children try to tear them off yourselves instead of letting me take them off of you." Lilly drops her hands and Mrs. Caplow returns her attention to the class with the instruction to the children that they are to "pretend that we are all asleep."

After the short rest period, Mrs. Caplow asked the children to watch her at the front blackboard.

She speaks to the class, "Okay, now boys and girls, look here. You know that now Christmas is past and we have had to take down all the Christmas decorations. We have taken down our Christmas tree, our Santa Claus, and now we need to make new decorations for our room. So today we are all going to try and make a snowman that we can use to decorate our room."

As the children were engaged in the construction of snowmen, I was able to walk among the group observing the performance of the four children.

Frank works on his snowman in a rapid manner, but his work is rather good. The circles for the head and body are not clear circles, but from the head and facial features there is no difficulty in distinguishing it as a snowman. The features he cuts neatly. The triangles are nearly perfect and the red hat is the "stovepipe" type.

Laura is working simultaneously on two snowmen. She has asked the teacher if, since one has to stay in the room to decorate the walls, she may make another to take to her mother. Mrs. Caplow consents. Laura's work is neat and precise. She handles the scissors well.

Lilly is having difficulty making her snowman. Her major trouble appears to be in her use of scissors. The large circle that is to be the body of the snowman is crumpled and quite jagged at the edges. It is difficult to tell that it is meant to be a circle. She drops her scissors quite often and appears to be growing angry with herself for her inability to control where she cuts.

LeRoy does not appear to be having difficulty with the scissors, but his figure is quite distorted and crumpled. He holds the paper in such a way that he bends it out of shape as he cuts.

I stood and watched as Lilly and LeRoy completed the body for the snowman. At this point Lilly asked if I would cut the hat for her snowman. Before doing so, I asked the teacher if she thought it permissable that I help the children at Table 3. She said that I should "feel free by all means since they need so much help anyway." I then cut a hat for Lilly and for LeRoy, Fred, and Susan who had asked me to do theirs also. When the bell rang for the morning recess, both Frank and Laura had completed their snowmen. LeRoy also had finished, but Lilly had not. She was having difficulty making the eyes and buttons. She soon finished and brought it to show to the teacher. Mrs. Caplow commented on Lilly's work: "Oh, Lilly, this is such a nice snowman, you did a very good job." This was the second time during the school year that Lilly was observed bringing her material to the teacher. On the first occasion she had been rebuffed. When Lilly received this compliment, she smiled and went back to her table to clear it of scraps and paste.

During this same observational period the teacher asked if I was getting to know any of the parents of the children I was visiting. I said that I was. She then stated what appeared to be her hypothesis about the educational success or failure of any individual child: "It really is the home that holds the key to whether or not the child learns." She noted the other teachers as well had known "for many years that no matter what happens in the classroom, the home is what really affects whether the child learns. You can have the best teacher in the world, but if the home life is miserable, the child is not going to learn anything."

This statement serves as additional support for a major contention of this study: that the teacher's perception of the academic potential of children was ultimately based on nonacademic criteria. In this instance, Mrs. Caplow stated that poverty and disorganized homes are the source of educational failure, that the child comes to school a failure before the first day of instruction—for his home has made him one. Thus there is really very little a teacher can do other than group children from these environmental circumstances as slow learners and leave them there where they "have no idea of what is going on."

January 17
Following the long unit on family life, Mrs. Caplow began a series of lessons on health and personal hygiene. As previously, she was to rely on film strips, short skits for the children to act out, and some visual aids. This morning there was to be a film strip.

Mrs. Caplow has the children come from their seats and form a semicircle on the floor so that they are facing the screen. She sits in a chair between the children and the screen. "Now, boys and girls, we are going to watch a film strip. I think you will enjoy it. Anne, do you remember how much difficulty you had getting your boots on for recess this morning?" Anne: "Yeah, they too small." "Well, Anne, why do you think they are too small?" "Because they don't fit." Mrs. Caplow: "Well, do you think the reason they are too small is because you have grown since you first bought the boots?" Anne: "Guess so." "All of you boys and girls," continues Mrs. Caplow, "are growing bigger and bigger every day. Now I want to show you a film about growing bigger and bigger. The title of the film is 'We Grow.' "

At this time Mrs. Caplow left the front of the group and went to the projector situated behind the children. As she began to thread the projector, she mentioned to me that the film she was about to show was "quite good" and that she was lucky to be able to reserve it. As she continued to work on the projector, she went on, "You should have been here yesterday. Laura brought a medical encyclopedia to school and wanted to show the class pictures of the reproductive system and the birth of children." At this point, she turned to look at several of the children who were talking among themselves. She said nothing to them and turned again to me. "You know, I believe Laura must talk over everything that goes on in the classroom with her mother because her mother is always sending material for her to have for show and tell. It's nice to have that kind of interest shown by the parents."

The film "We Grow" was the story of a white, blond, blue-eyed baby girl. It showed how she grew bit by bit until she began her first day of school, when it ended. The little girl was an only child, living in a ranch style suburban home, with parents who were always dressed in dresses and suits. She played on the lawn, which resembled a golf green, and wore pretty, bright clothes that were never dirty. The lack of congruity between the message of the film and the lives of many of the children in the classroom was evident from their inattention .

Lilly and Susan sit side by side, looking at a small mirror that Susan is holding in her lap. The two of them begin to giggle. Mrs. Caplow leaves her place beside the projector and walks to where the two are seated. She moves Lilly and her chair about three feet away from Susan. As Mrs. Caplow turns to go back to her seat, she notes that LeRoy and Fred are each holding a plastic army man. She walks over and moves Fred about three feet away. Then she returns to her seat.

At the end of the film, Mrs. Caplow instructs the children to move to the piano and form a semicircle. When the children do so, Laura and Frank are near the teacher while Lilly and LeRoy are both on the periphery. "Okay, now everyone stoop down and tuck in your head." The teacher and class are all near to the floor bent over as if in a fetal position. "All right, now we start to grow slowly, slowly, slowly, slowly." She is gradually rising. "This is just the way we grow. Slowly, slowly. We get bigger and bigger, taller and taller." At this time, Mrs. Caplow is standing straight with her arms stretched above her. "Isn't it fun to grow? Okay, now let's all sit down and be

sure our legs are in front of us. Keep your hands in your own lap."
She begins to play on the piano and sings a verse to the children:

I am growing up so tall,
I am growing up so tall.
I am growing up big and strong,
I am growing up big and strong.
I want to be a happy helper all day long,
I want to be a happy helper all day long.

The teacher repeats the verse with the children saying each line
after her. After another repetition, she asks the children to return to
their seats.

February 2
The class was to take a field trip to a local dairy. Mrs. Caplow had
asked the mothers of four children at Table 1 to accompany the group
—the mothers of Laura, Mary, Joe, and David. Since the bus held
forty-nine passengers and the number of students plus parents,
teacher, and myself equaled thirty-six, Mrs. Caplow had invited twelve
students from the afternoon kindergarten section to accompany the
group on the tour. I asked the criterion by which she had chosen them,
and she responded, "I wanted to get some children that are somewhat
verbal so they can come back and tell the rest of their class about the
trip." On the bus ride to and from the dairy, Laura sat with her mother,
Lilly sat with Susan, LeRoy sat with Fred, and Frank sat with Mike.

During the time that the children were to be in a line, as they were to
leave the room, board the bus, walk through the dairy, or return to the
room, Frank was to "supervise" the group and make sure "that everyone stayed in line." Mrs. Caplow said that as part of the unit on citizenship she had appointed Frank the "sheriff" for the trip. She stated that
the children had to learn to "respect the law" and that a sheriff would
symbolize the law to them. Thus it was Frank's duty to enforce Mrs.
Caplow's "order" that "the line was to be straight at all times." The
notes give indication of Frank's conduct as he attempted to keep the
lines "straight."

Before the class is to board the bus, Mrs. Caplow pauses and waits until Frank has straightened the line. Frank walks the length of the line repeating, "Boy, get where you suppose to." He often pushes the children as he speaks to them. Several times he also tells children from Table 3 that the teacher has made him the sheriff and displays the badge that Mrs. Caplow has given him to wear. Mrs. Caplow smiles as Frank comes to the front of the line and says that everyone is ready.

Frank continued to engage in this assertive behavior through the remainder of the trip. At no time was any comment made to him about the manner in which he pushed, shoved, and twice kicked different children to achieve compliance with his directives. A "sheriff" would supervise the class as a surrogate teacher on all the field trips that the children took during the rest of the year. The boy appointed to the role of sheriff was always from Table 1. No one else had the opportunity. When the rhetoric of "learning respect for the law" is stripped away, it is obvious that middle-class children were learning how to exercise effective control over those of the lower class while the lower-class children were learning how to shuffle in the face of superior power. Only once did a boy from the third table resist Frank's shoving. Mrs. Caplow immediately rebuked the child for pushing Frank in return and threatened not to take him to the dairy. The similarity to the manner in the larger society by which the middle class moralistically controls the poor with stringent means to insure "law and order" should be readily apparent. And as with the children at Table 3, losers are to be content with their lot.

February 5
Academically, the kindergarten year is to be one in which the student is prepared for formal learning that will occur in first grade. Kindergarten preparation consists primarily of having the students move through various series of "readiness material" designed to acquaint them with

the symbols and language of learning. In Mrs. Caplow's classroom, the children were not completing the material at the same pace. When she divided her teaching between the Table.1 group and that of the remaining two tables, there immediately emerged an unequal allocation of her time. The observational periods revealed a consistent pattern: Mrs. Caplow gave two to three times as much academic instruction to the Table 1 group as to the remaining two. Consequently, the first week in February found the Table 1 group approximately two and one-half weeks ahead.

The result of this widening gap in the completion of materials led to two noticeable interaction patterns in the class. The first was the solidification of the teacher's pattern of questioning only the Table 1 students when the students were assembled together. Often her questions would be related to some topic or event recently covered in the Table 1 readiness lessons which had not yet been reached by the remaining two tables.

Mrs. Caplow finishes the collecting of empty milk cartons and napkins. She tells the children to take out their crayons, for they are going to draw a picture of a tea party. The children at the first table begin talking among themselves about the lesson on a tea party they have just completed before the milk break. The remaining children take out their crayons, but appear less certain as to what they will be doing. Mrs. Caplow comes to the front of the class and begins talking with the Table 1 students about all the things they will want to be sure to include in their picture: a teapot, a table with a cloth on it, napkins, cake, spoons, and forks. None of the discussion extends to children at the remaining two tables though the entire class will be drawing the picture.

A second pattern of interaction which began to emerge as a result of the division of the classroom was the adaptive means by which the Table 2 and Table 3 students sought to learn material specifically taught to those at Table 1. Though the last two groups were often given other assignments while Mrs. Caplow was with the first table, the former group would either stop what they were doing completely and listen or else work only intermittently on their own assignment as they also tried to listen to Mrs. Caplow. They were not gaining the information through direct contact with Mrs. Caplow, but by the secondary means of overhearing what was being said in the other group. This "secondary learning" often involved discussion among the children at Tables 2 and 3 of the material that was being taught to Table 1 students. Not only did I observe this in the classroom, but in subsequent home visits to Lilly and LeRoy they would relate to me information taught in the class only to the Table 1 group. At times Lilly and LeRoy could relate what was being discussed in class in only a superficial manner, but there were other instances when they indicated a good grasp of the intent of the lesson. It is not as if the children at Tables 2 and 3 were ignorant of what was being taught in the other group, but rather that the patterns of classroom interaction established by the teacher inhibited the children at the two tables from verbalizing what knowledge they had in fact accumulated. The teacher assumed that if the material had not been formally presented to the two tables, they could not be expected to discuss it—though they were doing precisely that among themselves.

Mrs. Caplow passes to each of the students at Tables 2 and 3 a ditto sheet with numbers down one side and empty boxes down the other. The children are to draw the number of balls in the empty box corresponding to the number on the left side of the page. She instructs the children to begin and she then goes to the first table, where the children are going to listen to a recording. The recording has a number of instructions for the children to follow, and Mrs. Caplow passes out to the children the ditto they will be using in conjunction with the recording. The children at Tables 2 and 3 are engaged in their exercise. When the record begins, however, all the children at these two tables but Fred and Karen put down their crayons and begin listening. The recording speaks to the children and asks them if they have put on their shoes in the morning. Not only do the children at the first table answer "yes," but so do more than half at the other two tables. There are several other questions of this type and children from all three tables respond.

Lilly is up out of her seat and has walked over to the first table, where she is watching Marcia work on her paper. Marcia turns and hits Lilly in the stomach with her elbow, telling her to move away. Lilly returns to her seat. Mrs. Caplow observes the interchange but says nothing.

Mrs. Caplow speaks to the children at Tables 2 and 3, telling them to quit whispering among themselves and to do their exercises. Though I cannot hear all of what they are saying, they are talking about the lesson on the record.

At the end of the record, Mrs. Caplow asks the Table 1 students if they enjoyed it. Children from all three tables raise their hands.

February 15
Today's "new idea" for the class was to be a lesson on "sequential logical thinking." Mrs. Caplow asked the children to form a semicircle by the piano bench. On the periphery of this group, along with other children from Tables 2 and 3, were Lilly and LeRoy. LeRoy was so far to the rear that Mrs. Caplow had to ask him to move in closer so that he "could hear what was going on." LeRoy moved next to Art.

When LeRoy moves near Art, he takes out his billfold and shows it to Art. Mrs. Caplow notes that the two boys are talking among themselves and says, "LeRoy, what is that in your hand?" LeRoy makes no verbal response, but holds up the billfold so that she can see it. She responds, "All right, now let's put it away." He does.

The lesson on sequential logical thinking begins with Mrs. Caplow showing four small pictures to the class. Each of these pictures rep-

resents an episode in a sequential activity. The first set is the following four pictures: a chicken, an egg, an egg in a frying pan, and
an egg on a plate. The pictures are not shown to the class in this
sequence, but in a random fashion; and the children are then correctly to establish the progression of the activity. A second set of
pictures shows blowing snow, a boy rolling a snowball, a snowman,
and a snowman with a hat on. Finishing this second lesson, Mrs.
Caplow interrupts the class and notes that she forgot to call the roll.
She goes back to her desk and comes back to the piano bench with
the attendance record.

At the completion of the roll, Mrs. Caplow asks David to stand and
says, "David, can you tell Mr. Rist why you are wearing the star?"
David responds, " 'Cause I the sheriff." Mrs. Caplow continues,
"Can you tell him how you got to be the sheriff?" "By being a good
citizen." "David, what do good citizens do?" "They check up on
others." Mrs. Caplow: "Well, that's not all they do. LeRoy, what else
do good citizens do?" LeRoy makes no verbal response to the
question and Mrs. Caplow repeats the question for Frank. Frank
stands and says, "Good citizens obey all the rules." Mrs. Caplow
responds, "Yes, that is right, Frank. Good citizens obey the rules,
no matter what they are."

Mrs. Caplow then returns to her lesson and puts four pictures on
the flannel board. She asks the class, "What is this story about?"
Laura is the only one to respond and says, "That Miss Muffett." Mrs.
Caplow then says the nursery rhyme and asks the class to repeat it,
line by line. When the class has said the rhyme, she then asks them
to put the pictures in proper order. The next four cards are pictures
of the story of "Humpty Dumpty." Lilly is called upon to select what
she thinks is the correct card for the second position. She does not
respond and Laura calls out, "I know." Mrs. Caplow responds, "I
know that you know, Laura. But we should give others a chance,
also." Frank is called upon, and he correctly selects the card for
the second position. Lilly begins to swing her arms with Susan at

the rear of the group. Mrs. Caplow asks Lilly to come and sit by her chair. As Lilly rises, Susan stops waving her arms.

The children were each given a work sheet with eight small pictures on it, four on the story of Little Miss Muffett and four on Humpty Dumpty. They were to cut out the eight pictures and paste them in the correct sequence on a piece of colored construction paper. Both Laura and Frank worked very quickly and efficiently on this project, and were the first children in the class to finish the lesson. Both seemed to know the two nursery rhymes quite well. Lilly and LeRoy, on the other hand, had a great deal of difficulty. They cut the eight small pictures from the sheet but did not know the order in which to paste them on the construction paper. Mrs. Caplow began to walk toward the children at Table 3, and Lilly asked for assistance. Before Mrs. Caplow came to the third table, she paused to reprimand Virginia for speaking too loud at Table 2. When Mrs. Caplow came to Table 3, she began to help Susan and Karen. Lilly sat and watched Mrs. Caplow help the other two children. LeRoy also watched. Mrs. Caplow then came to help Lilly and asked Lilly to tell her the story for the Little Miss Muffett pictures. Lilly said she did not know it. Mrs. Caplow asked for the Humpty Dumpty story and Lilly said she did not know that story either. Mrs. Caplow quickly pasted the eight pictures on the sheet for Lilly without explaining the reason for the sequence in which she placed the pictures. LeRoy watched Mrs. Caplow paste the pictures on Lilly's paper and then did his in a similar manner.

After Mrs. Caplow left Table 3, she commented to me that both LeRoy and Lilly appeared to be displaying more "groupness." She noted that both children had begun to participate more frequently in the class, but their academic performance had not correspondingly improved.

February 20
For the first time since the eighth day of school Mrs. Caplow made a modification in the seating arrangement of the class. She divided

Table 3 into two smaller tables with the four boys at one table and the six girls at the other. The four boys were the farthest distance away from the blackboard where Mrs. Caplow gave most of the class instruction. The distance and angle of the table at which the four boys were seated was such that to see the teacher clearly when she was at the blackboard, they would have to push their chairs out and away from the table. On one occasion when LeRoy and Fred did so in order to see the instructions on the board of how to draw a circle, they were reprimanded and told to sit with their legs under the table. This, of course, precluded their seeing anything on the blackboard. When the exercise sheet was passed out on which the children were to practice making a circle, all four boys performed poorly.

February 27
In February of 1968, the St. Louis school board announced that it would seek voter approval of a bond proposal for the construction of several new schools and the extensive remodeling of others. Signs appeared in the windows of classrooms throughout the city urging a "yes" vote on the proposal. At Attucks School, the principal also called for a special emphasis on the bond proposal at the April PTA meeting. He encouraged the teachers either to have their classes present some entertainment at the meeting or to provide literature and decorate the individual rooms in a manner urging support for the bond issue. The principal stated in his memorandum to the teachers that he wished the April meeting to be especially interesting for the parents in order that they would become "motivated" to vote for the bond issue.

In the kindergarten class, Mrs. Caplow decided to have the children perform a "playlet" for the parents at the April meeting. The theme of the short play was to be the story of Little Red Riding Hood. The class began practicing for the performance eight weeks in advance of the April meeting. Today (the 27th) was to be the third practice session of the Little Red Riding Hood play. The children were seated in their chairs in a large semicircle in the middle of the room. As the children were to begin, Frank called to Mrs. Caplow that Mike "keeps his mouth open." Mrs. Caplow responded to Frank that it was "okay if Mike keeps his mouth open so long as he does not talk loudly." Laura had come to where I was seated and said, "I have the best part." Mrs. Caplow overheard Laura's remark and smiled. Laura had been chosen to play Little Red Riding Hood. Frank was chosen to play the woodsman who saves Little Red Riding Hood from the wolf at the end of the play. LeRoy was to be among the group of woodsmen at the beginning of the play who (in chorus) warn Little Red Riding Hood not to take the path through the woods to grandmother's house. Lilly was given the part of one of the children playing at the edge of the woods whom Little Red Riding Hood meets as she is about to go into the woods. Neither Lilly nor LeRoy had individual lines.

The class practiced the play for forty-five minutes. All the children were given some part, though only eleven had individual lines. The eleven were all the children at Table 1 and two girls from Table 2. When the rehearsal was completed, Mrs. Caplow asked the class to return to their tables and "put their heads down" for the next ten minutes. The children went to their tables though all did not rest. Several were coloring and three were looking at books from the library table. Lilly and LeRoy both had their heads down while Frank was coloring and Laura was looking at a book.

For the next several minutes, Mrs. Caplow and I discussed the play and the general performance of the children. She stated that she was pleased with the rehearsal and believed that the class could be ready by the middle of April. I then asked Mrs. Caplow if she kept papers the children completed in order to measure their progress over time. She said that she did not, but marked and returned them in order that the mothers might be aware of what activities the children were doing in the class. She also noted that when report cards were issued, she relied on what she could remember about the performance of the children in the past weeks.

The recess bell rang and Mrs. Caplow instructed the children to get their coats and line up at the door to the playground. When the children were in line with the girls first (and Laura as the first of the girls), Mrs. Caplow dismissed them to go on to the playground. She picked up the discussion we had been having and asked if I had noticed anything "different" in the home of either Lilly or LeRoy. I said that there appeared to be nothing out of the ordinary other than that both homes had new babies. (LeRoy's mother had recently had a son and Lilly's sixteen-year-old sister also had had a son three weeks previously.) She stated that her reason for asking was that both children were coming to school more shabbily dressed and dirty than generally had been the case before Christmas, that Lilly had a persistent strong odor of urine and that her hair had not been combed "in days." She said she did not "have any idea of what goes on in the homes of most of the children in the class." The only home she had ever visited was Frank's.

As I left the classroom while the children were still outside for recess, I was called by Nick, Lilly's brother. Nick was in the first grade. Nick walked to me and pointed to his first grade room. I asked if he liked first grade and he said "it okay." At this time a number of other boys began to gather around us. One of them asked me, "What you talkin' to Nick for? He a dumb-dumb." I said to the boy that Nick was my friend and that I had visited him in his home. The boy asked again, "Well how come you like him? He so dumb. He do all the stupid things in the room." Nick blurted, "I don't." I responded that I visited Nick and his family because I wanted to know them. I put my arm around Nick and we walked the length of the hall to the main entrance of the school. He asked when I was going to visit their home and I told him that I would be coming in two days.

Spring

Spring in St. Louis comes gradually. The warm days begin to intermingle with the chilly and soon the forsythia have a tinge of yellow and green about them. In the classroom, Mrs. Caplow began her spring activities with the children by flying a kite on the playground. There was also to be the planting of seeds in a sandbox in the room to watch "how plants grow." The bulletin boards were filled with pictures of tulips and a variety of other flowers. There was one picture of a white boy and girl in their new Easter outfits entitled, "Easter is Coming." The children were all asked to make a flower out of several different colors of construction paper, and these were then taped around the room above the blackboards. The class was well established in its routine, and the patterns of social organization created in the fall had retained their cohesion.

March 8

After the opening exercises, the teacher asked the group to come to the piano bench and form a semicircle to discuss the new garden that they would plant in the sandbox. As the children grouped themselves, Laura and Frank came to the very front nearly touching the bench. Lilly was near the center of the group holding hands with Susan, and LeRoy was on the periphery of the group seated next to John. Frank had with him a large sheet of paper approximately three by four feet on which was drawn a lion. The notes catch some of Frank's eagerness to come to the front and tell of his lion.

   Frank stands and says to Mrs. Caplow that he has a lion that he wants to show the class. Mrs. Caplow responds to Frank, "Not now, Frank." Mrs. Caplow then explains that the children are going to be able to watch a television program shortly on how seeds grow into plants. Frank stands impatiently on the side of the group. He has moved to the edge and stood up. Several times he calls out, "I got somethin' to show everybody." Mrs. Caplow makes no response to his statements. After several more outbursts, Mrs. Caplow stops and says, "All right, Frank, come to the front and show us your lion." Frank walks to the front of the group, smiling, and says, "Mrs. Caplow made a lion for me and I colored it." Mrs. Caplow responds,

"Well, that's good, Frank. Where do lions live?" Joe calls out, "In the jungle." Mary adds, "Lions are the king of the jungle." Mrs. Caplow then asks, "How is the weather in the jungle?" Joe responds, "It hot." Mrs. Caplow says, "Yes, it is very warm in the jungle." Mrs. Caplow explains to the class why she drew the outline of the lion for Frank. She tells them that Frank had asked for a picture of a lion, but she could not find one. Thus she drew the outline and let Frank take it home to color.

As Frank is about to sit down, Laura stands and says she also has something to show the class. Mrs. Caplow asks Laura to come to the front and show the class what it is that she has brought. Laura comes to the front and says, "I have a book." Mrs. Caplow asks Laura, "Do you know what kind of a book it is?" Laura responds, "It a Bible." Mrs. Caplow continues, "Yes, that's right. Do any of you know what these red and green ribbons inside the book are for? What are these called, these red and green ribbons?" There is no response from the class. "Some people use cardboard, but whatever they use they are called bookmarkers." She gives the book back to Laura and thanks her for bringing her Bible to class. During the time that Frank and Laura are in the front of the room, Lilly sits quietly with Susan holding her hand. LeRoy at the rear also sits quietly listening to what is going on at the front of the group.

When Laura was seated, Mrs. Caplow asked the class to stand and form a circle. All except for Lilly, Susan, and Ellen stood to form the circle. These three girls remained seated and the class began to create the circle around them. They did not move, and when Mrs. Caplow was ready to begin she saw these three still seated in the middle of the group on the floor. She went to them and softly asked if they would go and find a place in the circle. She was very pleasant with them and led them to a place in the circle. When Mrs. Caplow took her place in the circle she stood between Frank and Mary. Frank took hold of her hand, and the children began to play "Farmer in the Dell" with Mike as the farmer. He chose Laura as his "wife," who in turn chose Mary as the daughter. By the end of the song and selection of people, all in the circle were girls except for Mike. No boy was chosen for any of the parts.

At the end of Farmer in the Dell, Mrs. Caplow asks LeRoy to come into the circle and lead the class in the next game, called "Everybody Do This." This is a game where all the children on the circle imitate the actions of the person in the center. As the class begins to sing the "everybody do this" song, LeRoy begins to swing his arms. All the students and Mrs. Caplow do the same. When LeRoy finishes, he chooses Tom as the next person for the center. Tom then chooses Art, who in turn wants to choose Laura. Mrs. Caplow says that Art should choose someone else, since Laura participated in the last game. Art chooses Joe, who then chooses Frank. When Frank is finished, Mrs. Caplow says it is time to watch the television program on the growing of seeds. She instructs the children to gather around the television set. Lilly immediately grabs Susan's hand, and they sit together at the rear of the group. LeRoy does not sit down but goes to turn out the classroom lights. This task has usually been done by one of the students at Table 1. When the program is finished, LeRoy again jumps up quickly and turns on the lights. During the program the children display little interest. LeRoy goes to the rear of the group and begins talking with Tom. Lilly is speaking with Susan, and Laura is looking at Mary's new shoes. Frank is tracing the outline of his lion. Mrs. Caplow at one point asks Lilly to be quiet. When the program is over, the children line up to go to the restrooms.

During this slightly more than one hour of classroom activity, LeRoy's behavior was significant. When called to the center of the group to lead the game, he enjoyed himself immensely. He smiled and laughed as he swung his arms. His eagerness to participate extended to spontaneously taking charge of the light switch. He was the first child observed since Christmas to work the light switch who had not sat at

Table 1. His leading the group in the game was the first time I saw him as the center of attention during a class activity for the entire school year.

After the children had left the class for the playground, Mrs. Caplow made several comments about Lilly and LeRoy. She noted that LeRoy appeared to "be doing better in class. He tries hard and seems to like the other children. Sometimes his work is up to par, but there are other times when he simply sits confused or uncertain as to what he is to do. This is when he will watch the other children do their work and he does not do his own." Mrs. Caplow commented that Lilly was "sliding backwards." She said that Lilly had appeared to be doing much better during the winter, but that she was not doing well presently. When asked what criteria she used to determine that Lilly was not doing as well as previously, Mrs. Caplow responded that her clothes were much dirtier, her hair was uncombed, and that she had a strong body odor of urine. She added that Lilly's classroom assignments were not as well done and that Lilly was not participating in class to the extent she had before.

March 28

Mrs. Caplow was preparing to show the class a movie on various types of busses. As she prepared the projector, Laura came to where I was seated and said, "Mr. Rist, I have to go to the doctor after school. I have enlarged tonsils." Before I could make a response to Laura, Art interrupted and showed me his open mouth where he had lost a tooth. Laura left as Art began to talk. I then asked Art if he had his tooth and he pulled it from his pocket. As Art showed me the tooth, Frank pushed Art aside and said that his dog had "bigger teeth" than did Art. He also said that he thought his dog could bite "harder than Art can."

As the movie was about to end, an eighth grade boy came into the room with a message for Mrs. Caplow from the school nurse containing a list of nine children that she wanted to see in her office. Mrs. Caplow explained to me as she went to her desk for the medical records of the children that the nurse was giving each of the children an examination. She stated that this was the second group of nine students that the nurse had called to her office. Laura, Frank and LeRoy were among the nine children. Mrs. Caplow gave Laura the medical records for all nine children and told her to give them to the nurse. She also instructed Frank to lead the group to the nurse's office. The children left the room with Frank way in front of the remainder of the group. I followed, walking with LeRoy.

By way of examination, the nurse asked the children their ages and home addresses, taking their weight and testing their eyes. Both Frank and Laura could give the nurse their home addresses, but LeRoy could not. All three could give their correct ages. As the children waited to be called on by the nurse they sat on two benches. Frank left his bench and came to me. He asked me to lower my head so he could whisper into my ear. I did so, and he said, "Mr. Rist, you doin' fine." I replied that I thought he was doing fine also. He smiled and went back to his seat. Mike at about the same time left his seat and went to where LeRoy was seated. He pushed LeRoy out of his seat and sat down. LeRoy made no comment and went to another seat. Joe began to cry, apparently from fear of receiving a shot. Frank began to tease him about being scared of a shot and called him a "baby." Joe replied that he was not a baby. The nurse came to Joe and told him not to worry because there would be no shots. When the nurse had given the short examination to each of the nine children she dismissed them and told them to return to their room.

April 16

It was a balmy and wet spring day and the children were coming into the room for class. Several were quite wet, apparently having come to school without an umbrella or raincoat. Twenty minutes after the class bell rang Mrs. Caplow began the opening exercises. When these were completed, she asked the children to sit down. Frank did not sit down but walked to where Mike was seated. Mrs. Caplow asked Frank to take his seat and he then did. Mrs. Caplow began another familiar routine with the children—the weather calendar. Each day the children put on the calendar the correct date, the name of the day, and a symbol for the weather.

Mrs. Caplow asks who knows the name of the day. Art replies that it is Tuesday and Mrs. Caplow tells him that he is correct. She then asks him to come to the front and pin the card with the word "Tuesday" on the calendar. This Art does. Mrs. Caplow then pins onto the calendar a card with the number 16 on it. She then asks, "Who knows what number this is?" Laura calls out "16" and Mrs. Caplow acknowledges that Laura is correct, but says she will not take an answer from anyone who had not raised his hand. She calls on Fred from Table 3 to give her the name of the number on the calendar. Fred makes no verbal response, but comes to the front and stands by Mrs. Caplow. Frank begins to call out that "he don't know. He scared." Mary adds, "It sixteen, stupid." Frank tells Mary to be quiet. Fred then says "sixteen" and goes back to his seat. Mrs. Caplow points on the calendar to the weather symbol from the previous day, which is a cloud. She asks Frank, "What does the weather symbol say?" Frank responds, "It raining outside." Mrs. Caplow says, "Frank, you do not listen. Now be quiet." Frank gets up out of his seat and goes to the window. He looks out and says, "It is too raining." Mrs. Caplow responds, "Frank, come back and sit down. Now, listen to me." Mrs. Caplow calls on Joe and he correctly responds that the weather symbol means it is cloudy. She asks Joe what symbol they need on the calendar for the afternoon, and he correctly responds that the calendar needs an umbrella. Frank comes out of his seat to speak to Mrs. Caplow, but before he can say anything, he is told to go back to his seat. He goes back to his seat and calls out loudly, "Mrs. Caplow, Mike says we going outside for recess." Mrs. Caplow ignores Frank's comment.

Mrs. Caplow, upon completion of the opening exercises, introduced the class to Miss Brush, an apprentice teacher from Harris Teachers

College. Mrs. Caplow gave Miss Brush the name tags of the children and suggested that she call each of the children to come to the front for a name tag. Mrs. Caplow told me that she was going to let Miss Brush "take over the class" for the entire period. She had planned for Miss Brush simply to read stories and let the children color. Mrs. Caplow stated she wanted to be free of teaching for the afternoon in order to straighten the room for the PTA Open House to be held the same evening. Mrs. Caplow also noted that she had some forms concerning the bond proposal to be voted on in two days to prepare to pass out to each of the parents who would come to the room.

Miss Brush asked the children to form a semicircle on the floor by the flannel board. Laura and Frank came to the very front while Lilly and LeRoy sat far to the rear. During the reading of a story about the Easter bunny, the amount of whispering and talking among the children began to grow. Miss Brush asked the class to be quiet, but most of the children continued to talk. The noise continued to grow and Mrs. Caplow finally came to the flannel board. She told the children to return to their seats. Miss Brush appeared somewhat upset and Mrs. Caplow told her she should not worry because the class didn't "always do what they are told to do."

Mrs. Caplow took over direction of the class and had Frank pass out a sheet of lined paper to each student. She informed the class they would work on the title for the "Book of Sounds" they would be making. She said she had kept all the papers the children had done for the different sounds. Now they would begin to put them all together for a book of sounds. Mrs. Caplow began to write the heading for the title of the book on the blackboard. As was the case on many other occasions with blackboard work, the children at Table 3 could not see what the teacher had written.

Lilly stands up out of her seat. Mrs. Caplow asks Lilly what she wants. Lilly makes no verbal response to the question. Mrs. Caplow then says rather firmly to Lilly, "Sit down." Lilly does. However, Lilly

sits sideways in the chair in order to see the writing on the blackboard. Mrs. Caplow instructs Lilly to "turn around and put your feet
under the table." This Lilly does. Now she is facing directly away
from the teacher and the blackboard where the teacher is demonstrating to the students how to print the letter "O." There is no way
that Lilly can now see what the teacher is writing.

April 22

Since the beginning of January when the focus of the observations
shifted from the interactional pattern of the entire class with Mrs. Caplow to the observation of four children, I had made an attempt to note
as nearly as possible the simultaneous activities of all four children. I
attempted an alternative observational approach on the 22nd of April
when the focus of attention centered on individual students for periods
of ten to twenty minutes. All other students and the teacher were ignored except as they had contact with the single student under intensive observation. The two classroom activities during the observational
period were show-and-tell and a rehearsal of the Little Red Riding
Hood play to be presented at the closing exercise of the school in
June. Mrs. Caplow explained she did not believe that the children had
learned their parts well enough to perform at the open house the week
before and that the performance was going to be postponed until the
school closing program. (At the open house program the class sang
several songs instead.) The children were in a semicircle at the piano
bench, where they were about to begin a show-and-tell period.

LeRoy
1:08 p.m.
LeRoy is sitting quietly at the rear of the semicircle with his hands
under his chin and his legs crossed. He is intently watching Robert
tie his shoestring. LeRoy begins to try and tie the other of Robert's
shoestrings. He completes the tying and Robert makes a comment
to him in a soft voice. LeRoy nods in agreement. He looks out into

the hallway and sees two boys at the water fountain. He taps Robert
and points to the hall. Robert looks also. LeRoy points to Art's tennis shoes and tells Art that he also is wearing a pair of tennis shoes.
Robert tells LeRoy he is wearing a red undershirt. He pulls up his
shirt and shows it to LeRoy. LeRoy smiles. LeRoy pulls down the
neck of his own sweater and shows that he also is wearing a tee-
shirt. (During this time four children have been to the front for show-
and-tell.) At one point, Mrs. Caplow has the children repeat the
phrase "department store." LeRoy makes no response. When
Susan begins to tell of her trip to the zoo, he listens closely. When
she is finished, he yawns and stretches. When Mrs. Caplow asks the
class if a polar bear has a tail, he makes no response. As a number
of boys crowd to the front to see the small red truck Joe has brought,
LeRoy remains seated at the rear of the group. He clicks the toes of
his shoes together. Frank, who is seated in front of LeRoy, loses a
small red ball that he has been bouncing on the floor. It rolls back to
LeRoy. He picks it up and returns it to Frank. He watches as Frank
again begins to bounce the ball in front of him. While Mrs. Caplow is
asking the class about various animals in the zoo, LeRoy takes off
his shoe and then puts it back on. This he repeats twice. When Mary
begins to tell of her recent trip to the zoo, LeRoy again listens intently. He appears to enjoy Mary's description of several of the
animals.
1:19 p.m.

Frank
1:20 p.m.
Frank is seated in the middle of the semicircle between Joe and
Tom. He is propped on his knees playing with what he earlier told
me was a knife, but "not a real knife." He listens closely when Anne
comes to the front of the class and tells how she saw the funeral of
Dr. King on television. When Anne finishes, he stands up and goes
to the front of the class, taps Mrs. Caplow on the shoulder, and says,

"Dr. Martin Luther King was our leader." Mrs. Caplow makes no response to Frank and he returns to his seat. As Frank is about to sit, Mrs. Caplow tells him to "sit down and face the front." Frank sits propped on his knees. Mrs. Caplow then instructs the class to stand and form a circle. Frank returns to Mrs. Caplow, taps her on the shoulder, and again says, "Dr. Martin Luther King was our leader." Mrs. Caplow makes no response and he goes and stands between Joe and Rich. As the class sings, "The Farmer in the Dell," Frank does not participate, but does do the hand motions. When Mrs. Caplow is going to select the new cat, Frank raises his hand. Mrs. Caplow tells him to put down his hand as he is called on so often. He does put down his hand and begins to pick his nose as the rest of the class plays "cat and mouse." When the class plays "Farmer in the Dell" again, Frank begins to sing along. When the wife is about to take a child, he hesitantly raises his hand but is not called upon. When the game ends, Mrs. Caplow says the class will play one more, "Wee Willie Winkie." She asks Frank to be Wee Willie. Frank taps Mike and then beats him in running around the circle. When he gets safely into Mike's former place he tells Mike that he can run the faster. He is now standing next to Tom. He tells Tom to hold hands. At the end of the game he goes to Mrs. Caplow and shows her a small burn on his right hand. Mrs. Caplow asks Frank how he received the burn and Frank replies that he touched a hot plate at home. Mrs. Caplow tells the class that they are going to rehearse "Little Red Riding Hood." Frank goes immediately to Mrs. Caplow and asks if he can be the wolf. She says "no." Frank comes to me and shows pictures of two station wagons he is carrying in his pocket. He asks if they are like mine and I reply that they are similar. He wants to shake my hand but wants to use his left hand. Sensing what he wants me to ask him, I ask why he has to use his left hand. He then explains his burn. Mrs. Caplow tells the class to bring their chairs and form a large semicircle. Frank goes for his chair and as he returns, tells me he cut out a picture of Santa's reindeer and

pasted it on his wall at home. He tells Joe and Mary to quit talking or he will come and hit them. Frank sits and picks his nose as the class begins the rehearsal. When the entire class is to respond, he does not do so. He begins to draw figures in the air. He looks out the windows. Mrs. Caplow instructs the class to say the word "cape." Frank repeats the word, but when Mrs. Caplow tells the class to say it again, he does not. Soon Rich, who is seated next to Frank, is asked by Mrs. Caplow to correctly say the word "grandmother." Rich mispronounces the word. Frank corrects him softly and says it correctly. Rich tries to say it again, this time somewhat more correctly. When Mrs. Caplow asks the entire class to say the word "grandmother," Frank does not respond. Frank then tells Rich his shoestring is untied and smiles as Rich begins to tie it.
1:36 p.m.

Lilly
1:37 p.m.
Lilly is standing in the center of the large circle with her hands on Susan's hips. Lilly, Susan, Karen, and Anne are to be four bunnies who do the "bunny hop" and then are chased offstage by the wolf. When the girls are back in their seats and the wolf says that he wishes he had been able to catch a bunny so that he could eat it for supper, Susan and Lilly look at one another and smile. Lilly watches intently the scene between the wolf and Little Red Riding Hood. She pulls up her socks and then moves her chair in closer so that her view is not blocked by Susan. Ellen motions to Lilly that part of her hair is standing straight up on her head. This is a small pigtail that was braided on the top center of her head. Ellen begins to laugh and Lilly pushes down the hair. She puts her hand on Susan's shoulder, and both watch the wolf and Little Red Riding Hood. Lilly bites her lip as the wolf chases away the grandmother. Mrs. Caplow gives instructions on dialogue to both the wolf and Little Red Riding Hood. Lilly repeats each word softly to herself after the teacher.

When Susan indicates that she would like to play "pat-a-cake" Lilly says "no." When Mrs. Caplow tells the class to knock their knuckles on their chairs as if it were the wolf knocking, Lilly does so. Lilly laughs as Mike (the wolf) uses a high falsetto voice to imitate the grandmother in enticing Little Red Riding Hood into the house. She smiles as Mike puts on the apron worn by the grandmother. She moves to the side of her chair and holds her fist in such a way as to be ready to again knock on her chair when Little Red Riding Hood calls. However, this is not to be for several minutes and Lilly sits prepared before anyone else. When Mrs. Caplow gives further dialogue instructions to Laura (Little Red Riding Hood), Lilly repeats each of the words to herself. When Laura says the words, prompted by Mrs. Caplow, Lilly repeats them again. Lilly turns her head away from the play and looks at objects on the flannel board. Susan turns also and they begin to laugh at the various pictures of zoo animals on the board. They turn back to watch the play. When the wolf tries to eat Little Red Riding Hood and says the line "The better to eat you with, my dear," Lilly repeats the entire phrase softly. She puts her arm around Susan as they stand and watch the woodsmen kill the wolf.
1:49 p.m.

Laura
1:50 p.m.
As Mrs. Caplow tells the class to return to their chairs, having stood to watch the wolf being killed, Laura sits on one of the chairs in the center of the circle. Also sitting with Laura is Marcia. They begin to repeat the lines of the wolf and Little Red Riding Hood with Marcia taking the part of the wolf. When they get to the lines, "The better to eat you with," they laugh and Marcia begins to chase Laura. Laura then begins to sing softly to herself and snap her fingers. She stands by her chair when Mrs. Caplow tells the class to stand and be prepared to take the chairs back to their tables. Mrs. Caplow

calls for the Table 1 students to take their chairs first. Laura picks up her chair and carries it to her table. She does not sit down in her chair, but walks to the supply table where she picks up a piece of white drawing paper. She comes back to her seat and begins to fold it into smaller squares. She mentions to Mrs. Caplow that none of the children have been able to order their milk. Mrs. Caplow makes no response to Laura and instructs all the girls to line up for the bathroom. Laura goes with the rest of the girls from Table 1 to the entrance of the restroom. She has her piece of paper in her hand and continues to fold it smaller and smaller. Mrs. Caplow instructs the girls to line up at the door to the playground when they come from the restroom. Laura takes Virginia's hand and they are the fourth pair from the front of the line. Laura does not speak to Virginia, and stands examining her piece of paper. She drops her hand from Virginia's and again begins work on her paper. She now unfolds it and begins to refold it in a different manner. She looks up from her paper and tells Ellen that her hair looks like it is "melted." Ellen responds, "Girl, you crazy. My hair's not melted." Laura says, "It looks that way." Laura turns her attention back to the piece of paper and begins to fold it in the shape of a paper airplane. Mrs. Caplow dismisses the class.
2:00 p.m.

From an examination of the activities and interactions of the four children during this and two other class sessions (April 29 and May 6) it is possible to draw some tentative conclusions as to the adaptation of each of the children to the classroom milieu. There also were general patterns of behavior displayed by Frank and Laura from Table 1 that were not displayed by LeRoy and Lilly from Table 3, and vice versa.

For Laura and Frank, the classroom was not a place to fear, but one where they were allowed a great deal of physical mobility, received a disproportional amount of the teacher's attention and instruction, were

used by the teacher as models for the remainder of the class, and experienced a positive relationship with an adult. Specifically, Frank was
given an amount of mobility through the classroom not allowed any
other student. He had a continually high degree of interaction with
adults in the room, whether the teacher, student teacher, or myself. He
appeared to have learned how, in a sense, to "handle" adults. He
often openly disregarded Mrs. Caplow's directives and instead stated
his personal wishes, which were frequently granted. He sustained contact with other children during periods when there was to be individual
work done silently, and bantered with the teacher over the degree to
which he had to comply with class assignments. He also displayed occasional hostility and ridicule toward children at the other two tables.

Laura maintained a continually high degree of verbal interaction with
the teacher and was often quite close to her physically. She also had a
high degree of unrestricted mobility through the room and was the object of most of the affection displayed by Mrs. Caplow. She was given
a great deal of freedom and allowed to work on material not assigned
to the class. She also was able occasionally to ignore class assignments. She appeared to have highly internalized the pattern of the
class routine desired by the teacher. Like Frank, she also had a degree
of control over her own actions in the classroom. She did not always
comply with the wishes of the teacher and bantered as to the degree to
which she need comply.

For Lilly and LeRoy, the situation was quite different. Neither had any
degree of mobility in the classroom; neither had a high degree of interaction with the teacher or proximity to her; neither received much of
her teaching time; and neither was singled out for special praise and
treatment. Both exhibited (1) continual presence on the periphery of
the activities and seating arrangments in the class; (2) a low level of
interaction with any adult in the room; and (3) a strong solidarity with
other students at the same table. Both responded infrequently to the
questions and statements of the teacher. They appeared to learn a significant part of their material through a secondary mechanism whereby

the other students at the table became important in both discussion and sharing of information; and they were the subject of ridicule and derision from other students in the class, primarily from children at Table 1. There is no way of knowing, of course, just how the classroom experience was interpreted by these two children. They both displayed manifestations of withdrawing from the teacher, seeking closeness with fellow Table 3 students, and being only marginally involved in class activities. In their homes, both children expressed their liking for school and for the teacher. They both spoke with visible excitement and pleasure of some of the activities of the class (especially the field trips) and also of their class friends.

April 24
"Progress Reports" were given to the children at the end of each of the four ten-week sessions during the school year. On the front of the four-page yellow card was a letter addressed to the parents from the Superintendent of Schools. The letter was as follows:

To Parents: The Kindergarten provides activities which introduce your child to school life and help him learn to work and play well with others. Kindergarten experiences help him to grow in many ways and to develop important skills. All children, however, do not grow and learn at the same rate. You are urged, therefore, to study this progress report carefully so that you will know in which areas your child needs more time to grow or more encouragement and help. If there are questions concerning the report, you may wish to call the school and arrange to talk with the teacher. The best progress is made by the child when home and school work together.

On pages two and three of the report were listed the fifteen areas in which the child was evaluated. With each was an illustration of children engaged in the specific activity. Thus the first of the fifteen criteria was "I work and play well with others" and showed two children working together building with play blocks. The remaining fourteen areas of evaluation are listed as they appeared on the card.

2. I try to control my feelings.
3. I obey school rules.

4. I take care of my own materials and wraps.
5. I am a good listener.
6. I follow directions.
7. I work without disturbing others.
8. I finish my work.
9. I use crayons, scissors, paints, and paste properly.
10. I take part in singing and rhythmic activities.
11. I show interest in books, stories, and poetry.
12. I show improvement in the way I tell experiences and stories.
13. I speak so that others can hear and understand me.
14. I am making satisfactory progress in reading readiness activities.
15. I take part in counting and other number activities.

For each of the fifteen criteria, the teacher was to mark one of three grades, "Y," "S," or "N" (yes, sometimes, or no). There was space on the card at the bottom of page three for the attendance record of the child, including days present, days absent, and days tardy. The teacher was to sign her name at the bottom of the third page. On the fourth page at the top was room for the teacher to make "observations" about the performance of the child in the class. There was one space for each of the two grading periods in the semester. The parents were to return the card at the end of the first half of the semester, but at the end of the semester they could keep it. At the bottom of the card was room for comments of the parents.

On the 24th of April, the children returned the progress reports with their parents' comments on the teacher's evaluation of the first ten-week session of the second semester.

Frank

Frank had been given the "Y" mark on all fifteen criteria. He had been marked absent on nine of the forty-nine days. The teacher's comments read, "Frank has become an excellent pupil. He is alert and interested. His work is above average and his conduct is good. He works very well independently." Because of the fifteen "Y" marks, Frank was given a gold star on his card. Frank's mother had made the following remarks: "I am very pleased with Frank's progress at this time. I hope it continues. I am elated over his conduct! Let me know the minute it goes off, please."

Laura

Laura was given the "Y" evaluation on all fifteen criteria. She also was present all forty-nine days. She was given two stars, one gold for her performance and one blue for her attendance. The teacher wrote: "Laura is outstanding. She is unusually creative. It is a pleasure to have her in the class. She works very well independently." Laura's mother made no comment on the card.

LeRoy

LeRoy was given "Y" on eleven of the items and "S" on the remaining four. These last were: I finish my work; I follow directions; I take part in counting and other number activities; and I am progressing in reading activities. LeRoy was marked as present on forty-one of the forty-nine days for the quarter. The teacher's comments were: "LeRoy's work is fair. He tries hard but does not always seem to understand. Please help him and encourage him as much as possible." LeRoy's mother made no comment.

Lilly

Lilly received twelve "Y" and three "S" markings. The three areas in which she was evaluated as "S" were as follows: I show improvement in the way I tell experiences and stories; I am making satisfactory progress in reading readiness activities; and I take part in counting and other number activities. Lilly was marked as present forty-eight of the forty-nine days. Mrs. Caplow's comments were "Lilly has improved greatly. Please continue to encourage her." Her mother made no comment.

May 29

The teacher was not in the classroom when I entered. The children were variously occupied. Some were coloring, others were in the play-house, others were at the blackboard, and four or five girls were play-ing with the dollhouse. Lilly was at her seat coloring. I asked her what she was drawing, and she said in a low, barely audible voice that she was drawing a "ship bow." Ellen, sitting next to Lilly, immediately be-came excited and said, "Lilly sayin' a naughty word, Mr. Rist." Lilly responded, in a rather belligerent manner, "I ain't. I say ship bow." Ellen said, "You did not. You say shit bow." Lilly once more responded that she had not and then refused to talk any further with Ellen. She bowed her head and continued to color.

Mrs. Caplow returned shortly to the room and informed the class that they would begin practicing the Little Red Riding Hood play. She asked the children to take their chairs and form a large circle in the middle of the room. When the children were in a circle, she passed out a number of musical instruments that certain children were to use to accompany the class as they sang several songs. Most of the children who were given musical instruments sat at Table 2. As the instruments were distributed, Mike came to me and asked that I look at Lilly's dress. I asked why and he commented "because it so dirty." Lilly did not hear Mike's comments.

During the rehearsal, a girl from the eighth grade brought a three-year-old-girl into the room. Mrs. Caplow asked what she was to do with the child and the eighth grader said that this was her teacher's child and that she wanted Mrs. Caplow to take care of her until the end of the school day. In a disgusted voice Mrs. Caplow said, "All right," and took the child by the hand. She led her to one of the tables and gave her a piece of paper and a box of crayons. Mrs. Caplow told me that it happened periodically throughout the school year that she was expected to babysit for other teachers in the building. She stated that other teachers considered the kindergarten a "dumping ground" where they could all leave their babies. She was annoyed by this incident, and when she returned to the children in the circle, she was less friendly and patient with them.

June 6

During the first minutes after the children came in off the playground Mrs. Caplow allowed them "free time." She said that she did this because "in spring the children cannot settle down very well, and with the free time, they begin to calm down before the lesson starts. During the time the children were involved in a number of activities throughout the room while Mrs. Caplow painted a red and white playhouse, which was to be the grandmother's house in the play.

As I greeted Mrs. Caplow after first arriving in the room, she responded in a pleasant manner, but she appeared deeply disturbed. As I watched LeRoy and Frank at the toy chest, Mrs. Caplow came and began discussing the assassination of Robert Kennedy the previous night. She became increasingly upset as she talked and several times was on the verge of tears. She said that she could not understand why "the Arab had done what he did." She asked, "What would happen if all the Negroes who didn't like whites began shooting, or vice versa? That man probably had more opportunity in this country than any of my own folk." She broke off the conversation and went to the children. Shortly she returned to where I was seated. She spoke of the "general breakdown" in the society, the lack of respect for elders, for one another, and for property. She continued, "You know, I can even see it here in my own classroom. I try and have the children pick up after themselves and also help one another, but they constantly come back with the question, 'Why should I?' " She said that this was not the case when she was young and that everyone "pitched in" to help one another. "The children now are much more for themselves than they are for the group," she said. "If you can imagine how much stress this places in one little classroom, think of the entire nation. Why, there are two hundred million people and they won't work together." She was again on the verge of tears. She turned and went into the girls' bathroom.

I walked through the room as the children were busy with a number of activities and saw Lilly coloring. I asked Lilly what it was that she was drawing and she replied, "A parachute." Frank interrupted with "Lilly can't draw nothin'." Mrs. Caplow returned and had the class come to the center of the room for another practice session of the Little Red Riding Hood play. As the children took their seats, Mrs. Caplow spoke her only words of the hour to Lilly. She said, "Lilly, sit up straight." The rehearsal began with a welcoming song that was composed of the following words: "Mr. Miller and parents too, we welcome you to our program. It is the end of our kindergarten year and we will always hold our memories dear." The Pledge of Allegiance was next, and Mrs. Caplow told the children to place their right hands over their hearts. Seven of the children put their left hands over their hearts. Frank was told twice to put his hand over his heart but he did not. He stood with both hands at his side. After the pledge, the children began singing the "Little Red Riding Hood song." During the second stanza the recess bell rang. At the end of the verse, Mrs. Caplow dismissed the class.

June 13
Today there was no school. The children were excused for the day so the teachers could prepare the final report cards and submit all necessary forms to the office. On Friday the 14th, the children would be present for only half a day to receive their cards, turn in their books, and collect their belongings, papers, and projects. They also would go to their new classroom to meet their teacher for the coming year.

I met with Mrs. Caplow for nearly an hour to discuss aspects of the completed school year. She noted that of the twenty-eight children in the class, twelve were scheduled to remain in the central building while the others would be assigned either to a new school being com-

pleted or to one of the branch schools built to accomodate the overflow of students. She stated that Laura, Frank, and Lilly would remain
in the main buildings while LeRoy would be assigned to one of the
branch schools.

Mrs. Caplow also had the results of the IQ test she had given the
children earlier in the week. She gave the scores of the four children
selected for special observation as follows: Frank, 120; Laura, 111;
Lilly, 82; and LeRoy, 78. The variations in IQ scores among the four
students bears comment. There appear to be at least three possible
explanations for the differences in scores. First, the scores represent
the results of Mrs. Caplow's differential treatment in the classroom,
which contributed to the validation of the self-fulfilling prophecy. That
is, the teacher, by spending most of her teaching time with the Table 1
students, better prepared them to do well on the examination than the
students who received less teaching time. Secondly, the tests themselves may have reflected strong biases toward the knowledge and
experiences of middle-class children. Thus, students from such backgrounds could be expected to perform at a higher level than students
from low-income families. The test resulted not in a "value free" measure of cognitive capacity, but in an index of family background. The
third possibility is that Mrs. Caplow's seemingly intuitive judgments as
to which children in the class were "fast learners" and which were
"slow learners" may have been based on criteria unknown to me. Her
selections in this case may not have been subjective, but objective in
the sense of being based on nineteen years of teaching experience.
Yet not all those students in the Table 1 group did score higher than
those at Tables 2 and 3. There was no clear sliding scale in scores
from the highest to lowest correspondent to table assignment.

Mrs. Caplow then read the remainder of the scores of the children in
the class. When the list was finished, I asked, "Mrs. Caplow, from what
I am able to remember of the scores you have just read, it appears that
a number of them are low average or else below average. Why do you
think this is so?" Her response was:

"Well, most of these children are not above average. Some of them are even below average. I guess the best way to say it is that very few of the children in my class are exceptional. I guess you were able to notice this from the way the children were seated this last year. Those children at Table 1 gave consistently the most responses throughout the year and seemed most interested in what was going on in the classroom. The children at Table 2 and most all of them at Table 3, at times, seemed to have no idea of what was going on in the class and were in another world often by themselves. It just appears that some can do it and some cannot. I don't think it is the teaching that affects those that cannot do it, but some are just basically—I hate to say it—low achievers. You know, for some children, it takes time to learn what is expected of them in the school. A lot of them still haven't caught on at the end of one year of kindergarten. Some of these low scores I just can't understand because we spent a lot of time this year working arithmetic, comparisons, similarities, larger than and smaller than. This is just about all the IQ is made up of, too. Also I don't understand why the non-language scores were better than the language scores."

Following up Mrs. Caplow's last statement, I asked, "Why do you think it is the case that the children scored somewhat better on non-language tests than on the language tests?" Her reply:

"Well, I really don't know. It appears, though, that the children don't have ideas and also they have poor vocabularies. There is a set vocabulary to use for the test and whenever you give the instructions, you have to use specific words or else the test is invalid. It might be that some of the children didn't understand the words. This goes back to the environment because the children haven't heard the words before. You know, they're not very verbal at home. They get their needs fulfilled in ways other than talking. It is just the opposite with the children who scored very well on the test. They almost do too much talking and I have to spend my time trying to keep them quiet. Laura, for example, has great determination and lots of drive, but she is in some ways overly aggressive. But I guess it would be better for a child to be overly aggressive than passive and withdrawn. I would rather have a child try too hard than not try at all. It just seems that some children do not try. Laura, Frank, and Mike tried hard all year, but others do not seem inspired. I guess it is that the parents do not pay any attention to the children and take no pride in the work that the children bring home from school. The children just do not get encouraged. Did you notice at the play yesterday how so many of the children came so nicely dressed and clean and their hair was combed? And did you see how Lilly came? She was dressed in a dirty dress, dirty socks, and her hair wasn't even combed. But I am glad that she did come even though she did not look very nice. It must be that some parents just have a different set of values. The child can be no better than his association with his parents. Maybe some of the children will change when they get older, but most of them will be in a rut for their whole life."

The last question I asked Mrs. Caplow concerned the four children that she had selected—two doing well and two doing poorly: "Mrs. Caplow, would you care to discuss the four children that you selected for me and that I have been observing during this school year?"

"Frank, I think, is in some ways better than when he started. If kindergarten has helped him at all, it has been his social development. I think this will be a big help to him in the other grades, learning how to get along with other children. You know that Frank knew most of the material that we tried to teach this year in kindergarten so that I think the important thing for him was probably his social development.

"I think Laura gained new learning in kindergarten. Now she has learned to modify her actions somewhat to fit into the group. I like Laura very much for she has a great drive to do well. I sure hope that she keeps that drive to do well. Laura touches something very deep in me for she is such a creative child. There have been many times when she has done things on her own that show a high degree of creativity and ingenuity which I like to see very much in a child.

"As for Lilly, well, when she first came she was rather shy and withdrawn and didn't say too much. The early indications were that she was not going to do too well at all and that she was going to need special attention. It was possibly with your home visits that I began to notice that she began to blossom out and smile more here in the classroom. Lilly doesn't seem to be an unhappy child. It is so sad that some children are so miserable. They never smile. I think Lilly has changed some. She's different now in that she is more verbal and she talks to the other children in the classroom more than she did last fall.

"For LeRoy, he has good manners. I don't have to get after him to sit down or be quiet the way I do with Frank and Laura. You know, I have to speak less to Lilly and LeRoy than I do to Frank and Laura. LeRoy and Lilly aren't the kind that like to take over the way that Frank and Laura do. LeRoy is very quiet. He doesn't say too much but seems to enjoy school. But he has been out of school so much this year because of his asthma. I hope that doesn't continue in the next years for he could fall behind that way."

As Mrs. Caplow's final communication of the school year with the children's homes she gave each child the progress report for the semester, which the family was to keep. Besides her comments at the end of the school year to each of the parents, there was her last evaluation of the performance of the child. These are given for each of the four children.

LeRoy

LeRoy received eight "Y" markings on his card and seven "S" markings. The seven "S" markings were in the following areas: I obey school rules; I am a good listener; I follow directions; I finish my work; I speak so that others can hear and understand me; I am making satisfactory progress in reading readiness activities; and I take part in counting and other number activities. Mrs. Caplow's comments to LeRoy's mother read, "LeRoy will need more work on the readiness level. Please continue to help him whenever possible."

Lilly
Lilly received twelve "Y" and three "S" markings. The three "S" evaluations were for: I show improvement in the way I tell experiences and stories; I am making satisfactory progress in reading readiness activities; and I take part in counting and other number activities. The comments to the mother read, "Lilly has continued to improve. Please encourage her whenever possible."

Frank
Frank received fifteen "Y" markings and also a gold star. Mrs. Caplow's comments read, "Frank has satisfactorily completed the kindergarten program. It has been a pleasure to have him in the class."

Laura
Fifteen "Y" markings were on Laura's report as was a gold star. Mrs. Caplow's comments: "Laura's determination is indeed an asset and should always keep her near the top. She is a wonderful little girl."

When I finished examining the reports, I asked Mrs. Caplow if she would come to the first grade room with me, as I wanted to tell the first grade teacher, Mrs. Logan, that I hoped to be visiting her the coming year. Mrs. Caplow agreed and we spent a few minutes with Mrs. Logan discussing my plans to be back in the fall. Upon the return to the kindergarten room, I took a box of candy from my briefcase, gave it to Mrs. Caplow, and thanked her for her assistance during the year. I wished her a good summer and said I would be back to visit her in the fall. Her comment, "When you find the secret of how these children learn, let me be the first to know."

First Grade: The Pattern Remains

4

Though Mrs. Caplow had anticipated that twelve of the children from the kindergarten class would attend the first grade in Attucks School, eighteen of the children were assigned during the summer to the first grade classroom in the main building. The remaining children were assigned either to a new school a few blocks north of Attucks School or to a branch school to handle the overflow from the main building, or had moved away. Mrs. Logan, the teacher in the first grade classroom, had had more than twenty years of experience in the St. Louis public school system, and all the schools at which she had taught in the city were more than 90 percent black. During the 1968–1969 school year, I made four informal visits to the first grade classroom in Attucks School.[1] I made no visits to either the branch school or to the new school nearby to visit with children from the kindergarten class who had left their original school. During my visits to the first grade room, I made no attempt at taking notes on classroom activity. Rather, I would dictate my impressions and observations as soon afterward as possi-

[1] During the 1968–1969 school year, I was unable to conduct formal observations in the first grade classroom because of a teaching appointment out of the city.

ble. No structured observational sessions were conducted throughout the school year.

During the first grade school year there were thirty-three children in the classroom. In addition to the eighteen from the kindergarten class, there were nine children repeating the first grade and also six children new to the school. Of the eighteen children who came from the kindergarten class to the first grade in the main building, seven were from the previous year's Table 1, six from Table 2, and five from Table 3. Laura and Lilly were among them.

In the first grade classroom, Mrs. Logan also divided the children into three groups. Those children whom she placed at "Table A" had all been Table 1 students in kindergarten. No student who in kindergarten had sat at Table 2 or Table 3 was placed at Table A in the first grade. Instead, all the students from Tables 2 and 3—with one exception— were placed together at Table B. At the third table, Table C, Mrs. Logan placed the nine children repeating the grade plus Susan, who had sat at Table 3 in the kindergarten class. Of the six new students, Mrs. Logan placed two at Table A and four at Table C. The totals for the individual tables were nine students at Table A, ten at Table B, and fourteen at Table C.

The seating arrangement that began in the kindergarten as a result of the teacher's definition of which children possessed or lacked the necessary characteristics for success in the public school system emerged in the first grade as a caste system in which there was absolutely no mobility upward. That is, of those children whom Mrs. Caplow had perceived as potential "failures" and thus seated at either Table 2 or Table 3 in kindergarten, not one in the first grade was assigned to the table of "fast learners."

The initial labels the kindergarten teacher had given to the children had been reinforced in her interaction with those students throughout the school year. When the children were ready to pass into the first grade, their ascribed labels assumed objective dimensions. The first grade teacher no longer had to rely merely on the presence or absence of certain behavioral and attitudinal characteristics to ascertain who would do well and who would do poorly in the class. Objective records of the "readiness" material completed by the children during the kindergarten year were available to her, and on that basis she could form her first grade tables for reading and arithmetic.

The kindergarten teacher's disproportionate allocation of her teaching time meant that the Table 1 students had completed more material at the end of the school year than the remainder of the class. As a result, the Table 1 groups from kindergarten remained intact in the first grade, as they were the only students prepared for the first grade reading and arithmetic material. The children from Tables 2 and 3 had not yet completed all the material from kindergarten and had to spend the first weeks of school finishing kindergarten-level lessons. The criteria established by the school system as to what constituted successful completion of the necessary readiness materials insured that Table 2 and Table 3 students would not be placed at Table A in the first grade. The only children from the kindergarten who had completed the necessary material were those from Table 1.

It would be somewhat misleading, however, to indicate that there was absolutely no mobility for any of the students between the seating assignments in kindergarten and those in the first grade. All the students save one who had been seated at Table 3 during the kindergarten year were moved "up" to Table B in the first grade. The majority of Table C students were those who had to repeat the grade level. As a tentative explanation of Mrs. Logan's rationale for the Table C seating assignments, she may have assumed that within her class there existed one group of students who possessed so very little of the perceived behavioral patterns and attitudes necessary for success that they had to be separated from the remainder of the class. (Table C was placed by itself on the opposite side of the room from Tables A and B.) The first grade teacher's comments about the Table C students were reminiscent of the way in which Mrs. Caplow spoke of the Table 3 students the previous year.

Mrs. Logan appeared to perceive those who were placed at Table A as students who not only possessed the criteria necessary for future success, both in the public school system and in the larger society, but who also had proved themselves capable in academic work. Though the students at Table B lacked many of the "qualities" and characteristics of the Table A students, they were not perceived as lacking them to the same degree as those placed at Table C.

A basic explanation of the rationale of Mrs. Logan's seating arrangement is, of course, that she shared Mrs. Caplow's reference group and set of values as to what constituted success. Both women were well educated, were employed in a professional occupation, lived in middle-income neighborhoods, were active in a number of charitable and civil rights organizations, and expressed strong religious convictions and moral standards. Both were educated in the city teachers' college and had also attained graduate degrees. Neither of the two women had children. These similarities as well as the manner in which they described the various groups of students in their classes would indicate that they agreed on the indices of the "successful" student.

The number of children from Mrs. Caplow's kindergarten class who remained in Attucks School and made satisfactory progress through the grades dwindled each year. Of the thirty children who were in kindergarten, and the eighteen in Mrs. Logan's first grade class, only ten came to Mrs. Benson's second grade class. Of the eight who did not come with their cohorts, three were held back in Mrs. Logan's class to repeat the first grade and five moved from the school district. Both Laura and Lilly were in Mrs. Benson's class. LeRoy was not.

This was Mrs. Benson's second year of teaching and her first teaching second grade. The previous year she had taught third grade at Attucks School. She graduated from Harris Teachers College in June of 1968. She was married and had no children. She was living with her parents while her husband, a member of the armed forces, was overseas. On several occasions she expressed her pleasure at being able to teach at Attucks School as opposed to one of the older schools in the city. One of her very close friends from college was also a teacher at Attucks.

The First Days

September 4
On the first day of school, children did not come with their mothers to register as in kindergarten. Registration was done before the beginning of the school year, or took place at the school office if a child came after the year had begun.

The bulletin boards in the classroom displayed a variety of materials. On the left rear board was a red schoolhouse made from construction paper. The door to the schoolhouse was to serve as the monthly calendar for the class. Above the schoolhouse were the words "School House." On the right rear board was a large caterpillar made from construction paper, and below was a long poem entitled "The Caterpillar" taken from a magazine. The front left board was reserved for "Reminders." This board was for the use of the teacher, and she had tacked on it papers listing her playground supervision dates, the dates when audiovisual material was available to the class, the dates when the nurse was present at the school, and the first week's lunchroom menu. The final board on the front right contained the words "Fall Surprises" and five leaves of various colors.

Mrs. Benson enters the room at 8:23, and soon after her come five boys. They do not speak and go to sit at different desks. Mrs. Benson says, "Good morning," but the boys do not respond. She repeats her greeting, this time in a firm voice. Several of the boys respond with "Good morning." Laura, wearing a new bright yellow raincoat with an umbrella of the same color, enters with Mary. Laura goes immediately to the coatroom to hang her raincoat. The five boys and Mary follow Laura into the coatroom. By the time the bell rings at 8:30 a.m., there are fifteen children present in the room. Tom comes in shortly and one of the five boys calls out, "Look that ol' fool. He go got a haircut." Tom responds that because of his new haircut, his head is wet. The other first grade teacher (besides Mrs.

Logan) comes into the room and begins speaking with Mrs. Benson. She points to one of the girls seated near Laura and says she taught this girl the last school year. Mrs. Benson motions and the child comes to the front. The first grade teacher pats the child several times on the head and she then goes back to her seat.

At 8:40 a.m., there are twenty children in the room. Eleven girls are sitting on the right side of the room, seven boys and one girl on the left, and one boy in the rear. Among the girls on the right side of the room, the seats closest to the teacher are occupied by Laura, Mary, Marcia, and Virginia. Mrs. Benson begins calling the name of each child who has been preregistered for the class, and as each name is called, that child comes to her desk for a name tag. As the tags are passed out, the sex differentiation in the seating arrangement becomes complete. Carol, who had sat with the boys, goes to the right side with the girls after receiving her tag. David, who sat in the rear by himself, goes to the left side when he receives his tag.

Of the eight boys, four are known to me. David, Tom, and Joe were in Mrs. Caplow's kindergarten class, while the fourth is Nick, Lilly's brother. Among the girls, I recognize six: Mary, Laura, Marcia, Virginia, Karen, and Anne. A seventh girl who had been in Mrs. Caplow's class, but who is absent the first day, is Lilly.

Having passed out the tags to the children, Mrs. Benson introduces herself to the class. She says softly, "My name is Mrs. Benson. What is my name?" The children repeat her name. She continues, "I guess I will write that on the board." She writes M-r-s. and says, "That's an abbreviation for Mrs." She writes her last name and turns back to the class. "How many children are glad to be back in school?" All the children raise their hands. She asks, "How many children had a good summer?" All the children except Nick raise their hands. "How many children had a very good vacation?" Few of the children raise their hands. "I am going to give all of you an opportunity to tell of your exciting summer vacations."

Mrs. Benson asks Tom to come to the front to tell of his summer vacation. Before Tom can begin, Mrs. Benson tells him to return to his seat because she has forgotten to collect money from the children for lunch and for spending at the noon hour. Tom sits down. Fifteen minutes later, when she returns to the children's vacations, she begins with Joe. Tom is not called back to the front. Joe begins to tell of his experience flying on an airplane and the teacher asks him to speak louder. The school public address system has been on in the room since 8:15 a.m. playing popular music. Robert Goulet is presently singing the theme sing from *Camelot.*

When Joe finishes, Mrs. Benson calls on Jimmy, who describes his trip to Memphis, where he went to a fair and rode a "black widow." Mrs. Benson sees Curt speaking with Nick. Looking at Curt, she says in a firm voice, "Curt, what was it that Jimmy rode at the fair?" Curt does not respond and bows his head. She continues, "Jimmy, tell Curt what it was that you rode at the fair." Jimmy repeats he rode a black widow. After several other boys are called to the front, Mrs. Benson says that a girl "should have a chance." She calls on Mary, who relates how she made $25.00 modeling one evening for a television fashion show. She also talks of a birthday party she had. Mrs. Benson asks if she invited Laura to the party and Mary replies, "No." Laura is asked to the front and says that she took swimming lessons during the summer at the Y.W.C.A. Mrs. Benson asks if anyone else took swimming lessons and the whole class raise their hands. Mrs. Benson asks how many were at the "Y" with Laura and no hand goes up.

The first instance of what was to be a familiar pattern of behavior in the room occurred when one of the boys at the front turned toward Mrs. Benson instead of toward the class. Mrs. Benson responded by using black American English as she sought to have the child turn to the class. The teacher used black American English throughout the semester when she was disciplining or attempting to control the behavior of the children. When Mrs. Benson either rewarded or merely gave information or directions to the class, she spoke standard American English. But her use of the first was clearly associated with her exercise of control and discipline over the children.

Lou is asked to come to the front of the class. He begins speaking to the teacher. His back is to the class. Mrs. Benson says, "Boy, who you talkin' to? Look at the rest of the class when you talk, not at me." Lou turns and continues to tell of a trip to Mississippi.

Mrs. Benson's first encounter with Nick, who was to come to play the role of "class clown," occurred after most everyone else had had a chance to relate his summer experience.

Mrs. Benson says, "Nick, what did you do this summer?" Nick makes no response, but grins. Mrs. Benson asks again, but directed to the class, "What did Nick do this summer?" One girl says that Nick came to her house. A boy says that they played ball together. Mrs. Benson turns back to Nick and says, "Well, Nick, tell us about your playing ball." Nick is the only child who has not been asked to come to the front of the room to tell of his experiences. He remains seated at his desk. Nick responds to the teacher's question in a soft voice, "I play ball wit' my brother." Mrs. Benson asks who else Nick played ball with during the summer and Nick responds, "Nuthin'."

The first sign of interest among the children during the morning occurred when one girl said that she had done nothing during the summer. Mrs. Benson asked if she had even watched television, and the girl responded that she had. Mrs. Benson asked what significant event occurred during July and another girl in the class called out, "Go to the moon." Mrs. Benson said, "Yes, who went to the moon?" A boy responded, "Astronauts." A number of boys on the left side of the room began to talk among themselves about the moon landing. Though I could not hear all that was said, I did hear "rockets," "moon landing," "rocket ship," and "dust." The boys were enthusiastic and generated much lively discussion among themselves. Mrs. Benson raised her voice, "Carolyn, what did you do this summer?" The talk among the boys about the moon landing immediately ceased.

Another interactional pattern that I noticed in the kindergarten class and again during the first hour of the second grade school year was the teacher's failure to correct an incorrect response. On some occasions, the incorrect response was either allowed to stand or rewarded as correct. In this instance, it was the former.

Mrs. Benson tells the class that they are to draw something they did during the summer. She asks Joe what it is he is going to draw and he responds, "Summer." She passes out a box of crayons to each member of the class with the admonition to handle them carefully for they will have to last the entire school year.

September 5

On the second day of school there were sixteen girls and nine boys present. The boys again sat as a group on the right side while the girls grouped on the left, except for Lilly, who sat in the rear by herself. Briefly another girl joined Lilly, but Mrs. Benson soon took her across the hall to the first grade. Lilly remained by herself throughout the morning period.

After the children had taken their seats, Mrs. Benson asked, "Does everyone know the Pledge of Allegiance to the Flag?" All but five children raised their hands. She asked, "Does anyone not know the Pledge?" No one raised a hand. "If you know the Pledge, hold up your right hand." Lilly, along with six other children, held up their left hands. An equal number held up their right hands. Mrs. Benson asked, "What do we do to get ready to say the Pledge?" Laura responded, "We stand." "Yes. Let's everyone stand." She told the children to put their right hands over their hearts and she walked through the room to see if the children were doing so. She passed Lilly, who had her left hand over her heart and said, "Okay, that's good."

After the opening exercise, Mrs. Benson collected milk and lunch money. She asked Laura to take it to the main office. During the time that the money was being collected, Lilly had her head on her desk. Mrs. Benson began to call the names of each of the children to come to the front of the room for their name tags. Lilly did not go unnoticed.

Mrs. Benson calls Lilly's name. Lilly begins to walk toward the front of the room. Several of the boys see that she has no buttons on the back of her dress and that she is wearing a dirty white tee-shirt. The boys begin to laugh. Lilly looks at them, stares, and says nothing. At the teacher's desk, she picks up the wrong name tag and the teacher says to her in a firm voice, "Lilly, is that your name tag?" Lilly makes no response and her brother Nick comes to the front of the room and takes the name tag out of her hand. He picks up the correct tag and gives it to her. The teacher takes the tag out of her hand and pins it on her dress. She is the only child for whom the teacher pins on the tag.

Mrs. Benson left the room momentarily. When she returned, she noticed a leaf on her desk. She said, "Who brought me the leaf?" Mary responded, "Me." Mrs. Benson replied, "Who's me?" Mary said, "I'm me." The teacher said, "You're not me, you are Mary." Mary made no response. Mrs. Benson turned to the class and said, "This morning, I want to see how many of you can count to 100." Many of the children raised their hands and cried, "Me, me!" "I don't hear anyone who says, 'Me, me.' I only hear silent hands." Laura was called upon to begin counting to 100. While the children were counting, Lilly again had her head on her desk. She seemed to be asleep. She raised her head, though, when her brother Nick was called upon to count from 90 to 100. Nick said, "Ninety," and then grinned. He said no more and Lilly put down her head. Rose finished counting to 100.

Mrs. Benson says, "All right, now I'm going to see who can write their numbers from 1 to 100. Who in the room can write their numbers?" Lilly raises her head and her hand. Mrs. Benson calls on

Lilly to come and write from 1 to 10. Lilly walks very hesitantly to the front, staring at the boys on the left side of the room who had laughed at her previously. They begin laughing at her again. The teacher says, "Go on, girl." Lilly begins to write the "1" very high on the blackboard. The teacher erases it and tells her to write lower. Lilly then writes the "1" lower on the board. She steps back for the teacher to see it and the boys begin to laugh. She steps back to the board and begins the 2. She makes the top half of the 2 and pauses. She does not draw the line from left to right. The teacher asks if she would like to go and look at the number chart. Lilly walks to the chart, looks at it briefly and returns to the board. She picks up the chalk but does not complete the number. Nick begins to laugh. Mrs. Benson turns to Nick and says in a firm voice, "Boy, be quiet. That you sister. Who in the class can help Lilly finish the number?" Several of the children say, "Me, me." Mrs. Benson replies, "I can't see anyone who says 'me.' " The children are quiet and Mrs. Benson calls Mary to help Lilly. Mary completes the 2 and both girls sit down.

When the first eight numbers had been written on the board, Mrs. Benson asked the class if any of the numbers were wrong. Nick held up his hand. When called on to give the incorrect number, he made no verbal response and grinned. After each number, Mrs. Benson placed a comma. She asked the class what the name of the mark was that she had made behind each of the numbers. One child said, "Set marks." Mrs. Benson replied that they were not set marks and asked for other suggestions. Another child called out, "Check marks." "No, they are called commas, but we will talk more about that later." She asked Carol to come to the front and continue writing numbers.

After the children had written to 100 on the blackboard, she informed them she wanted each of them individually to write the numbers between 1 and 100 on a sheet of paper at their desks.

Mrs. Benson goes to the supply closet and brings out the individual

boxes of crayons the children have been given the previous day. She calls the name of each of the children who were present on the first day, and they come to her for their boxes of crayons. She passes out crayons only to the children who were present on the first day. When finished, she says, "Now, you can print your numbers in red or black. Print your numbers in red or black. Class, what colors can you print your numbers with?" The children respond, "Red or black." She asks again, "Class, what colors can you print your numbers with?" The class responds as before. Again she asks, "With what two colors can you print your numbers?" They respond, "Red or black." She replies, "Use only red or black." Two of the girls begin to talk softly about the assignment. One girl asks Virginia, "Did she tell us to draw picture?" Virginia replies, "No, girl, you dumb. She say to draw somethin' else." The children begin work on printing their numbers and only after Mrs. Benson begins walking among the students to determine their performance does she realize that five students are without crayons. She then gives crayons to this group, which includes Lilly.

Mrs. Benson's method of giving instructions to the class was to become a familiar part of the class routine. The repetition of the instructions three, four, or five times accompanied most directions related to academic activities. After the children had spent twenty minutes writing their numbers, Mrs. Benson passed to the class an exercise sheet in which numbers were to be written in smaller groupings. The paper had three horizontal lines through it. The first section was for the name, the second for the printing of the numbers 1 through 10, and the third to draw the number of "sticks" equal to each of the numbers directly above in the second section. After telling the children several times that their names were to be placed in the top "box," she began the instructions.

"Now, I want you to write numbers from 1 to 10 in the second box. Class, in which box do you write the numbers from 1 to 10?" The children respond, "Second." "In which box will you write your numbers from 1 to 10?" The class repeats its first answer. "You are going to write the numbers from 1 to 10 in which box?" The class responds, "Second." I note that three girls have already begun to write the numbers in the first box.

The Emergence of Classroom Organization

September 8

On the third day, Mrs. Benson established permanent seating arrangements. The class was divided into three groups. In the second grade class, all except two of those who had sat at Table A in the first grade were placed together on the left side of the room. At the rear of the room was the second group of students, which included the two former Table A students. In addition were those who had sat at Tables B and C during the first grade. Two students, however, who had sat at Table B in the first grade were not placed among those in the rear group. Rather, they were among the third group on the right side, which consisted of six students repeating the second grade plus two others returned from the third grade.

I asked Mrs. Benson why the two children (David and Anne) who had sat at Table A in the first grade were placed in the middle group in the second grade. She responded that she had placed them there in order that someone in the group "would be able to give the correct answer." She stated that she had very little confidence in the remaining students in the middle group and that she did not "want to waste time teaching them when no one would respond." Thus two children who should have been among those at the first table were placed at the middle table to fulfill the teacher's need for personal satisfaction.

The same question was posed about the two children (Carol and Nick) who had sat at Tables B and C respectively and were placed among the third group. She commented that she had been "warned" about Nick by the first grade teacher and had decided the "safest place for him was somewhere he could not bother those wanting to learn." The second child placed in the third group was Carol, and the teacher offered essentially the same rationale she had used for Anne and David. She stated that she knew teaching those in the third group would "mostly be a waste of time" and she wanted "at least one student in the bunch who could give a correct answer." There were nine students assigned to the first group by the window on the left side, eight assigned to the group at the rear, and ten assigned to the group along the right. Of the ten children remaining from the original kindergarten class, six were in the first group and four in the middle group.

By the time the children came to the second grade classroom, their seating arrangement appeared no longer to be based upon expectations of the teacher as to how they might perform. Rather, the assignments were based upon past performance. Available to the teacher when she formulated the seating plan were grade sheets from both kindergarten and first grade, IQ scores, a listing of the families on public welfare, reading scores on a series of diagnostic tests administered at the end of the first grade year, evaluations from the speech teacher, and informal evaluations from the kindergarten and first grade teachers.

When asked what was the single most crucial source of information utilized as she formulated the various groups, she replied that it was the first grade reading scores. She said that her goal was to divide the class according to "natural divisions" in these reading scores. The group by the windows on the left was designated as the "highest" reading group, the group to the rear was designated the "middle" reading group, and those on the right were labeled the "lowest." The high and middle reading groups were assigned second grade material, while those repeating the grade or returned from the third grade were to begin with material on a first grade level.

Except for the students placed in a reading group because of the teacher's desire to have "someone able to give the correct answers," the basic divisions of the previous year remained essentially intact. That is, there was no mobility from Tables B and C to the highest reading group. This is similar to the pattern which developed between the kindergarten and first grade. What mobility did appear each year was given those students who sat at the lowest table. They were, with few exceptions, moved in the following grade to the status of the middle group from the previous year. Thus, from kindergarten to first grade, Tables 2 and 3 become Table B. From the first grade to the second, Tables B and C become the middle group at the rear of the room. Each year there emerged a new low group designated as least capable and having the least potential for performance. In the first grade, a new group of students unknown to those from the kindergarten became the Table C students. Likewise, in the second grade, the lowest reading group comprised those repeating the grade or deemed unprepared for the third grade and returned. Through the time span of three grades, the most stable grouping appeared among those seated at Table 1, Table A, or in the "highest" reading group. The configuration of those who made up this group changed little in three years. Likewise, no one designated for this group by the kindergarten teacher was transferred out except for Anne and David.

As the children enter the room, Mrs. Benson asks them to put their wraps in the coatroom. When she sees Laura enter, she asks if the brown bag she is carrying contains her lunch. Laura responds, "No, this is for you." Laura hands Mrs. Benson the bag, and after she looks inside, she replies, "Oh, you brought us some leaves. How very nice of you." Mrs. Benson takes the leaves and places them on her desk. (Note the contrast in the way the teacher receives the leaves from Laura and the one Mary brought to class on September 5.) When the children are seated, Mrs. Benson asks them to rise for the Pledge of Allegiance. She notes that three children, including Nick, have their left hands over their hearts. She helps them switch to their right hands. But by the end of the Pledge, four other children have switched hands and have their left hands over their hearts. When the children are again seated, Lilly puts her head down on the desk. Within six minutes after the 8:30 a.m. opening, Mrs. Benson begins a penmanship lesson. (Note: This is to be the quickest observed movement of the class into academic material during the entire semester. The average length of time spent by the teacher and class in the morning organizational chores is slightly more than twenty minutes.)

When Mrs. Benson passes the paper for the lesson to the children, she instructs them to write their first names at the top of the page. Amy says to Mrs. Benson, "Girl, should I write my last name?" Mrs. Benson raises her voice noticeably and says, "Amy, do I call you girl or do I call you Amy?" Amy replies, "Amy." Mrs. Benson says, "All right, then, you call me by my name. What is my name?" "Mrs. Benson." Mrs. Benson responds, "Okay, now what is it you want?"

A standard direction Mrs. Benson gave to the class for each paper they wrote was to place a "heading" at the top of the page. The heading was to include the name of the child, the name of the school, and the date. On the front blackboard, Mrs. Benson wrote in one corner the word "heading," and below that she printed the word "name." On the third line was the name of the school and on the fourth the date. Laura was placed in charge of correcting the date on the board each morning. As Mrs. Benson continued her instructions, the principal began giving school announcements over the public address system. During the time he spoke, several of the children in the class continued to write on their papers. When the principal finished, Mrs. Benson spoke in a harsh voice to Marcia, "Marcia, I didn't tell you to write that yet." Alice called out, "What she write?" Mrs. Benson replied, "Alice, none of your business. But, Marcia, since you have already written it, don't erase it." (I later asked Mrs. Benson what it was that Marcia had written and she replied that it was the word "September.")

As the children continued to work on their papers, a new girl was brought into the class by the office secretary. Mrs. Benson interrupted the class to introduce the new student.

"All right, now, class, may I have your attention? We have a new girl in our class this morning. Her name is Shirley. Say "Shirley." The children repeat the name. Mrs. Benson continues, "Her name is Shirley. Her name is not 'new girl.' Her name is not 'hey, girl.' Her name is not 'that girl.' Her name is not 'hey, that new girl.' She has a name just like the rest of us. Her name is Shirley and she will sit by Anne. Anne, will you show Shirley what we are doing here in the class now?" Mrs. Benson gives Anne a piece of paper and a new pencil for Shirley. Anne immediately begins to show Shirley the assignment.

While the class was involved in the printing lesson, Nick was coloring on his piece of paper. He had begun to write the heading, but stopped. He took out his crayons and colored for thirty minutes. Mrs. Benson also was aware of his coloring. When I passed Nick's desk, she asked me to come to her desk. She took out a blue notebook in which she kept the class registration materials. She opened it to the section containing the materials on Nick. She pointed to his IQ score of 60 and then to both his mental age and his chronological age, which were stated at 4.8 and 7.9 years, respectively. She stated in a soft voice that she was going to attempt to have Nick placed in a special education class as soon as possible. She noted that there were several others whom she also wanted to place in special education. She called to Curt, who was seated in the rear of the room, and asked his age. He responded that he was nine. She commented, "He is another one that will have to go." (Note: At this point none of Curt's material from his previous school had been forwarded to Mrs. Benson. She did not know the results of any of the intelligence or academic tests given to the child. Two weeks later the material was sent from the main office and his IQ was listed as 121.) As I stood at the desk with Mrs. Benson, an older girl brought in a sheet for her to read. When she was finished, she initialed it and asked Laura to take it to the first grade teacher. Laura did so. Mrs. Benson began to discuss additional material she wanted the children to write on their papers.

September 11

The movement of children in and out of the class continued. The students now numbered thirty-one. There were twelve students in the high reading group, ten in the middle group, and nine in the low group. As the children entered after the noon recess, Mrs. Benson stood by the door and continually repeated, "Take your seat." When they were seated, she turned out the lights and said, "Your heads are down." She called the groups one at a time to hang up their wraps.

Mrs. Benson began to collect money from those students who wished her to keep it until the end of the school day. As she counted the change brought by Virginia, she heard Mary speaking to Tom. Mrs. Benson looked at Mary and said, "Mary, you disturbin' someone in the class who is trying to rest." Tom smiled and put down his head. Mary frowned and also put her head down.

Shortly, there occurred an interactional pattern between teacher and student that was to increase in frequency. As Mrs. Benson counted the change of another child, she called out, "Who's talkin' there in the back of the room?" Curt held up his hand and pointed at Stephen. Mrs. Benson said to Curt in a very firm voice, "Are you takin' care of him or are you takin' care of yourself?" More and more general questions were asked of the class concerning the behavior of other students. Questions such as "Who's doing all that talking?" "Who's making all that noise?" "Who can't keep his head down?" were frequent. A direct interpretation of her question would imply that she desired an answer. Thus children would point out a classmate who they believed fit the description. However, her responses to the children informing on one of their peers were not consistent. On some occasions, as here, she turned on the very child who gave the response. On others, she accepted the "squeal" and then reprimanded the child pointed out. There were other occasions when she would ask such a question and the class would not respond. She would repeat the question until one child offered a suggestion.

At the end of the organizational activities, Mrs. Benson turned on the lights and told those students in the high and middle reading group to continue on the arithmetic lesson that they began before the noon break. She instructed the children in the low reading group to take out their spelling books for a lesson entitled "spelling readiness." The lesson consisted of a series of pictures of two objects. The children were to establish whether the two objects in each picture began with the same letter.

The first picture shows a blond boy from the shoulders up and a baseball bat. Mrs. Benson calls on Alice for the answer and Alice responds, "Face and bat. No." Her answer indicates that she does not believe that face and bat begin with the same letter. Mrs. Benson looks at Alice and says, "Alice, that is not a face." Alice pauses, looks at the picture and says, "head and bat." "No, Alice, that is not a head and a bat." Another child calls out "Boy." Mrs. Benson says, "Yes. Now, what is the correct answer, Alice?" Alice responds, "Boy and bat." "Yes, Alice. That is a boy. That is not a head and it is not a face. It is a boy."

After the sixth series of pictures, Mrs. Benson asks the group if they agree with the answer given by one of the girls. Nick says that he does not. Mrs. Benson asks Nick why he does not agree and he smiles. He makes no verbal response to the teacher's question.

After the inappropriate response from Nick, on the seventh, eighth, and ninth series of questions the children began to call out the answers before Mrs. Benson could select a particular child for the answer. She became irritated and said, "Your mouth stays closed unless I call on you." The children remained silent for the following four questions and then began again to call out the answers.

At the end of this lesson, Mrs. Benson asked the entire class to take out a pencil. She passed out a sheet of lined writing paper. The class was told to write the correct heading for the day at the top of the page. As one child in the low reading group began to print his name, he crushed his paper slightly. Mrs. Benson observed that the paper was crushed and said in a loud voice to the entire class, "You know, this boy will not get his paper up on the board when we are finished because he's wrinkled it. I am not going to put any wrinkled paper up on this board." She then heard someone talking on the left side of the classroom and asked, "Who is that?" Mary pointed at Joe and Mrs. Benson said, "Joe, are you disturbing that row?" Joe frowned and shook his head. He looked back at Mary, who was smiling.

Within the class, Mrs. Benson had a policy of discouraging the children from sharing or borrowing from one another. Only infrequently did she approve of it.

As Mrs. Benson walked back to the blackboard, she noted that Virginia had not begun to write. "Virginia, what are you waiting for?" Virginia replies that she has broken her pencil. Mrs. Benson asks the class, "Is there anyone in the class who will loan Virginia a pencil?" Tom raises his hand and says that he will loan Virginia a pencil. Mrs. Benson gives him permission to leave his seat and go to Virginia's desk. On his return, Mrs. Benson looks directly at Tom and says, "Tom, you make sure you get it back."

In her admonition to Tom was the implication that if he did not seek out Virginia for his pencil at the end of the lesson, he would not have it back. Thus the rule of "no borrowing" may have been based on the assumption that the children did not have the integrity to return what they had been loaned. To avoid the anticipated claims of stolen materials, they were simply not exchanged.

Mrs. Benson continued with instructions:

After Mrs. Benson finishes writing all the letters of the heading on the board, she begins to walk around the room examining the papers of the children. On several of the papers she erases incorrect printing and helps the children to start over. With others she simply tells them to erase and begin again. As she walks through the room, she continually repeats, "You children *must* listen." Likewise there are several occurrences of the repetition of instructions. "Now, class, on what line did I say to write the name of the school?" Several of the children respond, "Second." She asks the question again, and the children respond as before. She asks the question for a third time and more children respond with the same answer. She walks to where I am seated and says with a sigh of resignation, "You know, it takes all day just to get these kids to write their names on the paper. They're so slow." She turns and again walks among the desks of the children on the left side.

September 16
After morning recess, Mrs. Benson began a reading lesson with the group on the right. She assigned arithmetic exercises to the remaining two groups of students. Lilly put her head down in her arms as soon as she finished the assignment. She stood at one point as if she were going to go to the reading table but sat back down and again put her head in her arms. A few minutes later she took out her box of crayons and began coloring. She worked at this only momentarily and put the crayons and paper away. Again she put her head down.

A teacher came into the class to borrow Scotch tape. She told Mrs. Benson that one of her students had eaten the cookies she had brought for lunch. She declared that she would "fix him, don't worry." As the teacher left, an eighth grade boy came in to ask Mrs. Benson's order for her lunch. He went to a small restaurant nearby and purchased the food for the teachers. (The boy was released 30–40 minutes early from class in order to have the food back to the school promptly as the lunch break began.) As he left, Mrs. Benson informed the class that they were going to make their first visit to the library.

Mrs. Benson mentions that the class is going to go to the library. Several of the children clap their hands with anticipation. Mrs. Benson says, "Now, we don't have to go to the library. Some people can cause us not to go. Nick, what did I say to do?" Nick makes no ver-

bal response and shrugs his shoulders. Alice whispers to him that
he should take his books off his desk. Nick does so. Mrs. Benson
asks the girls to "quietly line up." When the girls are in line, several
begin to lean against the wall. Mrs. Benson says to those girls in a
harsh voice, "Girls, get off that wall." She asks the boys to come
into the line behind the girls. As the boys move to the front of the
room, she says, "Get a partner and keep your mouth shut." Mrs.
Benson leads the class to the library.

When the group reaches the library, the librarian informs Mrs.
Benson that she is a week early. The library periods for the school
are not to begin until the following Monday. However, the librarian
consents to have the children come into the library. She instructs
the girls to sit on a large rug in one corner of the room. The boys are
to stand behind the girls. Mrs. Spring, the librarian, notes that Joe
has a piece of gum in his mouth. She asks him if he needs to go to
the wastebasket. He replies that he does not. She then asks what
he has in his mouth and he states that he has gum. Mrs. Spring:
"Well, don't you need to use the wastebasket?" Joe still does not
realize the implication of her question and again says "no." Mrs.
Spring, now irritated, says to Joe, "Boy, go spit that gum out." He
does.

Mrs. Spring informs the group when they come to the library they
are not to bring gum, candy, or sunflower seeds. Mrs. Spring explains to the class that they will begin coming the following week to
take books from the library. All the books that they will be able to
choose from are in the section marked with a large green "E."
Above the letter "E" is another sign which reads "Easy Books." On
the walls and on top of the bookcases are displays of jackets from
books in the library. Among the more than fifty jackets on display,
none has a picture of a black person. Many have pictures of white
children and white adults.

Mrs. Spring begins to list the materials available in the library. She
names books, records, puppets, pictures, and miniature replicas of

a number of animals. She asks the class what they can find in the library. The class responds correctly with the first four listed above. They also say "animals." Mrs. Spring says, "No, we don't have any animals in the library." At this point she picks up the replicas of the animals and puts them in a storage cabinet. Mrs. Spring comments that she has forgotten one other item in the library, and that that is filmstrips. Mrs. Spring asks the class to repeat the word "filmstrips" and the class does. She asks them if anyone knows what a filmstrip is, and there is no response. She says, "A filmstrip is a headful in a handful. Now repeat that." Several of the children say, appearing quite confused, "head in a hand."

The librarian has the girls come to the door and form a line. The boys come after the girls, and Mrs. Benson leads the group back to the second grade classroom. On the way back, Lilly walks at the very rear of the group by herself. She has walked very slowly, and the rest of the children walk past her.

When the children reached their room, Mrs. Benson told them they were to go to their seats and "be quiet." The noise level in the class, however, was high. The children were talking animatedly among themselves. Mrs. Benson said in a loud, harsh voice, "Someone did not hear what I said. I said to shut up." The noise level in the class diminished only momentarily and then returned to a rather high level. Mrs. Benson asked the girls to line up to go to the bathroom.

September 22

A phenomenon present in the kindergarten, but much more apparent in the second grade, was the continual interruption of the teacher and the class by persons walking into the room for any variety of reasons. During the first twenty minutes of observation on the 22nd, six interruptions were noted.

(1) 8:47 a.m.: A boy comes into the room with a pencil sharpener that Mrs. Benson has requested from the supply room.

(2) 8:58 a.m.: A boy comes into the room with three sheets of paper which he gives to Mrs. Benson.

(3) 9:02 a.m.: The office secretary brings a new student to the class.

(4) 9:04 a.m.: The assistant principal comes into the room. He whispers something to Mrs. Benson and leaves.

(5) 9:05 a.m.: The father of one of the children in the class enters to give lunch money to the student.

(6) 9:07 a.m.: The third grade teacher enters to borrow twelve sheets of green construction paper.

Mrs. Benson had begun to work with the class on the heading for a printing assignment at 8:42 a.m. With the interruptions, discussion of the lesson itself began thirty-three minutes later. The children worked intermittently through the interruptions to complete the heading. This list of interruptions is not atypical, except that it does not include the morning announcements from the principal, which were usually given at 8:50 a.m. They were this morning given at 9:25 a.m.—which was the seventh interruption in thirty-eight minutes, or approximately one every five minutes.

Earlier in the morning when the children first came into the classroom, there were none of the usual morning opening exercises. Instead, Mrs. Benson asked Tom to begin to sharpen the students' pencils. (Each day a boy was designated to sharpen pencils for all the students.) Pencil sharpening was supposed to be done at no other time during the day. If a lead was broken, the student had to borrow from a classmate. As Tom began, Mrs. Benson announced she had to leave the room. She gave no instructions to the children to be quiet or stay in their seats. She merely said, "I'll be right back." While she was out of the room, the noise level increased only slightly.

When Mrs. Benson returned, she asked why Laura was still standing at the pencil sharpener, where she had been when the teacher left the room. Laura explained that she had three new pencils to sharpen and that the lead of one had broken in the sharpener, so it had to be done again. Mrs. Benson made no further comment. Mary had finished her

heading and showed it to the teacher, who commented, "That's nice."
Mrs. Benson began to work on papers at her desk. The children were to continue work on their headings. The noise level slowly rose. She looked up from her work and said, "It doesn't take talkin' to put a headin' on the paper." The class was noticeably quieter. Mary looked around at the papers of students sitting near her and said to Mrs. Benson, "Some of the children have used three spaces for the headin' instead of two." Mrs. Benson replied, "That's because some children can't listen." Both Laura and Lilly had written their headings correctly, though the lines on Lilly's paper were not printed as darkly nor as straight as those on Laura's paper. Mrs. Benson instructed the children to write the numbers from one to one hundred on their papers. She continued working at her desk.

September 23
Twice during the morning lesson on language being taught the low group, Mrs. Benson asked a question of the group without receiving a correct answer. This was even after she had asked Carol, the child especially kept back from the middle reading group to insure that there would be one student who could provide the correct answer. When confronted with the situation, Mrs. Benson turned to students in the other two groups. These students were involved in a different lesson when Mrs. Benson interrupted them and asked for the answer to the question unanswered by the low group.

Mrs. Benson has written the word "fish" on the board. She asks the group if they know the word and several respond correctly that the word is "fish." She erases the "sh" and replaces the two letters with a "b." She asks how the new word is pronounced. Jim replies, "fit." Alice says, "fish." Lou offers, "bit." Mrs. Benson replies, "No, look at the word, f-i-b. This is the same thing as telling a story. Instead of them telling a story, they tell a [pause]. Carol, do you know?" Carol responds, "Somebody tells a story." Jim adds, "No, somebody tellin' a fob." Mrs. Benson asks, "A fob?" Jim responds, "Yeah." Mrs. Benson turns away from the group on the right to the remainder of the class and asks, "Anybody out there know what this word is? Liza, do you know what it is? Liza responds, "fib." Mrs. Benson replies, "Yes, hasn't anyone ever told you a fib?" Nick responds, "Not me." (Liza is in the high reading group.)

On the second occasion, the children in the low group were to define a word:

Mrs. Benson writes the word "colt" on the board. She says, "Now, who can tell me what a colt is?" Jim offers, "Somethin' you put on." Mrs. Benson replies, "No, that is a coat, c-o-a-t. I am talkin' about a colt, c-o-l-t." Alice says, "A colt is a slow." Mrs. Benson asks, "A slow?" Alice says, "Yeah." Mrs. Benson begins to draw a picture on the blackboard. She asks the group, "What is this I'm trying to draw?" Jim says, "A horse." Mrs. Benson replies, "So what is a colt?" Jim says, "A pig." Alice offers, "A cow." Carol says it is a "chicken." At this point Mrs. Benson turns to the children in the other two groups and says, "Does anyone out there know what a colt is?" Hal has raised his hand and is called on by Mrs. Benson. He says, "A baby horse." Mrs. Benson says, "Yes." Mrs. Benson then turns back to the group on the right and tells them it is the end of the lesson.

September 26

Interruptions of classroom activities from outside were continual. Thought patterns were broken, lessons were interrupted, attention wandered, and only short periods of concentration were possible as a result. On the 26th, I counted all outside interruptions during a thirty-five minute observational period. The dropping of a book, the talking of the children, or a coughing spell were not counted, though they also are factors that create interruptions. Such internal factors that contribute to disruption are inherent in placing more than thirty persons in one room for many hours each day. The most effective manner to control external interruptions would have been to lock the door, but fire regulations prohibited locked classrooms. The following account summarizes the repeated puncture of the classroom space:

12:45 p.m.
Bell rings indicating end of noon recess period.

12:51 p.m.
Children come into the room. Some go and sit while others talk or look at books.

12:56 p.m.
First interruption—teacher from the third grade enters and asks Mrs. Benson if she has a master key to the doors, saying that she has locked herself out of her room. Mrs. Benson suggests that instead of going to the office and asking the principal for a key, she send a boy outside to climb through the window. The teacher says she thought of that, but all windows are locked. Mrs. Benson suggests that she go and speak with Mrs. Logan, the first grade teacher. The third grade teacher leaves the room. Orlando enters the room and is called to the teacher's desk. Mrs. Benson then speaks with him for three minutes asking why he is late to class. He has to go and get his sister from the fourth grade to substantiate his excuse for being late to class.

12:59 p.m.
Second interruption—Orlando comes back to the room with his sister, who relates to the teacher the reason for his being late for class. The teacher tells the sister to "make sure" her brother is at school on time "from now on."

1:03 p.m.
Third interruption—principal turns on the public address system

and gives scores of the noon volleyball game in the eighth grade. He also tells the children that they can begin to bring their money to school to buy the tickets to the three children's concerts by the St. Louis symphony.

1:06 p.m.
Fourth interruption—student who does errands for the office brings slips to the room for Mrs. Benson to sign. She does so and the student leaves.

1:08 p.m.
Fifth interruption—second grade teacher, Mrs. Wright, comes into the room complaining that another teacher ate her sandwich at lunch. She sounds angry with the other teacher, who apparently ate the wrong sandwich by mistake. She states that the only thing she had to eat for lunch was the sandwich of one of her students who was not hungry. She also leaves a three-page memo with Mrs. Benson. The teacher leaves and Mary asks if she can take the memo to the next room. Mrs. Benson responds that she has not yet read it and Mary says, "Yeah, but I like to go around the school."

1:10 p.m.
Twenty-five minutes after the bell rings Mrs. Benson instructs the class to take out the workbooks they are using and finish their exercises. Mrs. Benson asks Rose from the high reading group to take the three-page memo to all the teachers on both the first and second floors. She instructs Rose to wait until the teacher has read it and then pass it on to the next teacher.

1:12 p.m.
Sixth interruption—three patrol boys come into the room asking the teacher if she has one of the school volleyballs. She says that she does not and they leave.

1:13 p.m.
Seventh interruption—fourth grade teacher comes into the room with money from two children who have brought it to purchase their symphony tickets. (Mrs. Benson and Mrs. Caplow are in charge of ticket sales on the first floor.) Mrs. Benson tells the teacher to keep all the money until the first of the next week when the principal passes the tickets out to her. The teacher leaves and Laura comes to the front with her book. She shows it to the teacher and is told to go ahead and finish the entire page of exercises. Mary comes to show her book and Mrs. Benson responds, "Go back and sit down; I don't want to be disturbed." Shortly Laura comes back to the teacher's desk and asks a question. Mrs. Benson replies, "That's right, honey. Now go back and finish the rest of the page." Laura goes back to her seat. Alice comes to the desk of the teacher and begins to ask a question. Mrs. Benson says, "Alice, that is irrelevant. Now go and sit down."

1:20 p.m.
Eighth interruption—a child from the fourth grade comes to Mrs. Benson with money to purchase symphony tickets.

The Formalization of Winners and Losers

September 29
I made eleven observations of the second grade students during their weekly half-hour library periods. The first of those periods was described in the discussion of September 16. To avoid the repetitious description of each of the periods, the observation of the library visit on the 29th of September is presented in some detail as representative of events which occurred during the library periods. The following excerpts should suffice to provide insights into the common and predominant experiences of the children.

Mrs. Benson says, "Okay, girls from the Tigers, come line up."

She repeats the instruction for the group of girls in the rear, referring to them as "Cardinals." The last group of girls from the right
are also called, as "Clowns." Mrs. Benson comes to me and explains that she has "gotten tired of not having any name for the
groups" so she has given each of the three reading groups a new
name. The boys are then also asked to line up, beginning with
"Tiger boys" and ending with the "Clown boys." Nick is the last
child to leave the room. He does not have a partner. Mrs. Benson
instructs him to turn off the lights as he leaves.

As the children enter the library, the librarian stands in the door
saying repeatedly, "Watch your lips." She also instructs the boys to
"pick up your feet. This is not a parade." She tells the children
where to sit, with the boys on the left and the girls on the right side
of the room. Mrs. Spring asks whether there are any children in the
class who did not receive a library card the previous week. One boy
holds up his hand and says that he is new. Another boy holds up his
hand and is asked by Mrs. Spring, "Are you new?" The boy replies,
"Uh, huh." Mrs. Spring replies, "Oh, no, we can't have talk like that
in my library. What is it you are supposed to say when you are in the
library?" "Yes, ma'am." Mrs. Spring says, "No, that is not good
enough. Say, 'Yes, Mrs. Spring.' " The boy repeats as instructed.

Mrs. Spring asks who has forgotten to bring his library book. Nick
says he forgot, and Mrs. Spring responds, "Oh, no, we can't have
that. You better bring that book back at lunch or I will put your name
on the list of those who forget today is Monday. You better bring
that book, hear me, boy?"

Rose calls out to Mrs. Spring, "Carol forgot her book." Mrs. Spring
turns to Rose in a harsh voice, "Oh, no, little lady. The next time you
open your mouth I am going to lose my temper. I am able to speak
for myself. Now you keep sittin' there and keep your mouth shut if
you want to stay in my library." Mrs. Spring asks Audrey where her
book is and Audrey replies it is at home. The librarian begins liter-

ally to scream at the children, saying, "What's wrong with you? Can't you remember anything? What's wrong with your mother? Can't she remember anything, too? Why didn't you bring your book? What are you trying to do, lose all of my library books? Are you trying to embarrass the whole room?" Audrey softly replies, "No, ma'am." Mrs. Spring retorts, "Never mind, you are embarrassing the whole room. I am disappointed in you." She turns away and Audrey, distressed, puts her head in her arms.

When the children have checked out their new books, they return to their seats. Lilly begins to show her new book to Shirley. Mrs. Benson, who is seated in the rear of the room, calls to Lilly, "Lilly, shut your mouth." Mrs. Spring sees two boys, Tom and Joe, showing one another pictures from their books. She says, as she claps her hands three times, "Hey, you two, turn around and use your books." The two boys separate and then close their books.

The time allowed to select a new book is short. The last four children do not have enough time, and Mrs. Spring simply gives them books to check out. She tells the class to line up to leave with all the girls before the boys. She hears Rose talking to Laura. She comes up behind Rose and claps her hands four times and says, "Oh, no, oh, no. You are going to close your mouth, little lady, or you and I are going to have a falling out right here. I have taken all from you that I am going to take today. If I hear one more word from you, it is all over."

The librarian says, "All right now, little people, you can go back to your room." I am the last person out of the library from the class. As I pass the librarian, she says, "Maybe I ought to give you one of these little kiddie books, too." I say I have plenty to read and leave.

An event not to be overlooked in the material on the library visit is the teacher's giving names to the three reading groups. By calling her high reading group "Tigers" (they had won the last World Series in

St. Louis), the middle reading group the "Cardinals," and the low group the "Clowns," Mrs. Benson made a telling summary of her perceptions about the various groups in her class.

With the introduction of "Tigers," "Cardinals," and "Clowns," there occurred a decisive split in the conceptual evaluation of the various reading groups. No pretense was made of implying gradations on one plane of performance. Rather, it was assumed that there were profound differences of perceived ability and potential that separated the students into two major groups. *To call a group of students "clowns" was more than a mere evaluation of their academic performance. It was a statement of their perceived worth as individuals.* They were viewed as belonging to an entirely separate category of persons—to paraphrase Matza (1966), those considered "disreputable" students. They were perceived as such because the stigma of poor records of academic performance, "undesired" behavioral and attitudinal characteristics, and low social class origins set them apart from the remainder of their classmates. They were losers.

October 6
A twice-weekly routine for the children was to take home all their completed papers. On Friday, October 3, Mrs. Benson instructed the children to "make sure all papers go home today to your mothers." As was to become clear during the Monday lesson, these instructions created a misunderstanding among the children, and the Clowns were denied a reading lesson because they had explicitly followed her directions.

Mrs. Benson walks to the front of the Clowns' section and says, "Clowns, take out your duplicating sheets. We are going to grade them now." Lou responds, "I took mine home." "Lou, you were not supposed to do that. You are never to take home any papers that are not graded." Lou continues, "But Friday you say to take all papers home." "Well, I meant that you were only to take home those papers that had been graded." Lou makes no response. Laura interrupts Mrs. Benson and shows her the paper she has finished. Mrs. Benson goes to her desk for a ditto, which she asks Mary to take to the office to have duplicated.

Mrs. Benson leaves her desk and brings her chair to the Clowns group. When she is seated, she finds that only two of the nine students have their ditto sheets. She asks the remaining seven children where their sheets are. They respond that they took them home. One boy says he lost his sheet on the way home. Mrs. Benson becomes irritated with the group and says, "Well, you are not ready. None of you are ready. You all better get those papers tonight and bring them back tomorrow so we can grade them. We can't read today because you are not ready. I am going to go and read with the Tigers. Tigers, get out your notebooks. The Tigers have their work. I am going to go and work with them." She gives no further directions to the Clowns, and they sit for the next twenty-five minutes watching Mrs. Benson teach the Tigers or with their heads down in their arms. Later in the period, several of the children begin to color in a coloring book Lou has brought from home. He tears out pages and shares with others in the Clown group.

October 9

At 12:50 p.m. the children began to enter the room. They went to their seats, and Mrs. Benson repeated several times, "All heads are supposed to be down." A number of the children put down their heads but others did not. The noise level was low. Mrs. Benson said, "Somebody isn't resting." Only two of the eight with their heads up then put them down.

Alice comes from her seat in the Cardinal group toward the teacher. Mrs. Benson says, "Sit down, Alice." Alice keeps coming toward the desk. Mrs. Benson repeats herself, but Alice walks directly to her. She speaks softly and explains that she lost her eraser on the playground and asks if she can go outside to find it. She also asks if she can take someone from the class with her. Mrs. Benson replies, "Okay, girl, but I doubt that you find it." Many of the children have been listening. When Mrs. Benson gives permission for Alice to go outside, a number of them hold up their hands saying that they would like to go along with Alice to look for the eraser. All the girls in the Clown group hold up their hands as do all but two girls in the Cardinal group. No girl in the Tiger group shows any desire to go with Alice to the playground. Alice, however, ignores the requests of all the girls with their hands raised and calls on Virginia from the Tiger group to accompany her. Virginia rises when Alice asks her to go, and they leave the room.

As the two opened the door to leave, a breeze blew through the room. A paper fell from the desk of Rose, seated in the Tiger group, and blew across under the desk of Lou, seated in the Clown group. Lou picked up the paper and held it for Rose. Rose came across the room to Lou, grabbed the paper from him and said, "Gimmee that paper, boy." She walked back to her seat.

Mrs. Benson says to the class, "All right, now everyone take out their spelling workbooks. Also take out a piece of crayon. Put all pencils and erasers away." Lou and Amy both ask Mrs. Benson what color crayon to use for the checking of the workbooks, but she makes no response. Hal, who sits in the Cardinal group, comes to Mrs. Benson's desk and explains that he has not been able to finish the lesson. Mrs. Benson replies, "There is not a thing I can do for you. There is just not a thing I can do. Go back and sit down. Every question that you have not finished you will have to mark wrong." Mrs. Benson begins to check the books of the Tigers and Cardinals, calling on Shirley from the Cardinals for the fourth answer. Shirley responds, "I don't know where you are." Mrs. Benson responds, "Well, what am I supposed to do for you, girl? Find out where we are." Mrs. Benson then calls on Laura, who responds correctly.

When they had checked the first ten exercises for the Tigers and Cardinals, Mrs. Benson asked all the class to close their books and put them away. None of the work done by the Clowns was checked. Mrs. Benson explained that since it was Fire Prevention Week, they were going to go to the gymnasium to hear a fireman talk to them. As the girls and then the boys lined up to go to the gym, Lilly was left without a partner. She walked by herself as the last girl before the boys. The same was to be the case as the class returned to the room at the end of the talk.

From a Different Perspective: The Teacher

In an attempt to learn more about Mrs. Benson's perceptions of the classroom, the students, and her role as teacher, four interviews were conducted during two weeks in October. Areas of concern discussed during the interviews included her satisfaction with her position; her students and the school; her perception of what was involved in the teaching and learning processes; values and attitudes that she brought into the classroom situation; and whether she held different expectations for the various groups of students in the class. The following excerpts are instructive:

Mrs. Benson, do you like teaching?
"Oh, yes, very much. I really enjoy working with children. I'd like for the children to be a little older. I would like to teach third or fourth grade. They seem to catch on quicker and you don't have to spend so much time getting them ready to do something. I sure do like teaching. But you know, I did not like Harris Teachers College. That place didn't do nothing for me. I was so glad to get out of there. When I look back now, I can't think of a single thing that I learned that I have used since I started teaching. When I left Harris, I thought I was not going to like teaching, but now I am into it, I really love it."

Mrs. Benson, do you believe it is easy to get through to second graders?

"It's not easy, no, because second graders have an attention span that is so short. They daydream a lot. They just stare out of the window for long periods of time. But by the third grade they are more settled down."

Mrs. Benson, nowadays, one hears a lot about the term "cultural deprivation." Do you believe this term applies to any of your second grade students?
"Yes, definitely. A lot of them had never seen the downtown before we took our bus ride. I think that most of these children get their cultural experiences through the school. They really wouldn't have any cultural education if it was not for the school because most of these children are in families that don't have the time, money, or interest in their children to take them places and do things with them. But I know that is not true for all my students—especially for my Tigers."

Mrs. Benson, do you have any perception that you and the children may come from different backgrounds?
"Yes, I notice that when I went to school kids were not as ragged as they are now. Now they are downright dirty. They come to school and they are absolutely filthy. I can never remember so many ragged kids as now. Some of these kids even come to school without underwear. I guess times must be harder now than they used to be."

Mrs. Benson, I suppose that people come to a profession like teaching with certain ideals. Would you say that it was true for you?
"I am sure I did, but I can't remember them. I just thought teaching was a very noble profession."

Mrs. Benson, what is the biggest thing that keeps you in teaching?
"I just love children and I like to teach. I enjoy what I am doing. There is never a dull moment in this room. Children are constantly changing. I guess it is the children themselves that keep me going."

Mrs. Benson, what do you find the most difficult thing to put up with?
"Discipline is pretty hard to stand around here sometimes. Some of
these kids just go wild."

In addition, specific questions were posed concerning the three reading groups in the class. Her responses were reminiscent of those of the
kindergarten teacher, Mrs. Caplow, two years earlier.

Mrs. Benson, how would you describe the Tigers in terms of their
learning ability and academic performance?
"Well, they are my fastest group. They are very smart."

Mrs. Benson, how would you describe the Tigers in terms of discipline matters?
"The Tigers are very talkative. Laura, Mary, and Virginia, they are
always runnin' their mouths constantly, but they get their work done
first. I don't have much trouble with them."

Mrs. Benson, what value do you think the Tigers hold for an education?
"They all feel an education is important and most of them have
goals in life as to what they want to be. They mostly want to go to
college."

The same questions were asked concerning the Cardinals.

Mrs. Benson, how would you describe the Cardinals in terms of
learning ability and academic performance?
"They are slow to finish their work . . . but they do get finished. You
know, a lot of them, though, don't care to come to school too much.
Hal, Audrey, and Edith are absent quite a bit. The Tigers are never
absent."
Mrs. Benson, how would you describe the Cardinals in terms of discipline matters?
"Not too bad. Since they work so slow, they don't have time to talk.
They are not like the Tigers, who finish in a hurry and then just sit
and talk with each other."

Mrs. Benson, what value do you think the Cardinals hold for an education?

"Well, I don't think they have as much interest in education as do the Tigers, but you know, it is hard to say. Most will like to come to school, but the parents will keep them from coming. They either have to babysit or the clothes are dirty. These are some of the excuses the parents often give. But I guess most of the Cardinals want to go on and finish and go on to college. A lot of them have ambitions when they grow up. It's mostly the parents' fault they are not at school more often."

Her responses to the questions concerning the Clowns lend credence to the interpretation that she viewed them as categorically different from the remainder of her class.

Mrs. Benson, how would you describe the Clowns in terms of learning ability and academic performance?

"Well, they are really slow. You know, most of them are still doing first grade work."

Mrs. Benson, how would you describe the Clowns in terms of discipline matters?

"They are very playful. They like to talk a lot. They are not very neat. They like to talk a lot and play a lot. When I read to them, boy, do they have a good time. You know, the Tigers and the Cardinals will sit quietly and listen when I read to them, but the Clowns, they are always so restless. They always want to stand up. When we read, it is something else. You know, Alice and Amy especially like to stand up. All these children, too, are very aggressive."

Mrs. Benson, what value do you think the Clowns hold for an education?

"I don't think very much. I don't think education means much to them at this stage. I know it doesn't mean anything to Lou and Nick. To most of the kids, I don't think it really matters at this stage."

Two additional questions were posed to Mrs. Benson:

Mrs. Benson, what do you believe will come of these children in life?
"I think they want to be better than their parents since their parents
had so many kids. They will try to make a better life for themselves
than their parents had. Most will want to go to college and finish
their education. But you know a few are not going to make it. They
are not going anywhere. But most of them are good kids. There is
such a strong emphasis on education to get the good jobs that they
will want to go on and finish, especially the Tigers. I know most of
them will want to go to college."

Mrs. Benson, you mentioned a few of the children are "not going to
go anywhere." Can you tell me more about that?
"For example, take Nick. He is not going to do anything. Lou might
straighten up. He likes to do his work, but it is always wrong. Curt
won't amount to very much and neither will Orlando. Amy tries, but
she just hasn't got it. Lilly is the type that will drop out and go to
work. She doesn't have the kind of clothes she wants and she is very
self-conscious about the clothing she wears now. The kids in the
class are always making fun of the clothes she wears now. Lilly will
probably drop out and go get the clothes she wants. But that is the
worst thing she could do. Getting an education is so much more
important. This is the way it goes for a lot of the students in the
class. They just are not going to go anywhere."

In the Classroom: Halloween to Christmas

October 31
Though there is no formal policy in the city schools that Halloween is
to be celebrated, custom has prevailed and a yearly event is the school
parade and classroom parties. In the second grade, Mrs. Benson had
asked the children to come in costume. Of the six children who wore
complete outfits, five were from the Tiger group. The sixth was Lou, a
Clown.

When I entered the room, Mrs. Benson was pointing a stick at a group of boys from the Tiger and Cardinal groups who were playing with one another on the floor. Mrs. Benson told them to "get off the floor and quit actin' like Clowns." She also commented, "Hal, I am surprised at you. You are actin' just like one of those Clowns."

Mary's mother, Mrs. Spiller, was the only mother to attend the party. She brought a punch bowl and a half-dozen cans of Hawaiian Punch. She also donated four packages of Oreo cookies. When the party began, she served punch and cookies to the children. After all had been served, Mrs. Benson told them to sit in their seats until everyone was finished. During the time the children were eating, Mrs. Spiller, Mrs. Benson, and I sat by the teacher's desk. The mother began to quiz Mrs. Benson about Mary. The first question was whether she believed "Mary was a sloppy child." Mrs. Benson replied that Mary was, at times, but it was because she worked so rapidly. Next, Mrs. Benson was asked if she had difficulty with Mary since she was an only child. Mrs. Benson said that she did not and that Mary was one of her best students. Mrs. Spiller commented that Mary had expressed a strong sense of competition with Laura on class activities. She related that Mary often came home with a paper which had only one error and would cry because Laura had a paper with no errors. "I think one of the best things that has happened for Mary," continued her mother, "is the competition with Laura. Now she works so hard to keep up with her. You know, it would be good if everyone had a Laura in their life, because then they would work so much harder."

Mary came to the front and introduced Alice (who was a Clown) to her mother. She told her that Alice was one of her "best friends." Mrs. Benson responded, quite surprised, "Why, Mary, I didn't know Alice was one of your best friends." Mary's mother said, "Oh, Mary has all types of friends." Neither Mary nor Alice made any response and both went back to their seats.

Mrs. Benson mentioned that she wished she could think of some games to play with the children now that they were finished eating. I suggested musical chairs. She agreed and began to organize the class. Several of the girls were sitting on the floor. She reprimanded them, "You are all acting like Clowns. Get up off that floor."

At the end of three games of musical chairs (in which six of the Clowns could not participate because there were not enough chairs), Mrs. Benson passed out small bags of Halloween candy to the children. She told them to go to their seats to eat the candy. The children complied. Mrs. Benson returned to her desk and again began talking with Mrs. Spiller. Mrs. Benson pointed out to Mrs. Spiller different children in the room, making short comments about each child. She noted that several of the Tigers were "very good students." She said that for Nick and Curt "there was no hope," and that she had applied to send both boys to special education classes.

The teacher was asked if she often had to "whip" the children. "Not too often because most of the time you can get them to do what you want just by talking to them." Mrs. Spiller responded that she had tried talking with Mary, but sometimes there seemed to be "nothing to do but whip her." Mrs. Benson agreed that sometimes "a whipping was the best thing for them." Mrs. Spiller inquired if Mrs. Benson had any special technique she used for whipping. Mrs. Benson responded that she preferred a ruler, because she did not have to hit the child "directly." The children were told that they could dance to records Mary and Joyce had brought for the party. Mrs. Benson and Mrs. Spiller remained seated in the front talking until ten minutes before the dismissal bell, when they began to straighten the room and dispose of the paper. The two women were calling one another "girl," dropping the formal address.

November 3

Mrs. Benson spent the majority of her teaching time with either the Tiger or Cardinal reading group. Once more, I observed her giving an academic assignment to the Cardinals and a nonacademic assignment to the Clowns.

Mrs. Benson instructs the Cardinals to take out their notebooks for a spelling lesson. Before leaving her desk to go back to the Cardinal group, she calls Alice to her. She gives Alice one sheet of paper to pass out to each of the students in the Clown group. She instructs the group that for the next 25 minutes they are to draw a picture of a "Thanksgiving dinner." Nick responds, "Huh?" Mrs. Benson turns to him and says, "Boy, I didn't say for you to talk, hear?" She takes her chair and goes to the rear of the room where she begins the lesson with the Cardinals. The Tigers are involved in a three-page arithmetic assignment.

During the lesson with the Cardinals, the performances of David and Anne, the two children held back, was consistently good. They answered questions when others in the group could not. Mrs. Benson persistently turned to these two students for answers after others in the Cardinals gave incorrect responses. For example, when she showed the group the table of contents in the book, she asked what it was called. She received responses of "magazine" and "stories" from other students before calling on David, who responded correctly. Likewise, when asking the group which was the page for the lesson, several incorrect pages were suggested before Anne gave the correct page number.

November 4
Today Mrs. Benson had scheduled the single field trip of the school year for the class. They were to be accompanied by the first grade. The itinerary, as planned by Mrs. Benson, was to drive first through the downtown section of the city and along the levee of the Mississippi River. The second half of the trip was to be a tour through a large park on the west edge of the city where the children were to see part of the zoo, a large bird enclosure, duck ponds, and the colors of the fall leaves. The bus was crowded, in fact, seven over the maximum capacity listed on a sign above the driver.

After driving through the city and along the riverfront, the group stopped at the historic Old Courthouse where, among other events, the Dred-Scott case of 1856 was argued. Here the children were allowed thirty minutes. They were accompanied by the teachers and were organized to walk in columns, two by two. Neither of the teachers was heard to explain to any students the significance of the building and what place it had in American history. In one of the court chambers, the teacher asked who sat in the large chair. No one in the class replied. "That is where the judge sits. Now, say judge." About half the group repeated the word.

The children during the first part of the tour were most excited by their short travel along the levee. They were interested in the boats and made comments about their various sizes. They appeared little impressed with the Arch (a six-hundred-foot steel structure built to symbolize St. Louis as the "Gateway to the West") though the teachers continually told them to turn away from the boats and look at it. Very few did so for any period of time. The fascination was with the river and the boats.

During the second part of the tour through the park and parts of the zoo, the children enjoyed themselves. They were pointing out things to one another, especially when they first observed ducks on one of the ponds. The teachers several times asked for quiet in the bus, but to little avail. The children also enjoyed their walk through the large bird enclosure in the park. They lingered as long as possible inside the cage and pointed out to one another features of the birds which appealed to them. Later, as the bus driver jokingly asked the class if they wished to spend all day on the bus and not go home until nine o'clock, all the children cheered their agreement.

The children appeared genuinely to enjoy themselves on the tour, in spite of excessive demands from both teachers for orderliness and quietness. Two examples of the way in which the teachers sought to maintain control over the children occurred in the Courthouse and in the bird enclosure. In the Courthouse, when the children were on the second floor, Mrs. Benson threatened to throw any child "over the side" who did not stop talking and move down the stairs near the wall. In the bird enclosure, the children were also threatened with being thrown over the side, but this time among birds "who will eat you up." The children were always arranged in a long column whenever they left the bus. When on the bus the teachers asked for silence, but often found themselves in competition not only with the interest of the children, but with the bus driver, who carried on conversations with as many children as could hear him.

November 14
On the 11th of November Mrs. Benson had sent home progress reports on the first quarter. All were returned by the fourteenth. The following is a summary of the reports and comments of the parents.

Among the Tigers, gold stars were given for academic performance to Laura, Diane, Liza, Joyce, Joe, Mary and Rose. Blue stars to recognize perfect attendance during the quarter were given to Tom, Virginia, Mary, Laura, Liza, and Diane. Mrs. Benson commented on eight of the reports in an identical manner. Her statement was as follows: "[Name] is progressing very nicely. Please continue to encourage him/her." For four children, Mrs. Benson made additional comments. "Tom is progressing very nicely, but works a little too slowly. Please continue to encourage him. Your help is greatly appreciated." On Diane's report, "Diane needs much encouragement to speed up her work. With greater speed in finishing her work, her grades could possibly be higher." "Rose is doing very nicely in her work, but needs more encouragement to be less talkative." Finally, for Liza, "Liza is progressing very nicely but works a little too slowly. Please continue to encourage her to do her best."

In response, five mothers of children in the Tiger group wrote short notes. Laura's mother said, "I was very pleased with Laura's report card." From Mary's mother, "We'll do our best in encouraging Mary." Virginia's mother stated, "I am very pleased about Virginia's report card. We'll encourage her more as well as help her." Joe's mother responded, "I am happy to know that Joe is doing well in school and I hope he will continue." Finally, Rose's mother wrote, "Mrs. Benson, Rose is very talkative here at home and I wish that you could help me keep her quiet. You may punish her whenever it is needed and I will try to improve on my part."

Among the Cardinals, only two students received gold stars for academic performance. They were given to David and Anne, the two children especially placed in the group by Mrs. Benson. Blue stars for perfect attendance were given to Hal, Lilly, and Doug. For seven of the Cardinals, the same comment was made to the parents as for the Tigers: "[Name] is progressing very nicely. Please continue to encourage him/her." Other comments were: "Roy is doing fine in his work but he works a little too slowly. Please encourage him to speed up his work. This might help pull up his grades." "Lena is progressing very nicely, but is absent a little too much. With better attendance there could be improvement in her grades. Please continue to encourage her in her work." For both Hal's and Dan's report, "Dan (Hal) is progressing nicely but is too talkative and playful. Please encourage him to play less and work more. Your help is greatly appreciated." To Joyce's parents, "Joyce has trouble following directions and in reading. She needs much more help in her studies. Please do all you can to encourage her to do better work." Finally on Lilly's report, "Lilly is progressing very nicely, but talks a little too much. Please encourage her to talk less and work more. Your help is greatly appreciated."

Responses were given by parents of four children. On Lena's card, "I hope Lena approves in her attendance, I'm very proud of her grades although she can do better." From the mother of Dan, "I am gois to do my best to make Dan study moor and quit play's and talk's." Anne's mother wrote, "I am very glad that Anne is doing well. We will continue to work with her on this end and hope you will do likewise." The last comment was from the mother of Doug. "Dear teacher, I hope Doug will continue to progress thank you."

No Clown student was given a gold star. Three students, Nick, Lou, and Amy, received a blue star for perfect attendance. Only one child, Jim, received the standard comment from Mrs. Benson. For Nick, Mrs. Benson commented, "Nick daydreams a lot, and therefore is very in-atentive [sic]. He doesn't follow directions and never finishes a paper. Please encourage him to pay closer attention to directions and work harder." To the parents of Lou, "Lou is very playful and inatentive [sic]. Please encourage him to be less playful and to work harder." "Amy works nicely but can't seem to follow directions. Therefore her work is usually wrong. Please encourage her to be more attentive and work harder. She also talks a little too much." On Jim's report, "Works nicely, but a little too slow. Please encourage him to speed up his work." To Orlando's parents, "Orlando finishes his work very hur-riedly and sloppily. He uses the rest of his time for talk and play. Please encourage him to work more and play less." "Alice is doing much better in her work. Please encourage her to do her best. She needs much help in arithmetic." "Carol takes very little interest in her school work. She needs much encouragement to do better in her lessons." Finally, to the parents of Curt, "Curt sometimes does nice work but tends to be very playful and talkative at times. Please encourage him to take his work more seriously."

Four parents of students in the Clown reading group wrote short notes. From Lou's mother, "Dear teacher, all I can say is whip him good about that playing and work." From Amy's mother, "Amy can do better and now I am going to tighten down on her." Jim's mother wrote, "He did ok, but could have did better." Finally, from Orlando's mother, "Will you please whip Orlando when he is playing and talking. I will see that he study more at home."

Other than the perfunctory remarks made to parents of more than half of the class, Mrs. Benson's comments centered on the behavioral aspects of the students' performance in the class. The three areas most often mentioned were talking, playing, and working too slowly on assignments. To ask the parents to encourage their sons or daughters to work faster, play less, or talk less implied that the parent had some influence on the processes of interaction and performance operant in the classroom. Mrs. Benson's continual statements that she received very little support from the parents of her students and that they do not appear to have interest in the class may in part be explained by the type of support and interest she requested. What Mrs. Benson most desired from the parents was their support in making their children quiet and passive. Her goals were to create a classroom with a more efficient organization, not necessarily to foster more learning. The parents were asked to participate in the behavioral modification of their children, but not in their learning development. The issue is whether, in fact, parents could have influenced their children while inside the classroom to suit Mrs. Benson. I suspect they could not—and that Mrs. Benson continued to receive "nonsupport" from the parents. Given her set of expectations, it could not have been otherwise.

November 26
During October, a professional photographer came to the school and took color pictures of each of the students. The parents were able to buy pictures for two dollars per set. Of this amount, fifty cents was donated to the school and the remaining dollar and a half was reimbursement for the photographer. The photographer returned the proofs to the school just before the Thanksgiving vacation. The children were not allowed to take the proofs home to show their parents before they bought them. The principal decided not to allow them out of the building, for he claimed that a large number of the proofs would never be returned. Each teacher was given the proofs for her class. The children were able to see them one time.

On the 26th, Mrs. Benson spent the first thirty-five minutes after noon recess individually showing the children proofs of their pictures. She explained that she was showing the pictures to the children "the slow way" because she had had "a hard morning and didn't feel like teaching any more today. Today just isn't the day to do any teaching." During the time she showed each child his picture, the light was off in the room. She also had the children practice the songs "Come, Ye Thankful People, Come," "My Country, 'Tis of Thee," and "America, America" for the Thanksgiving assembly that was to begin at 1:45 p.m. The program was being sponsored by the primary grades (kindergarten through third). During the practice of the songs, Mrs. Benson told several children that if they sang "that way on the stage, I come grab you right off there."

After the children sang each of the songs twice, Rose came to Mrs. Benson and asked if she and several of the other girls in the class could sing for the class. Mrs. Benson gave permission. Rose selected three other Tigers, Mary, Laura, and Virginia, to come stand with her in the front of the room. They began to sing "Come, Ye Thankful People, Come," but had completed only half of the song when Rose turned to Mrs. Benson and said they were going to stop because no one in the class would listen to them. Mrs. Benson spoke to the class in a loud harsh voice, telling them to "shut up and listen to the girls." When they finished, there was only scattered and very brief applause.

Mrs. Benson organized the class to leave the room. Laura, Mary, and Liza were excused from the class as they were the only second graders with speaking parts in the skit presented by the third grade students. The remainder of the second grade and all of the first grade students were to stand on the stage as a chorus. The kindergarten class was to perform an Indian dance which was a prayer for corn.

In the gymnasium were approximately three hundred students from both Attucks School and one of the branch schools nearby. The assistant principal greeted Mrs. Benson at the door to the gym with the words, "You are a little late, aren't you?" Mrs. Benson replied they were not late because the program was not to begin until 1:45 p.m. The assistant principal said that he thought the program was to begin at 1:30 p.m. In addition to the teachers, students, and school administration present for the performance, there were also a number of parents at the rear of the gym. From the second grade class there were the mothers of Mary and Tom. The program lasted for forty minutes. It opened and closed with a prayer.

December 5
Displays related to the seasonal activity of the year were a part of the second grade classroom as they had been in kindergarten. Mrs. Benson had extensively decorated the room for Christmas. There were three different pictures of the Nativity, two pictures of Santa Claus, and one of snow-covered fields. There was also a small artificial tree in the room on the library table. Mrs. Benson had placed an artificial poinsettia on her desk. Only two displays in the classroom were not related to Christmas. The first was the "Reminders" bulletin board she used for her notes and memos. The second board not in the Christmas motif was in the rear to the right. On this board in red letters on a yellow background were the words "We Try Harder." Below the wording were tacked six arithmetic papers, all graded with a gold star and a "100." The six papers all were done by children who sat in the Tiger group.

On the schedule printed by the Board of Education indicating the amount of time that the teacher should allocate to each activity through the day, ten minutes were set aside for "organization" when the children came in from the noon recess. In Mrs. Benson's room the "organization" of the class after the noon period averaged between eighteen and twenty-five minutes. The following account of the period gives some idea of the typical manner in which time was spent.

The bell rings at 12:45 p.m. The children do not arrive in the room until 12:52 p.m. When the children enter, Mrs. Benson is not present. They go to their seats, but not all sit. They are talking softly among themselves. Nick is told by Joe to stand near the door and watch for Mrs. Benson. He goes to the doorway and almost immediately comes back, followed by Mrs. Benson, who enters the room at 12:55 p.m. Alice goes to Mrs. Benson and shows her a can of soda that she is drinking. Mrs. Benson tells her to go back to her seat and try to finish it. Rose comes to the desk and asks Mrs. Benson if she may leave the room to look for her purse. Mrs. Benson nods that she may. Mrs. Benson asks the Tiger girls to hang up their wraps. The remainder of the class, she says, are to be resting. The noise level does not diminish. She says in a loud voice, "Somebody did not hear what I said, Lou." Immediately, Amy says, "Nick," but Mrs. Benson makes no response to either Amy or Nick. The Tiger boys, Cardinal girls, and then the Cardinal boys are asked to hang up their wraps. Hal does not leave his seat as quickly as do the remainder of the Cardinal boys. Lou calls out, "Mrs. Benson, Hal won't hang up his coat." Hal rises and walks by Lou's seat toward the coatroom. As he passes Lou, he says, "Forget you, boy." Hal calls from the coatroom that Doug has turned off the light. Mrs. Benson says, "I bet I am gonna make a lot of people absent if they don't hurry out of there." Rose returns with her purse. Mary and several of the other girls in the Tiger group tell Mrs. Benson the reason Rose always loses her purse is because she "is always chasin' boys." Mrs. Benson turns to the group of girls and says, "I would say that is none of your business." The Clowns as a group are told to hang up their wraps. Jim is asked why he does not have a reentry slip since he was absent during the morning session. Jim explains that he was going to be late for school and was afraid to see the principal, so he went back home. Mrs. Benson tells him he should come anyway and go instead to see the assistant principal. Alice shows Mrs. Benson she has finished the soda. Mrs. Benson tells her to put it in the wastebasket, which Alice does. At 1:05 p.m. Mrs. Benson asks Hal why he was absent yesterday and where his reentry slip is. Hal explains that he does not have a slip. Mrs. Benson says that they will have to take care of the slip during the afternoon recess. Money is collected from the children who wish Mrs. Benson to keep it until the afternoon dismissal. At 1:13 p.m. Mrs. Benson instructs the class to take out their spelling books to study spelling words.

December 10

At the beginning of the observational period, the Tigers were involved in completing an arithmetic assignment given earlier. The Cardinals were reading from a short play with Mrs. Benson, and the Clowns were making Christmas cards from construction paper, writing verses, and coloring scenes. In the Cardinal group, Hal, Lena, and Anne were standing and reading their respective parts from a short story about a family going to the store to buy food. While the children stood reading their parts, Lilly sat tying her shoestrings. She had been sharing her reading book for weeks with Lena, and when Lena needed the book for her part in the play, Lilly was left with no book in which she could follow. Lilly and Lena were the only two children in the Cardinal group who had to share.

When the three children finished, Mrs. Benson ended the lesson and walked to her desk. At this time a student from the seventh grade came into the room and asked if her teacher could borrow Mrs. Benson's book of classroom decorating ideas. Mrs. Benson gave the book to the child, who then left. As Mrs. Benson left the Cardinal group, Lilly immediately took out her reading workbook, *Come Along,* and began using a red crayon to answer questions on one of the pages. The only other student in the Cardinal group who began to work of his own initiative was David, who also was using his workbook. Shortly, Dan took out his arithmetic book and began work. Lilly put away her reading and took out her arithmetic book. Lilly and Dan began to talk softly between themselves about the assignment. There was nodding and also shaking of heads as they spoke to one another. Both were actively engaged. Lilly looked up from her work as Mrs. Benson said to Lou in a loud voice, "Somebody sure wants to be an example, don't they? Now shut up and get to work." Lilly turned back to her book. Mrs. Benson shortly told the class to clear their desks of all papers and pencils. Lilly did not clear her desk until she had first finished the problem she was completing. Dan asked Lilly if she was finished, and she nodded that she was. When Mrs. Benson told the class to open their

spelling workbooks to page fifty, Lilly repeated softly to herself, "fifty."
As Mrs. Benson read the assignment on the page, Lilly softly read
along, barely moving her lips.

During this observational period, Laura was absent, which provided
an opportunity for extensive observation with Lilly. The following are
notes from the period until the bell for noon recess.

Mrs. Benson instructs the class to repeat with her each of the
twenty words which will be on the upcoming spelling test. Lilly
speaks the words along with the remainder of the children.

For those children who believe they knew the words, Mrs. Benson
gives instructions on a new reading assignment that they may begin if they wish. As she reads the instructions, Lilly reads along
silently moving her lips. Mrs. Benson asks for an example of each
of the three parts of the new assignment. Lilly does not raise her
hand. Mrs. Benson gives the class a further assignment at the top of
the following page. In this section are four sentences in which the
children are to select the best word for the blank. On the first three
questions, Lilly does not raise her hand as Mrs. Benson asks the
class for the answer. On the fourth sentence, she does raise her
hand, but is not called upon. Intermittently she chews on the end of
her eraser.

As the final set of additional exercises, Mrs. Benson discusses the
four pictures at the bottom of the page. The lesson is to indicate
whether the picture next to each of the four numbers is to be described in the singular or in the plural. Picture one is of one rat, two
of two beds, three of one apple, and four of two hats. Mrs. Benson
asks the class what is the name of the animal in the first picture.
Lilly becomes excited and raises her hand high. She is standing
partway out of her seat. Mrs. Benson sees Lilly and asks her for an
answer. Lilly smiles and says, "That a rat." Mrs. Benson responds,
"Yes, it is. Now who can tell me about picture two?"

Lilly looks at her spelling words for a short while and then takes a piece of paper to begin the new assignment discussed by Mrs. Benson. She works intently and looks up only when there are interruptions or disruptions in the class. (One girl comes into the room to borrow a stapler and on another occasion Mrs. Benson hits Lou with her four-foot stick as she says to him, "Boy, you shut up while I am reading.")

Mrs. Benson begins a short reading lesson with the Clowns. Lilly continues her own work until her brother Nick is called upon by Mrs. Benson to read. She stops her work and watches her brother. Nick does not know the word "farm" and Mrs. Benson asks Amy to help Nick. When Amy pronounces the word, Nick repeats it to the teacher and Lilly also says it softly to herself. Mrs. Benson asks the entire Clown group to say the word "farm," and as they do, Lilly repeats the word. She goes back to her work and places the book upright on her desk so that she is hidden from view. The book remains in this position for the next five minutes until Mrs. Benson tells all the students in the class to put away their books and pencils.

The single instance of direct interaction between Lilly and the teacher bears some mention. When Lilly was able to respond to a question from her experience and knowledge, she was willing to participate. (On several visits to her home, I had observed rats in rooms on the first floor.) Her desire to show that she knew the correct answer was obvious: She had stood halfway out of her chair waving her hand, hoping to be called upon. When the question was within her sphere of previous experience, she was more than eager.

Further Notes on the Second Grade: Reward and Punishment

Throughout the length of the study in Attucks School, it was clear that both the kindergarten and second grade teachers were teaching groups within the same class in a dissimilar manner. That is, different behavior was directed toward children in different reading groups.

Variations were evident, for example, in the amount of time the teachers spent teaching, in the manner in which they granted select groups privileges denied to others, and in their continued proximity to the select groups. Two additional aspects of differential treatment are related to the teachers' use of reward and punishment.

Though the differences were "evident," I attempted a systematic evaluation to gauge empirically the part they played in the behavior of the second grade teacher. In order to examine more closely the degree of these variations over time, three observational periods were devoted to the tabulation and categorization of each individual behavioral unit directed by the teacher toward any child. Each observational period was three and one-half hours in length, lasting from 8:30 a.m. to 12:00 noon. The dates of the observations were the Fridays at the end of eight, twelve, and sixteen weeks of school—October 24, November 21, and December 19, respectively.

As a mechanism of evaluating the varieties of teacher behavior, a ninefold scheme of teacher-initiated behavior directed at students was developed. The teacher's behavior was tabulated as a "behavioral unit" when there was some manner of communication clearly directed toward an individual child, whether verbal, nonverbal, or physical contact. General instructions to the class were not tabulated. When, within the interaction between teacher and the student, there was more than one unit of behavior, for instance, the teacher both spoke to the child and touched him, a count was made of both variations. The following is a list of the nine variations in teacher behavior tabulated within the second grade classroom. Several examples are also included.

1. Verbal supportive—"That's a very good job." "You are such a lovely girl." "My, but your work is so neat."
2. Verbal neutral—"Laura and Tom, let's open our books to page 34." "Mary, your pencil is on the floor." "Hal, do you have milk money today?"
3. Verbal control—"Lou, sit down in that chair and shut up." "Curt, get up off that floor." "Mary and Laura, quit your talking."

4. Nonverbal supportive—Teacher nods her head at Rose. Teacher smiles at Liza. Teacher claps when Laura completes her problem at the board.
5. Nonverbal neutral—Teacher indicates with arms that she wants Lilly and Shirley to move farther apart in the circle. Teacher motions to Joe and Tom that they should try to snap their fingers to stay in beat with the music.
6. Nonverbal control—Teacher frowns at Lena. Teacher shakes finger at Amy to quit tapping her pencil. Teacher motions with hand for Rose not to come to her desk.
7. Physical contact for support—Teacher hugs Laura. Teacher places her arm around Mary as she talks to her. Teacher holds Anne's hand when she has a splinter in it.
8. Physical contact, neutral—Teacher touches head of Nick as she walks past. Teacher touches head of each student whom she wishes to go to the blackboard. Teacher leads Amy to new place on the circle.
9. Physical contact for control—Teacher strikes Lou with stick. Teacher pushes Curt down in his chair. Teacher pushes Hal and Doug to floor.

Table III, which follows, is presented with all forms of control, supportive, and neutral behavior grouped together within each of the three observational periods. As a methodological precaution, since the categorization of the various types of behavior was decided as the interaction occurred and there were no cross-validation checks by another observer, all behavior was placed in the neutral category which could not be clearly distinguished as belonging to one of the control or supportive categories. This may in part explain the large percentage of neutral behavior.

According to analysis of these data Mrs. Benson distributed rewards quite sparingly and also equally but utilized somewhere between two and five times as much control-oriented behavior with the Clowns as with the Tigers. Alternatively, whereas with the Tigers the combination of neutral and supportive behavior never dropped below 93 percent of

Table III. Variations in Teacher-Initiated Behavior for Three Reading Groups during Three Observational Periods

	Variations in Teacher-Initiated Behavior		
	Control	Supportive	Neutral
Observational Period #1[a]			
Tigers	5% (6)[b]	7% (8)	87% (95)
Cardinals	10% (7)	7% (5)	82% (58)
Clowns	27% (27)	6% (6)	67% (69)
Observational Period #2			
Tigers	7% (14)	8% (16)	85% (170)
Cardinals	7% (13)	8% (16)	85% (157)
Clowns	14% (44)	6% (15)	80% (180)
Observational Period #3			
Tigers	7% (15)	6% (13)	86% (171)
Cardinals	14% (20)	10% (14)	75% (108)
Clowns	15% (36)	7% (16)	78% (188)

[a]Forty-eight (48) minutes of unequal teacher access (because one group of children were out of the room) was eliminated from the analysis.
[b]Value within the parentheses indicates total number of units of behavior within that category.

the total directed toward them, the lowest figure for the Cardinals was 86 percent and for the Clowns, 73 percent. It may be assumed that the presence of neutral and supportive behavior would be conducive to learning while the presence of punishment or control-oriented behavior would not. Thus, for the Tigers, the learning situation involved infrequent control, while for the Clowns, control behavior constituted one-fourth of all behavior directed toward them on at least one occasion.

Research related to leadership structure and task performance in voluntary organizations has given strong indication that within an authoritarian setting there occurs a decrease in both learning retention and performance on assigned tasks that does not occur in a nonauthoritarian setting (Kelley and Thibaut, 1954; Lewin, Lippitt, and White, 1939). Further investigations have generally confirmed these early findings.

Of particular interest within the classroom are the early studies of Adams (1945), Anderson (1946), Anderson et al. (1946), Preston and Heintz (1949), and Robbins (1952). Their findings may be generalized as stating that children within an authoritarian classroom display a decrease in both learning retention and performance while those within a democratic classroom do not. In extrapolating these findings to Mrs. Benson's second grade classroom, one cannot say that she was continually "authoritarian" as opposed to "democratic" with her students, but that she more frequently used control-oriented behavior with one group of students, the group that she had defined as "slow and disinterested." On at least one occasion Mrs. Benson used nearly five times the amount of control-oriented behavior with the Clowns as with the Tigers. The Clowns were most isolated from the teacher and received the smallest part of her teaching time; the results noted here suggest that the amount of control-oriented behavior directed toward them was substantial enough to compound their difficulty in mastering classroom materials.

Here discussion of the self-fulfilling prophecy is relevant; for the question remains unanswered whether the behavior of uninterested students necessitated the teacher's extensive use of control-oriented behavior, or whether, to the extent to which the teacher utilized control-oriented behavior, the students responded with uninterest. If the previous experience of the Clowns was in any way similar to that of the Table 3 students in kindergarten and those at Table C in the first grade, I am inclined to support the latter proposition. To put it more bluntly, the teachers themselves contributed significantly to the creation of the "slow learners" within their classrooms. That, over time, an increasing number of students were brought into the teacher's sphere of high control-oriented behavior may help to account for a phenomenon noted in the Coleman Report (1966), which found an increasing gap between the academic performance of the urban black student and the national norms the longer the black student remained in the school system. During one of the three and one-half observational periods in the second grade, the amount of control-oriented behavior directed toward the entire class was about 8 percent. Of the behavior directed toward the Clowns, however, 27 percent was control-oriented—more than three times the amount for the class as a whole. Deutsch (1968), in a random sampling of New York City Public School classrooms of the fifth through eighth grades, noted that teachers devoted between 50 and 80 percent of class time to discipline and organization. Unfortunately, he failed to specify the two individual percentages, and thus it is unknown whether the classrooms were dominated by either discipline or organization as opposed to their combination. If it is true, as Deutsch's findings would suggest, that the higher the grade level, the greater the discipline and control-oriented behavior, many of the unexplained aspects of the "regress phenomenon" among black students in urban schools may be clarified.

On another level of analysis, the teacher's use of discipline and organization is directly related to her expectations of the ability and willingness of "slow learners." That is, if the student is uninterested in what goes on in the classroom, he is more apt to engage in activities that the teacher perceives as disruptive. Talking out loud, coloring when the teacher has not given permission, attempting to leave the room, calling other students' attention to something on the street, making comments not pertinent to the lesson, dropping books, falling out of his chair, and expressing impatience for recess, all prompt the teacher to employ control-oriented behavior. The interactional pattern between the uninterested student and the teacher becomes a vicious circle in which control is followed by further manifestations of uninterest, followed by further control, and so on. The stronger the reciprocity of this pattern of interaction, the greater, presumably, will be the strengthening of the teacher's expectation that the "slow learner" is either unable or unwilling to learn.

The Caste System Falters

A major objective of this study has been to document the manner in which there emerges within the early grades at Attucks School a stratification system, based both on teacher expectations about behavioral and attitudinal characteristics of the child and on a variety of socioeconomic factors related to the child's background. As noted, when the student begins to move through the grades, the variable of past performance becomes a crucial index of his position within the class. The formulation of the system of stratification into various reading groups gained a castelike character over time, in that there was no observed movement into the highest reading group once it had been established at the beginning of the kindergarten school year. Likewise, there was no movement out of the highest reading group. There was, however, the described movement between the second and third reading groups, consisting of the combination of those at the low reading table one year with the middle table to constitute the middle table the following year.

Though formal visits with the second grade class of Mrs. Benson ended with the Christmas vacation, informal visits to the class continued through the remainder of the school year. The organization of the class remained stable throughout the winter months with one notable exception. For the first time during observations in either the kindergarten or the second grade, there was a reassignment of two students from the high reading group to the middle reading group. Virginia and Joe were moved by Mrs. Benson during the third week in January from the Tiger reading group to the Cardinal group. David and Anne were reassigned from the Cardinal group to the Tiger group to replace the two moved out. I asked Mrs. Benson the reason for the move and she explained that neither Virginia nor Joe "could keep a clean desk." She noted that these two students constantly had paper and crayons on the floor beside their desks. She said that the Tigers "are a very

clean group" and that the two could not remain in the high group because they were not neat. David and Anne were described as "extremely neat with their desk and floor." When moved to the Cardinals,
Virginia and Joe were placed in the back seats of the group.

  With this incident in mind, we might rephrase the quotation from
Michael Katz's work given early in the book: "The acceptable, by and
large, take the best marks and the best jobs."

Poor Kids and Public Schools

6

We began this study with the contention that myths die hard in America. If what we have seen in Attucks School is representative, we can add that inequality will also die hard. What we have found is an interlocking pattern of institutional arrangements descending from the macrolevel of the city-wide school system to the social and cultural milieu of a single school to the various stratification techniques employed by individual teachers in their classrooms. The outcome of this multileveled organization is ultimately expressed by comparing the experiences of the Tigers to those of the Cardinals and Clowns or more precisely, comparing the experiences of Laura to those of Lilly.

Throughout the various levels of the St. Louis educational system we found commonly shared assumptions about "how things really are." The basic tenets may be summarized as follows: Middle-class students can learn, lower-class students cannot; white schools are "good," black schools are "bad"; control is necessary, freedom is anarchy; violence works, persuasion does not; teachers can save a few, but will lose many; the school tries, the home will not; and finally, only the naïve would dispute these beliefs, as the wise know. *The outcome of this set of attitudes, assumptions, and values is that the school as an institution sustains, in a myriad of ways, the inequalities with which children first come to school.* The school's response to issues of color, class, and control all mesh together to make two nets —one to catch winners and one to catch losers.

Teaching and Learning in Attucks School

A major goal of this study has been to demonstrate the means by which teachers' assumptions manifest themselves within the class-room setting. These assumptions transform themselves into expecta-tions for individual children, with the result that differential treatment is accorded various members of the same class. The single most influ-ential variable to which the teachers responded was the social class background of the student. Thus, the kindergarten teacher's expecta-tions as to who would emerge within the class as a "fast learner" and who would emerge as a "slow learner" clearly delineated the middle-class students from their peers. It is important to reiterate that when the teacher made her seating assignments on the eighth day, she had no formal measures of academic ability or cognitive development to aid in her evaluation.

With both the first and second grade teachers, the process of within-class differentiation resulted in patterns of classroom organization not dissimilar from those of the kindergarten teacher. The latter two teach-ers, however, created their tracking systems not on the basis of sub-jective interpretations, but by evaluating the previous test scores and readiness material completed by each student. The end result of this "objective" placement of students in different groups was the rein-forcement of internal class divisions instigated by the kindergarten teacher.

One outcome of within-class tracking was the creation of a pattern of segregation among the students based on the socioeconomic posi-tions of their parents. Among those defined by the teachers as ex-pected to learn were the students who came to school clean and neatly dressed, who came from homes intact and middle-class in attributes, who displayed interest in the teacher, continually sought interaction with her, and who quickly learned the routine of schooling. On the other side of the segregation barrier were the students who were often dirty and smelling of urine, who came from poor homes frequently headed by one parent, who did not seek interaction with the teacher, and who never appeared to grasp the subtleties of the school routine. The relative impermeability of the top group through the various grades gave it a castelike character violated only once in two and a half years.

In the examination of specific classrooms, there emerged at least two identifiable interactional processes which operated simultaneously. Both occurred between teacher and student and both evolved four distinct stages. Using the kindergarten as an example, the first involved the teacher and the students sitting at Table 1. Initially the kindergarten teacher developed expectations for different students in her class, some of whom she believed met the criteria essential for future academic success. Second, she reinforced through mechanisms of positive differential treatment those particular characteristics deemed important and desirable in that select group. In turn, the students responded with the behavior which helped them from the beginning to gain the attention and support of the teacher. Thus, the Table 1 students perceived that verbalization was an ability that the teacher admired and so persisted with high levels of verbalization throughout the year. The cycle completed itself as the teacher again focused even more specifically on the Table 1 students, in whom she found the behavior she desired. The end of this process was the creation of an interactional scheme in which certain early forms of behavior exhibited by the students came to be permanent behavioral patterns, continually reinforced by the teacher.

A concurrent behavioral process went on between the teacher and students placed at Tables 2 and 3. These students came into the class possessing a series of attributes, both behavioral and social, which the

teacher perceived as indicative of "failure" within her frame of reference. By reinforcing her initial expectations, she made it evident that
she did not consider them similar or equal to the students classified as
fast learners. Those marked as potential and probable failures responded accordingly. That is, because of the teacher's use of control,
her lack of verbal interaction and encouragement, her allocation of a
disproportionately small amount of her teaching time, and her various
techniques of exclusion, this group of students withdrew from classroom participation. The final stage was the cyclical repetition of solidi-
fying behavioral and attitudinal characteristics initially labeled unacceptable. Like the students in the first group, the anticipated failures
were not objectively tested before they were tracked.

Generally, one might assume that the students in the class as a whole
possessed the range of potentials and abilities necessary to cope with
the demands and routines of schooling. Yet without ascertaining those
potentials, the teacher responded on the basis of social class criteria
which inhibited two groups of students from changing positions—
those in the higher group who in fact did not have the potential and
those in the lower groups who did. This analysis should not be miscon-
strued to imply that segregation resulting from ability tracking in the
classroom on the basis of objective criteria would be acceptable.
What I do suggest is that the teacher by her actions may have created
a situation in which those in the higher group who might not have been
expected "objectively" to perform at the high level came to do so and
those in the lower group from whom one "objectively" would expect
more came to give less: all in accordance with the teacher's expectations.

From a different perspective on might argue that the teachers in Attucks School created their tracking systems not because they believed
their students to be so dissimilar that they required entirely different
treatment, but because they were quite similar. That is, the teachers
may have assumed that the conditions within the black community
were so strongly inhibitive to the development of successful middle-

class life styles that it became absolutely necessary to "save" those few whom they perceived as having even the slightest opportunity. The patterns of classroom segregation were created to protect the high group from the lower groups, with their interests in the "streets," their use of "bad" language, and their lack of regard for school. One teacher, in fact, stated that the school had two types of students—those with "street blood" and those with "school blood." The pathos and the sense of the tenuousness of success in the black community that are evident in these assumptions are not entirely without foundation. As Jencks (1972b) has so amply demonstrated, the middle-class black father has less than half the opportunity of the middle-class white father to pass on the benefits of his position to his offspring, in terms of both occupation and income.

Within the classrooms, one of the seemingly inescapable consequences of the segregation systems was that the children themselves quickly picked up what it meant to be on one side of the barrier or the other. Each group of students began to emulate the teacher's treatment of the other. The high group followed the teacher in their ridicule, belittlement, physical abuse, and social ostracism of the lower groups. In short, middle-class students were learning, very early on, the mannerisms and techniques of how to deal with the lower class. The lower-class students displayed patterns of deference and passivity toward those of the high group. They seldom returned the ridicule in kind and infrequently began any sort of conflict with the high group. *Thus the middle-class students were learning to control the poor, and the poor students were learning to shuffle.* The classrooms became microcosms of the larger society in which cultural values were transmitted and put into operation so as to legitimate the attitudes and assumptions necessary for the perpetuation of inequality.

An important part of this transmission of cultural values is the definition given to the activities of major institutions. The current institutional arrangements in this society favor the affluent and discriminate against the poor. This holds true whether one examines patterns of political

power, economic concentration, occupational mobility, or access to
the goods and services available in the society. Those who benefit are
not likely to clamor for change in the status quo. In fact, what often
emerges is an attempt to rationalize the inequalities as natural, inevitable, and desirable. This, in fact, has occurred in American schools.
The patterns of schooling function so as to reward the kinds of activities and interests characteristic of middle- and upper-income students
while ignoring or negating the contributions of lower-class students.

The rationalizations for this inequality take the form of defending
"standards" that are class based, of proclaiming a policy of "equal
treatment for all" which does no more than reinforce inequalities, and
of laying the onus for lack of success on the individual rather than on
the institution. Such assumptions attempt to undercut demands for
change in institutional arrangements by implying that the institution is,
in fact, benign and that any tinkering would only be detrimental. The
irony emerges when one comes to take an egalitarian position in defense of inequality. Such is the present state of American education.

It should be evident from all that has gone before in this study that
teachers play the central role in establishing and perpetuating the system of classroom segregation. The consequences and ramifications of
this are several. First, teachers create for themselves a paradoxical
position. On the one hand, they view themselves as teachers—as
those who seek to aid children to learn of themselves and their world.
Yet they respond to the socioeconomic differences in their students in
a way that precludes for some the very opportunity for learning. They
generate failure in some of their students while believing themselves
to desire success for their charges. The way out of this dilemma for
teachers and school systems in general is to assume that they have
done all they can in the face of overwhelming environmental (and
genetic) odds. As Kenneth Clark has noted (1969):

Educational officials and teachers have been persuaded—and particularly have persuaded themselves—that the causes of the educational retardation of Negro children are not to be found in the quality of

teaching or school supervision. They have explained this chronic problem in terms of the children's alleged personal deficiencies— hostility and aggressiveness towards authority, low attention span, lack of educational experiences prior to entering school, and low motivation for academic work. The parents are to blame, so the teachers say, because they have "no-books-in-the-home," because they lack interest in their children's school achievement. Some educators seriously offered as an explanation of student retardation the fact that these parents "do not attend PTA meetings." They assert that the community is to blame because it suffers all the pathologies of ghettoes— it has dirty streets, over-crowded and deteriorated homes, and provides no model of academic excellence and reward for children.

Secondly, teachers may be fairly equal in their use of praise and reward with their students and still reinforce differences through use of control. The second grade teacher, for example, gave nearly equal amounts of verbal reward to the Clowns and to the Tigers. Yet the pervasiveness of control-oriented behavior toward the Clowns effectively thwarted a positive learning situation. One might only surmise what consequences the reversal of this situation would have had on patterns of performance within the class.

Third, the teachers' seemingly immutable assumption of the class-based differences in children was grounded not in an attempt to be malicious, but in their belief that "some can do it and some cannot." On one level it is possible to agree with the teachers that profound differences do exist between children because of environment, genetic endowment, and interaction between the two. However, the issue is not so much whether differences do exist, for there are few who would argue that children all come from the same mold, but what, in fact, one does with such information. If one responds in such a way as to assume that initial differences will be manifest as eternal differences, then a determinist theory of man results in classrooms where attempts at minimizing such differences are viewed as useless exercise. In such classrooms, the teacher can do little more than follow the "inevitable." If, though, a teacher acknowledges that children come to the classroom with differences, but that they also are capable of learning of their world, then the teacher-student relation becomes of immense importance in the pursuit of academic performance and cognitive development. The stagnation of tracking systems can be broken only by redefining what is supposed to happen inside classrooms.

The teachers did not acknowledge the adaptations made by the students placed in the lower groups as having any function in the making of "successful" students. Faced with ridicule from teacher and peers, receiving on occasion as little as one-sixth of the teaching time of the top group, and subject to continual control-oriented behavior, the students developed among themselves patterns of secondary learning, of infrequently giving the teacher the response sought, and often giving no response at all. Teachers saw these reactions as further evidence that the students were "not yet ready" to handle the material being taught to the high group. The reinforcement of the self-fulfilling prophecy persisted when teachers thus misinterpreted student behavior initially instigated, in part, as a reaction to their own behavior.

Finally, and in defense of the teachers, it has not been a contention of this study that the teachers observed in Attucks School could not effectively teach their students. In my estimation, they taught quite well. *Competence, however, is not the issue. The issue is the unequal accessibility to students of that competence.* Students who came to the classroom from middle-class homes experienced a positive and rewarding learning situation where they were given large amounts of teacher attention, were the subject of little control-oriented behavior, held as models for the remainder of the class, and continually reminded that they were "special" students. Hypothetically, if Attucks School had contained only those students perceived by teachers as having the traits necessary for middle-class status and future success, I would anticipate that the teachers would have continued to teach well, and in these circumstances, to the entire class. The consequences of reserving their teaching for those whom they believed were destined to become winners necessarily resulted in the avoidance of those destined to become losers. And losers are what they became.

What is to be Done? Reflections on Policies, Priorities, and Options

What follows is predicated upon one basic assumption: that an advocacy of the rights and freedoms of children supersedes the need to legitimate or perpetuate any educational institution touching their lives. Thus it is not the system that must be preserved, but the integrity of the child; not the administrative positions, but the environment for learning; and not the necessity of adapting for institutional survival, but the gaining and sustaining of individual freedom.

Asking the question, "What is to be done with American schools?" is like opening a Pandora's box. The alternatives may range from a return to "traditional" emphasis upon such skills as reading and writing, to the creation of "discovery centers" where children would be free to plot and chart their own courses in what they seek to learn, to the ultimate disbanding or disestablishing of schools as a distinct institution. There is, of course, the additional possibility of allowing schools to continue as they are. To provide some delineation for a discussion of options in American education, the following propositions are offered as a context within which various policies and programs might be evaluated.

First, the school as a state-financed institution requiring attendance will be with us into the indefinite future. This does not rule out the continued existence of private, parochial, or "alternative" schools. But the realities of large and increasingly powerful teacher organizations; of communities with tens of millions of dollars invested in buildings, equipment and supplies; of parents who want someone else to "teach" their children; and of an industrial society which utilizes educational credentials as a means to sort and categorize persons for different social class positions, all lead me to believe that the bureaucracy of public schooling will persist. Further, the chief means by which this bureaucracy has retained its clients has been compulsory attendance. I do not envision schools becoming so free as to offer children and parents the option of whether or not to attend.

Ivan Illich (1971) has argued that schools should be "disestablished" or else society should be "deschooled" so that learning ceases to be the scarce commodity held by a few and distributed at their discretion. The end result, Illich argues, of such differential access to "learning" is the perpetuation of inequality between those who possess it and those who do not. I agree with his critique of education as "commodity," but as Gintis (1972) has noted, there is yet a step beyond negating the current educational systems. A new synthesis is reached by recreating in such a manner as to transform their functions. Gintis suggests that it is irrelevant to speak of "deschooling" when American society chooses not to talk also of the means by which to "de-office," "de-factory," or more generally, "de-bureaucratize." He proposes that the issue is not whether schools are going to wither away, but whom they will serve. Gintis assumes, ". . . Schools are so important to the reproduction of the capitalist society that they are unlikely to crumble under any but the most massive political onslaughts." Thus, so long as the current institutional arrangements in schooling continue serving the ultimate stratification functions they presently do, the central arena for educational change becomes the political arena. Political, for the aim is not to abolish, but to transform so as to work toward the creation of a new social system. He notes:

The only presently viable political strategy in education . . . is what Rudi Deutchke terms "the long march through the institutions," involving the localized struggles for what Andre Gorz calls "non-reformist reforms," i.e., reforms which effectively strengthen the power of the teachers vis-a-vis administrators, and of students vis-à-vis teachers. . . .
In other words, the correct immediate political goal is the nurturing of individuals both liberated (i.e., demanding control over their lives and outlets for their creative activities and relationships) *and* politically aware of the true nature of their misalignment with the larger society.

A second proposition, which follows in part from the first, recognizes that, as Jencks (1972b) has written, "schools serve primarily to legitimize inequality, not to create it." As was manifestly evident in Attucks School, the inequalities, for example, with which Laura and Lilly came to school were reinforced, not reduced. The social class configurations of the larger society were mirrored and affirmed in the patterns of organization within individual rooms. Jencks notes: ". . . Schools serve primarily as selection and certification agencies, whose job is to measure and label people, and only secondarily as socialization agencies, whose job is to change people." (p. 135)

A wide range of major research findings, including the Equality of Educational Opportunity Survey, a study of the ninety-one high schools included in the Project Talent survey, and the Census Bureau studies of social mobility and income distribution, all provided Jencks with evidence. Given the seminal importance of Jencks' work, it is crucial to recapitulate his major findings and implications for American education. They may be summarized in five points:

1. Access to the resources of schools is distributed quite unequally, being directly related both to social class position and length of time spent in school. Access also varies with race, whites benefiting more than blacks.

2. "We found that both genetic and environmental inequality played a major role in producing cognitive inequality. We also found that those who started life with genetic advantages tended to get environmental advantages as well, and that this exacerbated inequality. . . . We found no evidence that differences between schools contributed significantly to cognitive inequality . . ." (pp. 253–254)

3. The family background of an individual was more influential in determining how much schooling he received than either intelligence (measured by IQ) or quality of schooling.

4. The occupation one eventually attains is directly affected by educational background, and educational background is influenced by family background. Thus family background becomes the more important of several factors ultimately influencing occupational status.

5. Education influences the options one has for first entering a particular occupation, but it does not have much effect on earnings or competence within that occupation.

The implications of these findings for the future of American education and for the issue of inequality in general create the basis for a third proposition: that reform within the schools can ultimately have only marginal effect on the inequality that exists outside schools. *Consequently, if one wishes to reduce the present inequality in American society, it is more advantageous to attack it directly than to attempt to amelioriate it through manipulating the institution of school, which is only tangentially related to the creation of that inequality.* If one wishes to make the situations of adults more equal in income, opportunities for mobility, and job security, then it is necessary to address oneself to the consequences of differential family backgrounds in terms of socio-economic variables rather than school curricula, teachers' credentials, size of gymnasiums, presence or absence of language laboratories, number of foreign languages taught, and the like. As Jencks summarizes:

There seem to be three reasons why school reform cannot make adults more equal. First, children seem to be far more influenced by what happens at home than by what happens in school. They may also be more influenced by what happens on the streets and by what they see on television. Second, reformers have very little control over those aspects of school life that affect children. Reallocating resources, re-assigning pupils, and rewriting the curriculum seldom change the way teachers and students actually treat each other minute by minute. Third, even when a school exerts an unusual influence on children, the resulting changes are not very likely to persist into adulthood. (pp. 255–256)

Applying these findings to the realities of what occurred in Attucks School, the best hope for those who sat at the Clown table lies not in anything that might be done for them within the classroom (though for humane reasons alone, change is necessary), but what might instead be done about the social class position of their families in American society. It is here that Attucks School weaves itself into the national pattern of generating educational winners and losers. Schools do not exist as agents of change, but as institutions which have been created to sustain, reinforce, and affirm existing structural and ideological arrangements. They have been created to reflect this society, not to transform it. It should not be surprising, then, if the income differential between the top fifth and the bottom fifth of American workers is 600 percent, that schools would mirror such inequalities. The point is that inequalities in the political and economic spheres of this society intrude into the space of the schools and are there reinforced. Consequently, the elimination of massive differentials in income and salary, in the control of property and assets, in the accessibility of mobility, in the possibilities for securing meaningful employment, and finally, in the ability to pass on the benefits of one's labors to one's children must be dealt with as the political realities they are, and not as the pedagogical issues they are not.

If we accept the correctness of these three propositions—that compulsory public schooling will be with us for the foreseeable future; that the organizational arrangements inside schools legitimate current patterns of inequality, but do not create them; and that reforming schools does not necessarily imply dealing with the inequalities of the larger society—then we might consider the following implications. First, we can liberate ourselves from the shackling myths of what schools are supposed to be doing, both for the benefit of the students and for the larger society. We can put down the notions that schools are the "great equalizer" that provides everyone equal access to the mobility escalators. Rather, we can recognize the realities of how schools reinforce social class differences and act to preserve the current arrangements. There is little possibility of transforming the schools to the point where they do not serve this legitimatizing function if it is not first acknowledge that in fact they do.

Second, given the central stratification functions which schools serve for our economic system, it may be the most we can hope for—short of a major restructuring of economic institutions—that schools be organized in such a way as not to exacerbate the inequalities present in the society. I seriously doubt that schools are in a position to overcome the current economic and political inequalities, but it may at best be possible to withdraw schools from their legitimizing function through such means as the refusal to label any child by whatever negative traits he or she might have and the refusal to establish tracking systems. These types of changes may not appear to be systemic, and they are not, with regard to the magnitude of inequality in American society. But then again, the schools are not at the root of adult inequality. Thus we arrive at the fact that resolving school problems does not present itself as necessarily an effective means to resolving societal problems.

Third, the foregoing allows us to begin to approach schools as an end in their own right, not as a mechanism designed to serve some alternative motives. We can begin to ask questions about how the time that children have to spend in schools should be organized so as to maximize the benefits for them. If schools are no longer assumed to have to provide the means to reach mobility escalators, because such escalators are not even primarily related to schooling, then what one does with twelve years of a child's life takes on a new dimension. Bereiter (1972), for example, suggests that we split the current elementary school system into two, one part of which will provide training in spelling, reading, calculation and writing, while the second will provide child care areas where the child is free to explore as he wishes without the pressure of an adult attempting to "teach" something. Once we disabuse our thinking of the mythical functions of schools, we can begin to meet the needs of children in a humane way that does not require them to be more than simply children.

As we give up our grand illusions, we can set goals which more realistically fit what can be accomplished by teachers and students doing something together. Perhaps the most basic goal would be to provide outgoing students with the necessary means to function in this society. I am thinking particularly of insuring that within those twelve years, children learn to write, to spell, to do arithmetic, and to read. In San Francisco a lawsuit has been brought against the city Board of Education by a youth who was graduated with a fifth-grade reading level from a city high school. A good argument can be made that if one is going to be forced to attend a school, then that school should be held responsible for accomplishing what is is supposed to do—in this case teaching a high school graduate how to read at the level of high school graduates.

Establishing this sort of criterion for schools would dramatically switch the emphasis from a concern with the initial *input* of the child, for instance, I.Q., social class background, and father's occupation, to the *output* of the school. In short, schools should be called upon during the years of their hold over students to equalize in basic areas of competence those initial inequalities in academic performance with which children first come to school. Schools may not be able to transform the occupational hierarchy of this society, but they can be expected to perform so that the children of low-status parents can read a book as well as the children of high-status parents.

There are no universal antidotes one can offer to insure that all schools will become humane and rewarding places in which teachers and students can spend time together. The task of the future will be to examine the schools, if necessary one by one, to ascertain the needs, the values, and the dreams of those who will be inside their walls. Charles Silberman (1971, p. 208) believes that such schools are possible:

Schools can be humane and still educate well. They can be genuinely concerned with gaiety and joy and individual growth and fulfillment without sacrificing concern for intellectual discipline and development. They can be simultaneously child-centered and subject-centered. They can also stress esthetic and moral education without weakening the three R's.

I should like to think that the time is at hand for learning if Silberman is correct. Depending upon one's perspective, the current arrangements in schools are either working very well or not at all. If one believes that the recent graduate in San Francisco or Lilly in St. Louis deserves, nay, has the inalienable right to leave the school equipped to do what the schools say should be possible, then the current system is simply unacceptable. If we, as a society, choose to shake loose of false assumptions, surreal expectations, and the consequent crippling of many young participants, we can begin to create settings where, because it is the humane thing to do, children are respected; where learning is valued; and where equality is pursued. In short, we can strive to create a new synthesis of words and deeds.

Bibliography

Adams, R. G.
1945. "The Behavior of Pupils in Democratic and Autocratic Social Climates." Abstracts of Dissertations, Stanford University, Stanford, Calif.

Allport, G. W.
1954. *The Nature of Prejudice.* Reading, Mass.: Addison-Wesley.

Anderson, H.
1946. *Studies in Teachers' Classroom Personalities.* Stanford: Stanford University Press.

Anderson, H., Brewer, J., and Reed, M.
1946. "Studies of Teachers' Classroom Personalities, III. Follow-up Studies of the Effects of Dominative and Integrative Contacts on Children's Behavior." *Applied Psychology Monograph.* Stanford: Stanford University Press.

Baratz, S. and Baratz, J.
1970. "Early Childhood Intervention: The Social Science Base of Institutional Racism." *Harvard Educational Review,* 40.1: 29–50.

Bereiter, C.
1972. "Schools Without Education." *Harvard Educational Review,* 42.3: 390–413.

Bowles, S.
1972. "Getting Nowhere: Programmed Class Stagnation." *Society,* 9.8: 42–49.

Clark, K.
1969. "Interview." *Bulletin of Council of Basic Education,* 14 (November).

Cohen, D., Pettigrew, T., and Riley, R.
1972. "Race and the Outcoming of Schooling," in *On Equality of Educational Opportunity*. F. Mosteller and D. Moynihan, eds. New York: Random House.

Coleman, J. S.
1966. *Equality of Educational Opportunity*. Washington, D. C.: United States Government Printing Office.

Connor, W. and Smith, L.
1967. *Analysis of Patterns of Student Teaching*. St. Louis: Washington University, Graduate Institute of Education.

Crain, R.
1968. *The Politics of School Desegregation*. Chicago: Aldine.

Deutsch, M.
1968. *The Disadvantaged Child: Studies of the Social Environment and the Learning Process*. New York: Basic Books.

Doyle, J.
1969. "St. Louis, City with the Blues." *Saturday Review,* 39.7: 90–94.

Eddy, E.
1967. *Walk the White Line: A Profile of Urban Education*. Garden City, N. Y.: Doubleday.

Fuchs, E.
1969. *Teachers Talk: Views from Inside City Schools*. Garden City, N. Y.: Doubleday.

Gintis, H.
1972. "Toward a Political Economy of Education: A Radical Critique of Ivan Illich's *Deschooling Society*." *Harvard Educational Review,* 42.1: 70–96.

Gittell, M. and Hollander, T.
1967. *Six Urban School Districts: A Comparative Study of Institutional Response*. New York: Praeger.

Goffman, E.
1959. *The Presentation of Self in Everyday Life*. Garden City, N. Y.: Doubleday.
1961. *Asylums: Essays on the Social Situations of Mental Patients and Other Inmates*. Garden City, N. Y.: Doubleday.

Goodman, M.
1964. *Race Awareness in Young Children* (revised). New York: Collier.

Gouldner, A.
1954. *Patterns of Industrial Bureaucracy*. New York: The Free Press.

Henry, J.
1963. *Culture Against Man*. New York: Random House. (Note especially Chapter 8, "Golden Rule Days: American Schoolrooms.")

Illich, I.
1971. *Deschooling Society*. New York: Harper and Row.

Jackson, P.
1968. *Life in Classrooms*. New York: Holt, Rinehart and Winston.

Jencks, C.
1969. "A Reappraisal of the Most Controversial Educational Document of Our Time." *New York Times Magazine* (August 10).

1972a. "The Coleman Report and the Conventional Wisdom," in *On Equality of Educational Opportunity*. F. Mosteller and D. Moynihan, eds. New York: Random House.

1972b. *Inequality: A Reassessment of the Effect of Family and Schooling in America*. New York: Basic Books.

Jensen, A.
1969. "How Much Can We Boost IQ and Scholastic Achievement?" *Harvard Educational Review,* 39.1: 1–123.

Katz, M.
1971. *Class, Bureaucracy, and Schools: The Illusion of Educational Change in America*. New York: Praeger.

Kelley, H. and Thibaut, J.
1954. "Experimental Studies of Group Problem Solving and Process," in *Handbook of Social Psychology*. G. Lindzey, ed. Reading, Mass.: Addison-Wesley.

Kohl, H.
1967. *Thirty-Six Children*. New York: New American Library.

Kozol, J.
1967. *Death at an Early Age*. Boston: Houghton Mifflin.

Leacock, E.
1969. *Teaching and Learning in City Schools*. New York: Basic Books.

Lewin, K., Lippitt, R., and White, R.
1939. "Patterns of Aggressive Behavior in Experimentally Created Social Climates." *Journal of Social Psychology,* 10: 271–299.

Liu, B.
1967. *Population by Census Districts, St. Louis City*. St. Louis: Health and Welfare Council of Metropolitan St. Louis, Metropolitan Youth Commission.

Matza, D.
1966. "The Disreputable Poor," in *Class, Status, and Power*. R. Bendix and S. M. Lipset, eds. New York: The Free Press.

Merton, R.
1957. *Social Theory and Social Structure* (revised). New York: The Free Press.

Mills, C. W.
1959. *The Sociological Imagination.* New York: Oxford University Press.

Montagu, A., ed.
1970. *The Concept of Race.* New York: Collier.

Moore, G. A.
1967. *Realities of the Urban Classroom.* Garden City, N. Y.: Doubleday.

Morris, F. L.
1971. *The Jensen Hypothesis: Social Science Research or Social Science Racism.*
Los Angeles: Center for Afro-American Studies, University of California.

Mosteller, F. and Moynihan, D. P., eds.
1972. *On Equality of Educational Opportunity.* New York: Random House.

Preston, M. and Heintz, R.
1949. "Effects of Participatory versus Supervisory Leadership on Group Judgment."
Journal of Abnormal Social Psychology, 44: 345–355.

Proshansky, H. M.
1966. "The Development of Inter-group Attitudes," in *Review of Child Development
Research.* L. W. Hoffman and M. L. Hoffman, eds. New York: Russell Sage.

Proshansky, H. M. and Newton, P.
1968. "The Nature and Meaning of Negro Self-identity," in *Social Class, Race, and
Psychological Development.* M. Deutsch, M. Katz, and A. Jensen, eds. New York:
Holt, Rinehart and Winston.

Riessman, F. and Gartner, A.
1969. "Paraprofessionals: The Effect on Children's Learning." *The Urban Review,*
4.2: 21–22.

Rist, R. C., ed.
1972. *Restructuring American Education: Innovations and Alternatives.* New Bruns-
wick, N. J.: Transaction Books.

Robbins, F.
1952. "The Impact of Social Climates Upon A College Class." *School Review,* 60:
275–284.

Saint Louis Board of Education
1956. *Official Proceedings of the Board of Education.* St. Louis: Board of Education.

1957. *Official Proceedings of Board of Education.* St. Louis: Board of Education.

1967. *Social Studies Curriculum Guide.* St. Louis: Board of Education.

1969. *Scorecard.* St. Louis: Board of Education.

Saint Louis Board of Education, Harris Teachers College
1967. *Apprentice Teacher Program.* Saint Louis: Board of Education, Harris Teachers College.

Semmel, H.
1967. "Race and Education in Saint Louis and Saint Louis County, Missouri." Paper prepared for United States Commission on Civil Rights, Washington, D. C.

Silberman, C.
1970. *Crisis in the Classroom.* New York: Random House.

Sjoberg, G., Brymer, R., and Farris, B.
1966. "Bureaucracy and the Lower Class." *Sociology and Social Research,* 50.3: 325–337.

Smith, M.
1972. "Equality of Educational Opportunity: The Basic Findings Reconsidered," in *On Equality of Educational Opportunity.* F. Mosteller and D. P. Moynihan, eds. New York: Random House.

Smith, L. and Geoffrey, W.
1968. *The Complexities of an Urban Classroom.* New York: Holt, Rinehart and Winston.

Taeuber, K. and Taeuber, A.
1965. *Negroes in Cities.* Chicago: Aldine.

Thernstrom, S.
1964. *Poverty and Progress.* Cambridge, Mass.: Harvard University Press.

Waller, W.
1965. *The Sociology of Teaching* (originally published, 1937). New York: Wiley.

Index